Hanged
For Three
Pennies

Hanged For Three Pennies

The Breedon Books
Publishing Company
Derby

First published in Great Britain by
The Breedon Books Publishing Company Limited
Breedon House, 44 Friar Gate, Derby, DE1 1DA.
2000

ISBN 1 85983 191 5

Printed and bound by Butler & Tanner Ltd., Selwood Printing Works, Caxton
Road, Frome, Somerset.

Colour separations and jacket printing by
GreenShires Group Ltd, Leicester.

Contents

Introduction

THIS HISTORY of the death penalty in Derbyshire would seem to be the only one that so far has attempted to tackle the whole subject. As far as can be ascertained, other studies have dealt with certain aspects or specific periods. While the period covered ranges from the 14th century to the 20th, there is nothing more certain than that details of many executions have been lost. From 1732 onwards, thanks to the old *Derby Mercury*, the list can be said to be complete. Before that time, the researcher has to fish in different waters, knowing full well the final catch will not be absolute.

To avoid this being simply a listing with some details of the county's executions, while it would be of interest to researchers, it is necessary to give something of the national background. Just why were there over 200 capital offences serving the nation's gallows in the early 19th century? Some explanation is necessary, and it is an absorbing one. Murder a man or pick his pocket, either offence could, and did, see huge crowds in Derby turn up to watch the perpetrators swing on the Fatal Tree.

That extraordinary, peculiarly English episode, known as the Bloody Code (1770-1830), was worth exploring since it revealed that for several years the hangman was busier in Derby than at Tyburn or Newgate. Lasting some 60 years, it made the ghastly sight of the gallows and gibbet almost a routine event,

much commented on by foreign visitors whose own countries were by then pursuing far more enlightened penal policies.

Before the Code, information is somewhat scarce although such well-known incidents such as the Padley Martyrs, the Bakewell Witches and the martyrdom of Joan Waste are well documented. Also dealt with is the little known execution of the Bracy gang, when no fewer than ten highwaymen were hanged at the same time, probably by a man who had hanged his own father and brother. Those apart, the centuries are silent and must be considered against the national background.

The Pentrich Revolution of 1817 is dealt with at some length. While the rising itself was an utter failure, the motive and the background against which the march was planned were of considerable historical significance, taking place as it did at one of the most crucial periods in English history. The trial and executions were to ensure that Derbyshire's role in the story of capital punishment was that little bit different to most other counties.

After the sudden collapse of the Code in 1830, there was effectively only one capital offence, that of murder. From then until 1907, the year of Derbyshire's last judicial killing, the history is little more than a recital of the 19 who ended their lives struggling at the end of a rope. From being a national debate, the question of capital punishment had ceased to arouse any considerable emotion. After William Slack achieved his footnote in local history as the last person to hang in Derby, the county's role in England's archive of capital punishment was ended. The end was inauspicious and, looking back, almost incidental to what had gone before.

Whether we like to think it or not, most people are attracted to the morbid and the macabre. The evil that men do lives after them, and our infinite curiosity ensures that it will continue to do so. For the author, that interest was first aroused many years ago when he heard the death sentence pro-nounced at a murder trial at Stafford assizes. Although it was clear that the condemned man, one of life's unfortunates, would not hang, the court was eerily hushed as the judge spoke the awful words. It is a memory that will never be erased.

If what follows may at times seem unduly sympathetic to some of those who hanged, despite their terrible crimes, it is because capital punishment surely has no part in any society calling itself civilised.

Edward Garner
Derby
April 2000

Out of the Shadows

WHEN Harry Pierrepoint placed the noose around the victim's neck and then sent him crashing through the scaffold's trapdoors, he had done more than routinely send a murderer to the next world. For the dead man was Edward Slack of Chesterfield, and he was the last person to be judicially executed in Derbyshire. The date was 16 July 1907, and the venue His Majesty's Prison, Derby, a massive, sombre place of stone sprawled like a barrier across the top of Vernon Street. Later they took away Slack's body, smothered it in quicklime and buried it without ceremony in a graveyard exclusive to murderers. The execution shed resumed its role of garaging the prison van. Pierrepoint, England's principle hangman, returned home to Yorkshire.

While there is no problem in putting a date to the end of capital punishment in Derbyshire, assigning a beginning is obviously impossible. The earliest recorded execution is 1341, a year when no fewer than six people were executed. Hanging was the fate of two men and a woman for murdering a King's purveyor. Later their bodies were gibbeted on Ashover Moor, presumably, since that was the custom, close to the scene of their crime. Three men were hanged at Chapel-en-le-Frith for robbery with violence, again, followed by gibbeting or, less starkly, 'held in chains'.

Further evidence of those early times comes from Ilkeston. A gibbet was listed in Farey's *General View of the Agriculture and Minerals of Derbyshire of 1815*, although there was no mention of when it was last used. It stood tall and stark on the banks of the Erewash River and according to another source, the Derby historian Woolley, the former Lords of the Manor of Ilkeston had the judicial privilege of executing felons. This could mean that a gibbet had been there since the 14th century. John of Gaunt, possessor of vast estates in the region, granted the people of that town the right of paying half tolls at Nottingham market, provided they maintained the gibbet. There is perhaps a distinction between a gallows and a gibbet, even though the terms are often interchangeable. The former, generally a stout beam between two uprights, was for hanging people. A gibbet was a tall post, with an arm projecting at its top from which executed felons, secured in chains or a metal jacket, were suspended. Although there are broadsides and ballad sheets showing people being executed on gibbets, they were as a rule too high for such use.

A whisper is heard at Hanging Bridge, just west of Ashbourne. There is no positive evidence of how that name was come by, or that of Gallowstree Lane a little further on. Folk memory has seemingly survived while any written record has been lost.

With the death of William Woderove of Hope in 1431 comes the first detailed case of murder. In September, accompanied by Robert Eyre of Padley, he was riding from Chesterfield to Hulme. A quarrel broke out and in an attempt to soothe matters Eyre appealed to Woderove: 'Friend, you well know that we are kinsmen and called honest men, and therefore it is disgraceful for us to fight and for the whole country to hear us quarrel.' (This conversation in all likelihood was added by some Victorian amateur history enthusiast, a not unknown practice). Woderove, far from mollified, dismounted, drew his sword and struck Eyre on the head. But for a large piece of cloth fastened there, Eyre would likely have been killed. He then dismounted, retreated to the protection of a hedge and, drawing his

sword, faced his attacker. In turn, Woderove was struck on the head. The blade went deep and two days later he died. Eyre was arrested and indicted for murder by John Dunbalen, one of the King's coroners for Derbyshire. At the subsequent trial in Derby, Eyre was found not guilty and acquitted. In returning their verdict, the jury laid the blame for Woderove's death on a Welsh labourer, Peter Swordman of Brecknock. He was arrested and, although no record survives, can be presumed to have hanged for the crime.

Going back further in time, Derbyshire's penal chronicle will have to be assumed against the backdrop of history. How serious crimes were dealt with before the Romans came to England can only be guessed at. They brought with them the axe, but that was a punishment reserved for offenders from society's upper strata. For the lower orders, common hanging, believed to have originated in Persia, would be quite sufficient. After the Romans came the Anglo-Saxons and in AD695 a thief was executed, the first known occurrence in England. How he was done to death we are not told. Several methods were available: burning, stoning, hanging, drowning, beheading or, if in hilly country, thrown from a great height.

Today we live in a society from which capital punishment has (only recently) been totally banished. Therefore, it comes as a surprise to learn that a similar state of affairs prevailed nearly 1,000 years ago. William the Conqueror put an end to executions, except for treason. *'I also forbid that anyone be slain or hanged for any fault, let his eyes be put out and let him be castrated. And this command shall not be violated under pain of fine in full to me.'* Those administering justice could, if appropriate, amend that edict by ordering the chopping off of hands or feet, or maybe the removal of nose and ears. Interestingly, the word 'murder' comes from this period, being a derivative of 'murdrum', a fine imposed on anyone foolish enough to kill a Norman. Compensation was very much a feature of criminal law, seen as giving more all-round satisfaction. Henry I restored the death penalty and in 1120 laid down that thieves could be summarily hanged. Since theft with its many guises was by far the commonest crime, employment prospects for hangmen improved no end and never really looked back for the ensuing seven centuries.

Throughout the career of capital punishment, the Church always gave its support. Indeed, studies in recent years have demonstrated that had it not, then the death sentence most likely would have withered and died far sooner than it did. When the need for Biblical approval arose, for example on the question of dissection or gibbeting, churchmen could be relied upon to tease out the necessary authority. Even the barbaric hanging, drawing and quartering was countenanced, thereby earning it the sobriquet of 'Godly butchery'. Whereas the Bible could be quoted as being against execution, citing that Cain slew Abel but was not himself executed, others were pointing out that Haman built a gallows 50 cubits high from which to hang Mordecai.

The Church was part of the Establishment; it drew much of its power and acceptance by supporting the State, of which it could be regarded as a department. Capital punishment becomes more understandable when it is accepted that laws were made not only to ensure the authority and well-being of the State but also to keep the masses in line. Primarily, the law (serving the State) protected property and wealth, and those two commodities were in the hands of relatively few (including the Church) and jealously guarded. They also made the laws. The common enemy always was the lower orders. Their numbers at first were troublesome. As the country's population grew, then increasingly they were regarded as more a threat.

Came the Tudors and executions entered their most voracious period. Between 1530 and 1630 it has been estimated that something like 75,000 were put to death. Henry VIII strengthened his grip through judicial slaughter. During his reign, 1509 to 1547, it is calculated that 2,000 were executed each year, a figure perhaps difficult to accept, although the rate was unquestionably high. Was it recognition of the executioners' workload that the Merry Monarch permitted them to work on Sundays, the only incumbent to show such consideration? Death by boiling in water was for a few years included in the list of approved killing methods.

While executions had always been public spectacles, the Tudors deliberately turned them into happenings designed to attract the multitude. The Grand Guignol of street theatre would not be an inappropriate description. Gradually a ritual became established that would, with the occasional shift of scenery, remain in place for 300 years. Tyburn, London's principal execution site, became and remains still a name grimly synonymous with legal butchery. The capital, naturally, sent more to the gallows. It followed that the rites, the official processions, the religious observances, the speeches, the final confession, the curious folk beliefs, and then the actual killing were more conscientiously and grandly performed there than their provincial equivalents. Nonetheless, regional hanging days adhered to a familiar pattern, if not always so strictly or with such emphasis. While spreading the message of deterrence might be thought the prime reason for those haggard displays, the underlying motive was always to demonstrate authority. Public slaughter highlighted in easily and quickly understood tableaux, the State's right to exercise power over the individual even to the extent of depriving of life when necessary. State interpretation of circumstances deemed what was necessary.

That the State carefully guarded its licence over life was illustrated in an incident involving the head of one of Derbyshire's most powerful families, Sir George Vernon of Haddon Hall. Born around 1508, he died in 1567. Last of the male Vernons and father of Dorothy Vernon of romantic myth, he was called, with justification, King of the Peak.

A servant reported that the badly beaten body of a pedlar had been discovered. Last seen alive, he had been entering the house of a local toll-keeper. Evidence, however, was not strong. Vernon decided to see if the perpetrator could be flushed out by 'bier proof', an old superstition claiming that if a murdered corpse was ever touched by its killer then the fatal wound would bleed again. A colourful drawing in the famous *Lucerne Chronicles* of 1513 depicted a husband, naked and tied by the waist, being led to a coffin containing his murdered wife. Touching her knife wound caused it to weep blood, thus proving his guilt. Vernon had the pedlar's corpse brought to Haddon and laid out beneath a sheet in the main hall. Among those summoned to the investigation was the toll-keeper, vehemently denying any involvement. Sir George pulled back the sheet, ordering that everyone present would individually touch the body. For the toll-keeper it was too much. He fled from the hall; Vernon ordered his men to follow. The fugitive succeeded in getting through Bakewell, but his pursuers were never far behind and they captured him near the toll-gate at Ashford-in-the-Water. They hanged him in a field close by. For years, the site was called the Galley or Gallows Field.

Such high-handed action reached the ears of authority in London and the King of the Peak was ordered to the capital to explain himself at court. After all, the toll-keeper had been entitled to a trial in a court of law, not by superstition. Anyway, powerful men needed to be reminded and restrained from time to time. Vernon successfully argued his case and, suitably cautioned, returned to Haddon. This episode demonstrates the Tudors' policy of bringing about the transition from private vengeance to Crown authority. It must be remembered that the Tudors were responsible for establishing a national bureaucracy that welded England into a nation. Not so many years before, Vernon's summary justice would have raised little serious comment; he had been reminded that there now was a superior authority.

Had the pedlar's murderer been arraigned before the assize court at Derby then his execution would have been attended by far greater ceremony than the hurried lynching at Gallows Acre. Immediately after the court's verdict he would have been either dragged to the gallows on a trundle, a form of sledge, or bundled into an open cart on which his coffin already waited. Crowds raucous for the ritual circus would have lined the way, jeering or cheering, blaspheming and swearing, as the mood dictated. Accompanying dignitaries represented authority, while priests persistently urged the condemned man to confess his sins, to pray and seek the repentance necessary if his soul was to attain the immortal state. It would also be expected of him to renounce his wickedness and ask the crowd to recognise the justice of his situation.

Finally, the public confession. There can be no disputing that many of these admissions were the fruits of clergymen's efforts; either that or many highly articulate felons ended their lives strangling on the hangman's noose. Printed 'dying confessions' (known in the trade as 'lamentations') first made their appearance in the 16th century. Evidence exists that some were the result of monetary understandings between clergymen and printers. If the hundreds of extant confessions are to be accepted at face value, then the good life could have been achieved and maintained from the outset by eschewing low company, loose women and strong drink. Sadly, life has never been that simple.

As with the preceding ceremonies, the gallows, too, evolved. At first, it was nothing more than a tree with a convenient branch or a plank suspended between two trees. Depending on the degree of business, or when the Tudors got into their stride, more permanent structures became necessary. At first a simple thing, two wooden uprights with a stout crossbeam from which to suspend the victim, or maybe three placed in a triangle to accept three crosspieces. Such a construction, known familiarly as the Triple Tree or the Three-Legged Mare, was erected at Tyburn on the outskirts of London. A dozen suspended corpses was by no means a rare sight. While unlikely that Derby ever warranted such hanging accommodation, there must have been more demand than usual in 1537 when two gallows were built which, it could be inferred, were permanent features to replace the *ad hoc* plank between two trees arrangement.

Earliest executions were little more than the condemned mounting a ladder and death summoned by the hangman kicking it away. Sometimes the victim jumped off in the faint hope of a quick finish. The only calculation entered into was the height of the victim; the more relevant body weight remained ignored until the latter part of the 19th century.

Executions spawned their own vocabulary. The condemned, or 'gallows apples', rarely hanged. They were 'turned off', 'launched into boundless eternity', 'topped', 'despatched', maybe they 'danced to death', 'walked on air', 'took a leap into the dark', or mundanely 'stretched'. Officially, deaths were almost always 'quick', 'immediate', or maybe 'after a short time'. A 'gallows bird' was the corpse. Gibbeting may have sounded less dreadful when termed 'held in chains'. Those with a criminal bent were wont to be described as a 'hang-in-chains'. Such avoidance of stark reality found Home Secretaries in later years turning down appeals against sentence with the notation: 'The law to take its course.'

In reality, death was painful and tardy. Five minutes or more was not uncommon. Also, it was death by strangulation, by its nature never a speedy conclusion. The swifter despatch by dislocation of the cervical vertebrae and rupture of the spinal cord lay a long way off. Of all people, it was the hangmen who eventually devised and perfected reliable and quicker methods of drawing the final curtain, including the most effective placing of the noose's knot: under the angle of the left jaw. Clergymen seem not to have protested at the too-often distressful death agonies; the same comment applies to doctors who later were to attend executions. Everyone would have been only too aware of the appalling agonies

suffered by victims as they groped for air, frantically clawing at the narrowing noose in futile efforts to ease the terrible pressure. Families and friends would rush forward and attempt to hasten matters by clinging on the victim's flailing legs and forcibly pulling him down – a task at which hangmen might assist. Such horrifying scenes rarely, if ever, were dwelt on in newspapers or ballads and broadsheets. (In the 1930s, the Home Office instructed that all judicial deaths took place over a 'very short interval'.).

Placing a white hood or cap on the victim's head was introduced in the 18th century and soon became customary at all hangings. It should not be thought such headwear was an act of kindness, however. By the time the scaffold was reached, the condemned man would have been only too aware of what awaited, even in the inebriated state many often were. In the cart taking him there, he would have sat or stood on his coffin, sometimes with the strangling rope tied about his waist. The noise of the boisterous, jostling, noisy, often half-drunken crowds would not have diminished the gallows' outline, nor the hangman waiting for the rope, or drowned the mournful monotone of accompanying clergyman. No, the cap was for the benefit of the spectators. Officialdom did not want the contorted face of death to be seen.

Awful things happened. Eyes, ears and lips became discoloured and swollen. Eyes turned red with blood and popped forward, at times almost quitting their sockets. The face became misshapen. But what the cap could not hide were the screams, nor the staggering around the scaffold, the pathetic wrestling with the executioner or the body slumped from fainting or lapsing into unconsciousness. Should the victim lose the use of his legs, then they sat him on a chair and carried on with the court's sentence. Nor would the cap staunch the expulsion of bodily fluids, the urinating, the blood-flecked spittle. Such nastiness was never reported in street literature and, later, the newspapers. The *Derby Mercury*, like many of its contemporaries, might mention an occasional lapse into bad behaviour (rarely described) being content to routinely claim that, as ever, death was quick. Individual eyewitness statements preserved a more realistic picture of hanging day horrors.

Executions drew the crowds, as they were intended to. In the 19th century, Charles Dickens attended several. 'No sorrow, no salutary terror, no abhorrence, no seriousness; nothing but ribaldry, debauchery, levity, drunkenness and flaunting of vice in 50 other shapes', he observed. Other sources show that scathing description equally applicable at any time throughout the long reign of public hangings. While not so eloquent, even the *Derby Mercury* eventually frowned:

'*...but we fear that the many, as executions are now conducted and spoken about, are induced to regard the punishment rather as the fate of a hero or martyr; while the less sentimental care so little for the awful spectacle, as to look upon it with the same feelings as they would gaze upon a brutal fight, and indulge all*

sorts of libidinous ribaldry, and ferocious ruffianism, and obscene mirth under the very shadow of the gallows itself...for never did we see such a revolting assemblage of low rascals and repulsive woman as on that occasion.'

The spectacles never deterred. They were a part of community activities, the eagerly awaited highlight of a fair day. That fair days frequently hosted executions was no coincidence. A hanging fair, or 'collar day', meant bigger crowds. And, in turn, that meant more business for traders. Whatever the name of the day, it was a hideous business to set before the people. A considerable time would pass before the lesson sank in, that the death penalty was a momentary thing, devoid of any restraining value. Watchers were corrupted by what they saw: an act of extreme violence that taught and inured people to violence. In the end, the law itself was being mocked.

* * * * * *

TIME'S withering passage made it inevitable that Derbyshire's known catalogue of capital punishment for the 16th and 17th centuries and the earlier part of the 18th is cogently unrepresentative and incomplete (see *Appendix A*). An example is Cromwell's Commonwealth (1649-1660), 11 years of increased penal severity (particularly for theft) and capital punishment. Not a single execution is noted for Derbyshire. That has to be the aftermath of lost sources, not astonishingly good behaviour or undetected crime. However, details have survived of two most notable incidents outside that period. Both about people dying for their religious beliefs, essentially for holding them at the wrong time.

On 1 August 1556, a congenitally blind woman of 22 was burned to death at the stake for the offence of heresy. The place was Windmill Pit at Derby, close by the turnpike on Burton Road, about a mile from All Saints' Church. Joan Waste's fundamental error was to continue publicly embracing Protestantism after the Catholic Mary I came to the throne. Her reign (1553-1558) was not a good time to hold opinions conflicting with those of Rome. Many did, and nearly 300 were put to death. Joan was the eldest daughter of William Waste, barber and rope-maker of All Saints' parish. Growing up, she took to visiting Derby's disgusting gaols, a task not without risk to health. At the debtors' prison, Joan befriended John Hurt, an elderly man of 70. Each time she called, he would read out a chapter from the New Testament. At other times, she made her way to John Pemerton, clerk to the parish church, or other like-minded people, listening attentively as they too read from the Scriptures. With that highly developed memory the blind often acquire, Joan Waste, as well as making her way unerringly through Derby's narrow streets, could also quote great lengths of the Bible and debate theological interpretation.

In the relatively tolerant reign of Edward VI (1547-1553), her religious espousal was not too hazardous an undertaking. With the arrival of Bloody Mary the atmosphere changed. Her determination to establish Roman Catholicism meant the end of Joan Waste, who steadfastly refused to abandon her convictions. Obvious and vocal, clashing with the ecclesiastical hierarchy was inevitable. To them she was a heretic, a capital offence.

In answering charges against her, Joan faced the Diocesan Bishop, Ralph Baine, and his fanatical chancellor, Dr Anthony Draycott. The latter was the one she had to fear. When Bishop Baine showed an inclination to perhaps accept her sincerity, the chancellor sharply reminded him: 'My Lord, you know what you do? you may in no case answer for a heretic.' Pointedly, Dr Draycott asked if she would renounce her faith. Joan sealed her fate by the reply that she could not and accepted whatever judgement was passed. The climate of the times allowed only one verdict, guilty. That meant death at the stake. On her last day, Joan Waste was taken to All Saints' Church, to endure a venomous diatribe from the lips of Dr Draycott. There was no trace of com-passion or sorrow over her imminent destiny. She was blind 'not only in her bodily eyes but also in the eyes of her soul'. The good doctor pointed out that while 'her body should be presently consumed with material fire, so her soul should be burned in hell with everlasting fire…' He warned the congregation not to pray for her. It was unlawful.

So Joan Waste was led away to Windmill Pit, guided by her brother Roger's outstretched hand. Dr Draycott did not attend the incineration; he returned to his room at an inn and retired to bed. Apparently his victim, for she surely was nothing less, died with commendable dignity.

Death by burning, usually reserved for women, was not just a matter of lashing the individual to a stake and setting fire to bundles of faggots piled up about its base. It was customary to first strangle the victim. The executioner passed a rope through a pulley some way up the stake and slipped its noose around her neck. Some preferred the victim to stand on a stool and kick it away at the appropriate moment. As an aid to combustion, tar was smeared over the body. A barrel or two filled with tar would also be added to the pyre. At a signal the executioner hauled on the rope and, hopefully, the condemned would die. Once life was thought extinct, the faggots were lit. Unfortunately, death at times followed its presumption. Flames severed the rope and the living victim dropped screaming into the flames.

There is no extant contemporary local archive referring to Joan Waste or her martyrdom. The sole source rests in Foxe's *Book of Martyrs*, first published in Latin in 1559 at Basle and in its final and enlarged form (in English) in 1563. Often reprinted and 'edited' to suit prevailing prejudices, it became a familiar sight in succeeding centuries in churches throughout England and Scotland. That the author was John Foxe (1517-1587), a Lincolnshireman, could be a warning, not to reject Joan's story, but to be wary. Foxe, martyrologist and ordained in his later years, was cast in the same fanatical mould as Dr

Draycott but with the Protestant glaze. When Mary I came to the throne, Foxe thought it prudent to leave England, taking up residence in Frankfurt and later Strasbourg. There he remained, delaying his return until Mary had been dead two years.

Foxe, therefore, had not been in England when Joan died. Of course, that would not necessarily mean the reports he received were unreliable, but might have over-emphasised certain aspects. Churchmen were as adept at propaganda as anyone. However, the character and motives of this zealous anti-Catholic must perforce raise reservations. One biographer thought him 'temperamentally incapable of writing what is now called scientific history'. Even amongst Foxe's contemporaries there were those who questioned his credibility, or indeed if he even possessed any. In the *Book of Martyrs* he recognises only evil and cruelty in the 'Romische Prelates', and lingered over vivid descriptions of torture.

Also to be borne in mind is that when Joan Waste stood indicted before Bishop Baine and Dr Draycott it was an ecclesiastical court which, while it could condemn her, lacked the authority to sentence her to death. That decision resided with the Privy Council and, and as far is known, no record has survived. Nonetheless, it can be accepted that Joan Waste did die at the stake. The execution's relative isolation might be sufficient testimony in itself: a broadcasting of Mary's ruthless determination to subject her kingdom to Rome's thrall.

Mary died in 1558, to be succeeded by

Elizabeth I. Under her, the kingdom shifted over to Protestantism. That meant conflict with Rome and, more immediately, Catholic Spain. In 1570 the Pope excommunicated her. More lenient than Mary, Elizabeth did not cause Catholics to suffer to the same degree as had Protestants, although they were viewed with suspicion and at times treated severely. With Elizabeth's exclusion, Rome held England's Catholics as being no longer bound in allegiance to her. Catholic families had now to be most circumspect; too overt and the authorities could respond harshly. Even so, Elizabeth still inclined to tolerance; she was wary of abstract theology. In 1584, she declared that 'never a Catholic should be troubled for religion, so long as they lived like good subjects'. Two years later, however, nerves tautened with the uncovering of the Babington Plot to free the imprisoned Mary Queen of Scots. Anti-Catholic feelings hardened further in 1588 with the knowledge that Spain was preparing to launch its Armada for the invasion of England. The loyalty of English Catholics came under closer scrutiny: was it to the Pope or to England? Disguised priests travelled the country to celebrate Mass at secret centres. Understandably, Elizabeth and her ministers were not inclined to linger in debate over the question. Weaved into this complex tapestry was the tragedy of the Padley Martyrs.

The Fitzherberts were a long established Catholic family, which had suffered much for its faith. In 1588, Padley Hall near Hathersage was one of their residences. Held under tenancy by John Fitzherbert, younger brother of Sir Thomas Fitzherbert, it was considered a place safe enough for peripatetic priests to hold Mass. A dangerous practice as was discovered when, on 12 July, the Earl of Shrewsbury, Lord Lieutenant of Derbyshire and fourth husband of the spectacularly ambitious Bess of Hardwick, arrived with his men in a series of speculative raids. His lightning enterprise netted him John Fitzherbert and, hiding in a chimney, two priests, Father Nicholas Garlick of Glossop and Father Robert Ludlam from Radbourne. For them, their capture could not have been more ill-timed. Spain's Armada was now heading towards England. Shrewsbury had the three prisoners, along with some household members, bound and escorted to Sheffield Castle. Later, they were transferred to Derby gaol.

Awaiting trial, the three met with a third priest, Richard Simpson. A Yorkshireman from near Ripon, Father Simpson had been arrested earlier that year and sentenced to death. For some reason, there had been a stay of execution. On 23 July the three priests were sentenced to death for the offence of having taken Orders abroad and subsequently returned to England, 'in defiance of Her Majesty's Statute'. Fitzherbert, for having sheltered Garlick and Ludlam, was also sentenced to die but was spared. He remained imprisoned until August 1590 when he was transferred to London's Fleet Prison. Gaol fever claimed him the following November.

The priests spent their final hours together

while in the Channel the English navy fought a running battle with the Spanish. According to some accounts, they shared their cell with a woman who had committed murder and, too, was awaiting execution. They reconciled her to God and before dying, she professed her new faith. On the morning of 25 July, large crowds gathered about St Mary's Bridge where the sentences were to be carried out, on its east, or town side. First to approach the scaffold was Father Simpson and, noticing him hesitate, Father Garlick exchanged places. Father Ludlam brought up the rear.

Unlike the condemned woman, the priests' punishment was not to be by straightforward hanging. They were to be hanged, drawn and quartered, a fate reserved for those guilty of offences that directly threatened the State, usually translating as treason. Death was the ultimate aim, but the nightmare ritual preceding that merciful release was with the deliberate intention of humiliating and mutilating the dying body. First, the victims were tied on hurdles and dragged by horses to the scaffold area. To deny them clear air or any vestige of dignity, they were pulled backwards, their heads declined downwards. Although each hanged, they did not do so sufficiently long enough to die. Still breathing, the three were cut down. What followed was total barbarity. First their private parts were exposed, cut off and burnt before their eyes, symbolising they would leave behind no unworthily begotten generation. Then came the removal of the bowels and other intestines, and their ritual ignition. Finally, the executioner's axe rose and fell, chopping off the heads in which the victims' mischief had been born. Still the sentence had not been completed. Each mutilated corpse had to be hacked into four, soaked in preserving solution and thrown into wicker baskets, to be carried off on hurdles to different locations. At each stop, some mangled piece would be stuck high up on a pole so all those passing would know that something dreadful had happened at Derby.

That same night, a small group of brave people removed some of the priests' bloodied remains and hurried them away for a decent and secret burial. Their actions were observed by a night watchman, who saw something of interest in another direction. Over the next few nights the remaining pieces were gathered in and interred. Nicholas Garlick's head, it is believed, lies buried in Tideswell churchyard.

Nearly 230 years would pass before Derby heard its next, and last, bloody sentence for treason.

A year after the Padley Martyrs' execution, another priest died. Father James Clayton, a native of Sheffield, studied in France for the priesthood, was ordained in 1584 and returned to England in 1585. By Christmas 1588, he was in Derby ministering to gaoled Catholics; their misdemeanours are not known. Such an undertaking was obviously risky and probably inevitable that he would be recognised eventually as a seminary priest. Arrested and charged with high treason, Father Clayton was condemned to death. He was found dead in his cell, a victim of gaol fever, on 22 July 1589.

ONE individual essential to this history has so far remained persistently anonymous. While there are details available, albeit sparse, of executions from the 14th to the 18th century, nothing is known about those who carried them out. They lurk unremarked in the shadows of the gallows. First published in 1732, the *Derby Mercury* dutifully recorded hangings for nearly two centuries yet waited until 1843 before first naming an executioner. That was Samuel Heywood, an Appleby man, who came twice to Derby and despatched four murderers to the next world.

Given the task hangmen performed on behalf of the State, this lack of identity might be thought understandable. Many would have preferred a degree of anonymity. Although there were individuals who gloried in their dreadful calling, they generally were busiest at Tyburn and their names known to all. Some would have journeyed to the provinces where men possessing their crude skills and disposition were perhaps scarce, but information is lacking. Killing someone who locally may have been well regarded, or at least sympathetically, by hundreds if not thousands of spectators would be best done as anonymously as was possible, probably behind a mask. No one ever held hangmen in high regard. They travelled unobtrusively and departed as quickly as they were able. To take life so deliberately and crudely, although sanctioned by State and Church, required some special characteristic many could not even begin to understand. Executioners dwelt at the edge of society. The abhorrence with which they were regarded to some extent served as their protection.

Not only were hangmen anonymous, they were invisible. While not naming them is perhaps understandable, this evasion even extended to their duties. Newspapers reports, the various forms of street literature describing hangings shied away from giving any account of the hangman, even to the point of just mentioning his sinister presence. We can read of an accused's trial, his life and crimes, the ministrations of the divines, the journey to the gallows and the execution, but the actions of the executioner remain unspoken. From the final speech at the gallows to being 'launched into boundless eternity', there was a universal ignoring of the man who pinioned the victim, perhaps supported him, pulled the white cap in place and slipped the noose around the neck. While it was not until the 1840s that the *Mercury* first gave the hangman's name, any description of his involvement waited until executions were no longer public events, but private matters conducted behind prison walls.

Periodically, someone attempted to put the hangman's role in perspective. One was Sir William Meredith who, in 1771 during a parliamentary debate on capital punishment, reminded the Commons:

'Some who hear me are perhaps blaming the judges, the jury and the hangman; but neither the judge, jury or hangman are to blame; they are but ministerial agents; the true hangman is the Member of Parliament; he who frames the

bloody law is answerable for all the blood that is shed under it.'

Hangmen were inclined to paraphrase Sir William's argument when questioned about their occupation.

Of England's executioners from the earlier period, the name of Jack Ketch remains supreme, if only as the hangman in the Punch and Judy shows. Ketch had a long career (1663 to 1686), and in addition to hanging ordinary felons officiated at the execution of the high-born who, having fallen foul of the law, had their heads chopped off. Hanging was considered a social disgrace, best reserved for the lower orders. Other duties included mutilation, flogging, branding, burning at the stake, and *peine forte et dure* (pain strong and long). The latter replaced starvation, having the advantage of being quicker, and more familiarly was known as pressing.

While sometimes causing death, pressing was not a death sentence as such, since its purpose was to force a defendant refusing to plead before a court, to answer either 'guilty' or 'not guilty' to whatever the accusation. Refusal to plead was legally termed 'mute of malice'. Property and its safeguarding were generally behind the silence. If an accused pleaded, then the risk was run of the property becoming forfeit; reticence ensured its protection.

The sentence ran as follows:

'That you be taken back to the prison whence you came, to a low dungeon into which no light can enter; that you be laid upon your back on the bare floor with a cloth around your loins but elsewhere naked; that there be set upon your body a weight or iron as great as you can bear, and greater. That you have no sustenance save on the first day three morsels of the coarsest barley; on the second day three draughts of stagnant water; on the third day bread as before; the next day water as before; until you die.'

To endure such inhuman punishment for even a single day would have demanded awesome courage. Most quickly entered a plea and took their chance in court. Those who persisted rarely lasted more than a few days, although a Nottingham woman is on record as surviving 40 days before being pardoned on a charge of murdering her husband. Pressing fell into disuse around 1735 and abolished in 1772. After 1827, refusals were entered as 'not guilty' pleas.

Only one case of pressing is known for Derbyshire. In 1665 a young woman died in a room at the County Hall in St Mary's Gate after declining to plead or give any evidence. In other words, the court considered her 'to be mute of malice', a phrase that has led some to believe, somewhat illogically, that the authorities had done someone to death only to belatedly realise that she was a mute in fact. Those suffering torture by weights gave ample evidence of their ability to talk. They answered questions, screamed, shouted, wept; did anything but enter a plea. The same story turns up in other parts of the country.

Returning to hangmen, a predecessor of Ketch was Derrick, a 'thorough-paced villain' according to a contemporary account, who held office from 1598 to 1610. Whether he devised some special form of gallows, by perhaps lifting up the victims, is not established but the name is perpetuated in mechanical devices designed to raise heavy objects. While those appointed executioners from perhaps the mid-19th century onwards were not necessarily disreputable or even former criminals, basic standards before then rarely applied. Some were as nasty as those they despatched. One was the notorious John Price. The last time he stepped on to a scaffold was to be hanged himself, in 1718, for murdering a woman. As a warning, his remains were afterwards held in chains.

Only one Derbyshire hangman has ever been identified with certainty. Deservedly he could be ranked alongside Ketch, Derrick and Price. John Crosland embarked on a long career around 1660 by executing his own father and elder brother. All three had been found guilty of horse stealing, a common felony. According to the Derby historian, William Hutton (1723-1815), the court 'entertained the cruel whim' of offering each of the accused a pardon, on condition they hanged the other two. In declining, the father said he could not take away the lives of those to whom he had given life. The elder son also rejected the offer, declaring he would not wish to be the remaining branch of a family he had destroyed. Such qualms failed to trouble John Crosland. The manner in which he carried out the task impressed officials and shortly afterwards he was appointed Derbyshire's own executioner. News of his abilities spread and

from time to time neighbouring counties employed his services. Hutton claimed that if a hanging did not go according to plan and the victim struggled for too long, then the diligent Crosland completed the job, 'with violence'. Presumably, that meant yanking down hard on the victim's kicking legs.

Crosland would have earned a reasonable if not respectable income. Hangings apart, his duties included administering whippings, branding thieves with a hot iron, and officiating at the stocks and pillory. He may have carried out the pressing of the young woman already referred to.

One exceptional pay-day that must have come his way was in August 1679, when no fewer than ten highwaymen were done to death. The total would have been higher had not two others turned King's Evidence. As it is, the multiple hanging qualifies as Derbyshire's known biggest. Derbyshire antiquarian Thomas Bateman's library catalogue lists a halfpenny broadsheet titled *Trial and Condemnation of 12 Highwaymen in Derby*, which gives a comprehensive account of the Bracy gang. The golden era for highwaymen lay between 1660 and 1710, almost coincidental with Crosland's odious career.

Led by Richard Bracy, a Nottingham man, the gang seemed to have come into being around 1677 and must have been one of the more successful operating outside the mecca of all highway robbers, the main roads coming out of London. The gang operated all over the Midlands, but their main targets were Derby, Nottingham and Newark. Highwaymen were desperate individuals, and none came more so than Bracy. He took to the road at 18, with an established criminal record. As a boy he had been imprisoned for theft, and at 17 was believed to have murdered a servant girl. According to the broadsheet, he would torture his victims if they were less than helpful. One who was not intimidated by him was Lady Jane Scroop. Her coach had been stopped by the gang outside Nottingham. Having collected £600 off her, Bracy decided to add rape to her humiliation. She proved more than a match for him. Lady Jane slammed the coach door so hard that the highwayman tumbled out on to the road. Startled by all the commotion, the horses bolted, carrying her away to safety.

While a little is known about Bracy, only the names, all reputed to be local men, of his followers have come down: John Baker, John Barker, Roger Brookham, Daniel Buck, Joseph Gerrat, Thomas Gillat, William Loe, Thomas Ouldome, Richard Piggen, John Robottom and Andrew Smedley. Their first known outing was on the house of John Monday (Mundy?) at Morton, to the north of Alfreton. They 'bound the Esquire and all his Family in their beds and using great insolence by threats to make them confess their Treasures'. Intimidation proved effective, for the robbers left Morton carrying gold and silver worth more than £1,800.

For a while the Bracy gang enjoyed considerable success. They ranged everywhere, on one raid striking at Ockbrook just outside Derby. There was nothing romantic about them. They were cold, brutal and callous, killing when it became necessary. They were at an inn planning a raid, when they were overheard by a potboy. Seizing him, the robbers disregarded his frantic entreaties for mercy and slew him. The body was buried in a cellar.

For nearly two years, the Bracy gang preyed on the Derbyshire and Nottinghamshire roads. Downfall began when Richard Bracy was ambushed at an inn kept by his wife. A Justice of the Peace was informed of the highwayman's presence by one of the servants. Getting an armed party together, the JP had the inn surrounded. There was a brief pistol fight and Bracy was taken. For three months the remaining 11 gang members carried on with their robberies, but they missed Bracy's leadership. One by one they were caught. All 12 were arraigned to appear at the August assizes in Derby. John Piggen and John Baker gave evidence against the other gang members and so escaped the gallows. Ten were hanged in what may have been the biggest multiple hanging in the county's history.

Crosland died around 1705, having carried out his duties into 'extreme old age…Loving none and beloved by none, he spent a life of enmity with man.' As he walked the streets of Derby, children would scamper after him, hurling abuse. Hearing the hangman's name silenced crying babies. No one mourned his going. While volunteering to kill his father and brother can only be regarded as weird, if not actually unique, agreeing to execute others to earn a reprieve was by no means unheard of.

Lincoln witnessed such an incident in 1786, while York, notorious for its busy gallows, was not without examples. In Ireland, a woman's offer was taken up. Derbyshire would produce at least two more volunteers, long after Crosland had gone off to plead with St Peter.

One murderer, while perhaps avoiding Crosland's clutches, did not escape the death penalty. The story behind the naming of Gibbet Moor, rising behind Chatsworth House, while familiar enough is almost certainly an exaggeration. A vagrant called on an old woman's cottage near Baslow, and begged some food. She replied that there was nothing for idlers the like of him. Unfortunately, she was cooking bacon at the time and the tramp, enraged by her retort, grabbed the pot of boiling fat and forced the liquid down her throat. She scalded to death. Arrested and tried, the man was sentenced to be gibbeted alive. And, the tale goes on, the Earl of Devonshire down at Chatsworth, could hear the man's screams as he struggled against death in his iron cage. So distressed was the Earl that he used his influence to bring about the end of that savage penalty. Although no date can be fixed for the incident, it would have taken place between 1618 and 1694, the era of the four Earls of Devonshire.

There is no reason to doubt the murder nor that a vagrant was executed. The story's probable origin is that he was hanged and then gibbeted. The hangmen bungled (an occupational habit) and what was presumed a corpse spluttered back to life on Gibbet Moor. An incident not without parallel. In 1777, near Durham, a highwayman's execution was similarly mishandled. To put him out of his misery the guard of a passing stagecoach shot him dead. There appears to be no authentic or acceptable reports of sentences of live gibbeting.

Towards the Bloody Code

S O FAR there has been a general lack of detailed local information concerning executions. However, as the 18th century advanced, more and progressively reliable sources began to appear. Newspapers made their appearance, supplementing the already well established ballads, broadsheets and chapbooks. Execution sheets, usually more descriptive (while not always reliable) than the more expensive newspapers, were immensely popular and remained so until the end of public hangings. Sales in the tens of thousands were by no means uncommon. Spectators crowding round the gallows seemed never to tire of such publications, albeit remarkably similar in content and style. That they appeared within minutes of the hanging could only mean that printers expected no hitch in rituals well honed by time and practice. Sales were equally brisk through the remarkably efficient countrywide distribution network travelled by itinerant ballad singers and hawkers.

An entertaining account from early 19th century Derbyshire tells us:

'These sheets were carried round the villages and sold at one penny each the first and second days after the Assizes were ended, afterwards coming down to half that amount…I remember once an edition being carried through our village by a vendor who was not only very early with his news-sheet but in a hurry to be gone. He arrived with a large bundle on his arm shortly after noon, and very quickly supplied the wants of our straggling roadside village. The sheets were perused and re-perused at the 'smithy-shop', and the merits of each sentence discussed – in some cases the case was re-tried; but it was some hours before some one, slightly sharper than his fellows, discovered that the early edition was a quantity of unsold stock of the previous editions of the previous midsummer!…When there was a murder in that list (happily not frequently), these vendors reaped a large harvest, for a supplementary sheet was issued which

An early example of an illustration for a broadside or execution sheet.

described very minutely the incidents of the murder, the antecedents of the murderer and his victim, with a motive for the crime. If the sentence of death was carried out there would appear 'The last Dying Speech and Confession', whether a speech and confession had been made or not. Sometimes a doggerel would appear detailing in verse, which might be sung or said, all the horrors. But worst of all…was the canvas daub, which in horrid colours and most minute untruthfulness pictured the crime in all its phases. A descriptive ballad was sung and sold by the owners of the canvas, who generally did a roaring trade.'

Unfortunately, this popular form of literature was printed on poor quality paper using similar property ink. Consequently, survival rate was low. The result is that old newspapers have now become the primary, most readily available and continuous source of information. In the early days, the *Derby Mercury*, as did other provincial newspapers, relied heavily on national and international news. Local matters were accorded maybe a column or two at the most. Derby, remember, was then a relatively small country town where everyone knew what was going on anyway; the wider, less accessible news was what people demanded. However, always reported and gradually more in depth were the twice yearly assizes trying the more serious criminal and civil cases. The latter were pleaded before the Nisi Prius bar, while the Crown bar tried the former.

Derbyshire assizes went back to the 12th century, the earliest sharing the same court with Nottinghamshire. Derby's burgesses were unhappy with such an arrangement. In time they succeeded in getting the court moved to Sawley, that venue being mutually convenient. By the end of the 14th century, the county had won the right to hold its own assizes. Judges and their colourful retinues travelled periodically to assize towns, which eventually were organised into regional circuits. In 1558 the Midland Circuit came into being, with Derbyshire included. The system survived until 1971, when the assizes were replaced by Crown Courts.

As a rule, the assizes were held around each March and July. The arrival of the judges and their officials was an event of great civil and social importance, surrounded with appropriate pomp and circumstance. Derby's commercial interests ranked the court periods as one of their busiest times, together with the hanging days which, unhappily for some, followed closely on, often being a fair day. Accompanied by the Sheriff and as many local dignitaries as could get themselves included, the judges and their entourage were met on the road and escorted into town. Not welcomed was the ragged army of pickpockets and beggars that invariably followed on. The noisy, colourful arrival was followed by a special service at All Saints' Church to mark the formal opening of business, with some suitable text chosen from the Scriptures. Religious duties dispensed with, there was then the solemn, stately procession of bewigged and gowned judges, officials and dignitaries to the courthouse. An important and august occasion now sadly removed from the county calendar.

Criminal cases were heard before a judge and jury and the defendant had to plead or, in some cases, run the risk of being subjected to *peine forte et dure*. Before any prisoners were tried, the judge advised the Grand Jury – an assembly of 12 men of property – on the cases listed on the calendar, guiding them on points of law where necessary. That jury would retire to consider each case and establish if, in its opinion, each prisoner had a case answer. If not, then he would be released. It says something for the system that such decisions were by no means rare. Should more evidence be needed, then the charge would be held over until it became available. Those having a case to answer then appeared before the judge, who sat with a trial or petty jury. Not until as late as 1898 could an accused give evidence on their own behalf. Before then, any statement made was not on oath and therefore could not be admitted into the proceedings. Witnesses would give evidence, for and against, while the accused's version of events had to be presented through his legal representative.

In the remote times, those found guilty on capital charges were hanged on gallows erected close by the courthouse. Since executions were carried out in public, there arose the need for recognised sites that would accommodate the largest numbers of spectators. Judicial killings were officially regarded as deterrents, a belief never borne out in reality. If gibbeting were included, then the corpse would be taken down and usually shifted to a site close to the scene of the original crime, although near the dwelling of the deceased's victim was sometimes, though rarely, preferred.

Before the building of the County Hall in Derby's St Mary's Gate in 1660, the assizes were held in the original guildhall or town house on the Market Place. Plague was an ever-present threat and the court was obliged to remove to safer locations on at least two occasions. Once was to Chesterfield in 1608 and when the judges left town five men and a woman were heading for the gallows at Tapton Bridge. The second time was in 1645. Then the pestilence was not thought so virulent since the court moved merely to other premises in Derby, in Friar's Close, a private estate once part of a Dominican friary in what is now Friar Gate. There was at least one execution: Richard Cockrum swinging for

killing a man called Mills, a servant at the Angel Inn in the Cornmarket. Cockrum's hanging is of particular note, being the first recorded as taking place on Nuns' Green, an area of common land on Derby's west side.

Printers of ballads and broadsides detailing murders, trials and hangings, would use the itinerant army of singers and musicians to sell their publications. This etching dated 1760 shows 'Singing Sam of Derbyshire' who undoubtedly would have supplemented a precarious income with such sales.

The area was first given to the nunnery of St Mary in the 14th century and after the Dissolution was mostly designated as commonage. It was a place where the ordinary people grazed their livestock, held their fairs, wagered on cockfights, or fought rival parishes. Clearly, it was the most obvious place for hangings, somewhere where the lower orders popularly gathered. After all, executions were intended as a deterrent. That a man named Okey was executed outside the Town Hall in 1599, crime unspecified, does not really detract from the presumption that the Green was where the gallows was principally sited until the early 19th century. Derby's ballad sheets and newspapers were curiously coy about identifying the killing ground. They were quite content to say that the prisoners were conveyed by cart 'to the usual place', or, more, menacingly, 'to the Tree' (always the capital T). There they remained suspended in death, 'for the usual time'. The latter, lasting an hour, was a crude but effective precaution against premature burial, having the additional advantage of airing the deterrent.

One of Derby's last few remaining notable buildings, the County Hall was looked on in legal circles as Pride of the Midland Circuit. Closure came in 1989. (At the time of writing it remains closed and sadly in sore need of renovation.) Apart from the courts, the building was also used for elections, the more important public meetings, not to mention as a gymnasium where sword fencers might practise. Extensively altered in 1828, society balls and dinners were added to its more traditional functions.

There were other, more morbid activities. For a period during the Bloody Code, the bodies of murderers were delivered there, straight from the scaffold. In a room dominated by a large table, surgeons publicly cut up the cadavers while their students and the curious looked on. Dissections, essential to medical advancement, could be most unpleasant. Surgeons everywhere complained about the dirty, smelly condition of bodies that had been living people little more than an hour before. As each body (known as a 'thing' in the trade) was sliced up, its various component were held up and their structure and function explained. To facilitate those unable to view the initial dissection, the bits and pieces remained on public display for a day or so, before unceremonious burial somewhere other than a churchyard, possibly beneath the gallows.

The first newspaper report of an assizes was in 1731, when the short-lived *The British Spy* or *Derby Postman*, informed its readers that on 9 April, William Billings had been hanged. Displaying an alarming lack of journalistic skills, the newspaper failed to supply any details of Billings, his crime, trial or execution (although promising to reveal more in the next edition, it never did). However, the comment was made that he 'behaved very unacceptably at the place of execution'. In fact, that criticism was one of the rare occasions when a Derby newspaper commented on a victim's behaviour when experiencing the last remaining moments of life. As a rule, readers were left with the impression that the condemned were quite subdued, dutifully repentant and died quickly. Other sources (from other scaffolds) dispel that notion.

While reluctant to go into details of a hanged man's last agonies, Derby's newspapers were not quite so inhibited when publishing accounts of executions elsewhere. The *Derby Mercury's* reporting is to be discussed later. In 1727, the *Derby Postman* printed an intriguing verse immediately after a report on proceedings at London's Newgate, but under the heading: 'Derby, 15 June'.

Joseph Reeves, of Conscious Thieves,
Most tir'd with this life, Sir,
On Sunday last, was try'd and cast,
Then hang'd, and left his Wife, Sir.
No Stay-tape strong, could do him wrong,
No binding made of Hair-lace;
But surly Hemp, which met the Pi…p, (sic)
And flew him on the Stair-case.
Even so may all his Cabbage Kindred die,
Whose Yards and Sheers doe Honesty defy.

Quite what it meant is a mystery; a murder, a suicide or an execution? Or a form of double entendre, on target in its day, but now beyond our understanding? Records around that period are intermittent; the only hanging known for 1727 was that of an unnamed man for horse stealing.

Derby had few recorded hanging days, traditionally Mondays, in the first half of the 18th century. That agreed with an overall national drop (outside London) in prosecutions, particularly for offences against property. Fifteen times the High Sheriff looked for an executioner, but only once for (joint) murderers. Among other felonies, some were choked to death for horse stealing, highway robbery, counterfeiting and, a rarity, a woman for rick burning, a subject of which more later. Traditionally, a hangman's fee was set at 13½d (about 6p today).

Certain, sometimes quite bizarre gallows customs and rituals evolved over the years. Long-held was the belief that the touch of a hanged man's hand would cure warts or similar skin blemishes. Women rushed forward to rub the suspended corpse's hand on the afflicted part. Children suffering from broken or fractured limbs, cuts and bruises, would be lifted up so that a dead man's sweat could cure them. The notion that possessing a piece of the execution rope improved the complexion persuaded other women to haggle with the hangman, to his pecuniary advantage. After-sales was an important part of his income, particularly selling off the deceased's clothing. There were the years when a hangman could negotiate a deal with either the representatives of anatomists seeking fresh corpses, or a victim's family, seeking to give him a decent burial. A most curious ritual, which has defied explanation, was that of some bystanders waiting until the body had been taken away and then slowly and silently shuffling their feet on the ground immediately around the gallows. Shavings from the hanging beam itself were much sought after; putting them in a bag hung around the neck was held to be a remedy for ague.

* * * * * *

THE sad story of the joint murderers, John Hewitt and Rosamond Ollerenshaw, might not have excited so much interest had it not involved one of Derby's more extraordinary criminal characters, the infamous Ellen Beare. If gossip of the day was well founded, or the evidence more compelling, then she too would have sat on her coffin in the open cart bound for Nuns' Green. The enormous excitement aroused over the case prompted Samuel Drewry, owner of the recently launched *Derby Mercury*, to publish a separate broadsheet containing the murderers' confession. Hewitt and Ollerenshaw had signed that document and handed it to Drewry on condition that 'no other' printer published it. Such exclusive rights deals were not uncommon nor was financial collusion between printer and clergyman attending the condemned. Cheque book journalism in its infancy. Broadsides were much sought after on hanging days and Drewry's venture was reported (by the *Mercury*!) as 'now very much bought up'. Additionally, the sheet carried the court proceedings, taken down in shorthand, as well as much background detail. Unfortunately, none have apparently survived. However, the *Mercury* printed reports while the local historian Hutton, a young boy at the time, was witness to some of the events.

John Hewitt, around 30 and a butcher by trade, lived in Stepping Lane with his wife, Hannah. Their marriage of seven years had been blessed with a daughter, whose presence did little to halt a deteriorating relationship. Hewitt kept his wife short of money and treated her violently. Hannah sought solace in drink, mostly at the Crown Inn on Nuns'

Green. Her husband frequented the same place, but not with her. One of the public house's great attractions was Ellen Beare, wife of the landlord, Ebenezer, a man seemingly bereft of personality. Hutton claimed that 'he bore no weight in the family, he was never mentioned'. Even his inn was referred to as 'Mrs Beare's', and customers addressed by her maiden name, Ellen Merriman. The lady herself was a popular mine host. A handsome woman of 30 with an education superior to her calling, she possessed an engaging manner that appealed to customers and gained their confidence.

Ellen Beare's popularity owed much to activities beyond dispensing good cheer. If Hutton is to be believed, and her trial and newspapers support him to some degree, she could perform abortions, provide the means to dispose of wives becoming troublesome to their husbands, and, intriguingly, was 'remarkably expert at procuring qualifications for men'. Employed by the Beares as a serving maid was Rosamond Ollerenshaw. A young woman, she formed an attachment for John Hewitt and willingly accepted his timeless story of a husband burdened with an unsuitable wife. Hutton stated that Hewitt was something of a ladies' man and Ellen Beare apparently was also attracted to him. While she could entertain no future with him, the maid could and did. So landlady, butcher and maid hatched a scheme to dispose of the troublesome, drunken Hannah.

Whether through fondness of the bottle or shortage of money to purchase food, Mrs

Hewitt presented a permanent pathetic image of someone sorely in need of a good meal. Ellen Beare, all fuss and concern, invited her to sit down and have some pancakes she herself had just made. Rosamond would serve them up. That was the last food the butcher's wife ever tasted. Within a short time she became violently ill and was sick in the inn yard. A pig ate the vomit and expired. Three hours later Mrs Hewitt collapsed and died. Such a sudden death aroused official suspicion, more so since Mrs Beare was involved. The surgeons were called in, who opened up the body and discovered arsenic. Ellen Beare, John Hewitt and Rosamond Ollerenshaw were arrested and remanded to the March 1732 assizes. Derby buzzed with excitement. At last Mrs Beare had gone too far; or so it seemed.

Hewitt and Ollerenshaw stood trial for murder, were found guilty and sentenced to death. Ellen Beare, too, had appeared in the dock but was committed to the July assizes, remanded for further inquiries into possible felony and murder. Three days after the execution the Mayor of Derby ordered the digging up of her garden at the Crown Inn. Whatever information was being acted on, it proved reliable. Probing shovels exposed the bones of a child aged between seven and eight months.

Those failing to gain admission to the court joined the enormous crowds milling around St Mary's Gate. Following the verdicts, rumours circulated that Rosamond Ollerenshaw had unwittingly saved Mrs Beare's life. When the judge asked the serving maid if her mistress was privy to the poison or ordered her to administer it, Hewitt trod on her foot indicating that she should agree. Rosamond took the pressure to mean her answer should be 'no'.

On the morning of their execution, 29 March, the couple sat miserably in the condemned pew at St Michael's Church and listened while the Revd William Lockett preached a sermon on the text, 'Be ye also ready', always a popular choice under such circumstances. Hewitt, dressed in a dark grey suit adorned with black cuffs and trimmings, comforted Rosamond for whom he clearly retained some affection. Dressed in a drab dress, her face remained almost hidden behind a large hat. When the time came to move she could barely stand. Hewitt put an arm around her waist and gently led her out the church and into the waiting cart. 'A vast number of people' swarmed around the vehicle as its horse drew it to its terrible destination. More spectators crammed and jostled in the streets leading to Nuns' Green. Also in the cart was the Revd Lockett, with a second clergyman, the Revd Henry Cantrell of St Alkmund's Church. Both relentlessly pursued the couple's immortal souls with a homily on another favoured text, 'Repent and be converted.' Hewitt had been handed a tract titled, *An account of the life and death of Thomas Savage who was executed for murder*, which he carefully read as the cart bumped and rattled along. Whether Savage was another unfortunate who had travelled the same route remains a mystery.

The Tree was reached. As their cart stopped, the two murderers stood up, stripped off their clothes to reveal they had already put on shrouds, a sight which only added 'to the awfulness of the occasion'. The practice of previously donning funeral garb was sometimes identified as a tradition among Roman Catholics, although evidence implies it was more widely adopted. Rosamond, by now incapable of standing, sagged limply as the hangman slipped the noose round her neck. Spectators swore she died even before the cart moved away. Hewitt kicked and lunged at space and after many agonising minutes, joined her. Their lifeless bodies were left dangling for an hour, turning slowly to and fro, before being taken down by the hangman and removed for burial.

With John Hewitt and Rosamond Ollerenshaw disposed of, attention turned to Ellen Beare. That formidable landlady stood at the bar of the July assizes, to answer three charges. First, for endeavouring to persuade Nicholas Wilson to murder his wife and handing over poison for that end. Secondly, with procuring an abortion for Grace Belfort of Nottingham by means of an iron instrument (a skewer, claimed Hutton, adding that her fee was five guineas), while the third charge was of destroying the foetus in an unnamed woman. Not mentioned were the bones exhumed at the Crown Inn.

On the first two charges, Mrs Beare was found guilty; the third was not proceeded with. Her punishment was to stand in the pillory for an hour at the next two Derby market days and in addition serve three years in prison, an unusually long term for the times. On 18 August, she was dragged to the Market Place and locked into the pillory. Large crowds had gathered to witness and ensure her misfortune, armed with eggs, rotting fruit and vegetables, and well filled chamber pots. By law, stones were not allowed, a rule often ignored. Hutton, one of the crowd, memorably recalled remembered that even 'the stagnate kennels were robbed of their contents and became the cleanest part of the street'. However, the mob was to be denied its fun. The pillory was in such a poor condition that the prisoner had no difficulty in breaking free. Leaping down into the astonished crowd, she fled down the Morledge. After her went the furious spectators, hurling their stinking refuse, while 'new missiles produced new ammunition; she appeared to be a moving heap of filth'. She was soon captured and among those who hurried her back was the late Rosamond Ollerenshaw's brother. But the stipulated hour had passed and so Ellen Beare was returned to prison, to contemplate her second appearance.

A week passed and the woman led to the pillory presented an unexpected sight. No longer the handsome woman in her prime, but an old-looking, swollen and decrepit crone. Having secured the creature in the repaired pillory, the attendant examined her more closely and discovered that Mrs Beare had dressed in several layers of clothes and tied a pewter plate round her head. Away came those safeguards and for an hour she struggled, screamed and raged helplessly against the crowd's fury and stinking missiles raining down. Then, back to prison and three years' enforced retirement. Such is the fickleness of human nature that when she was released in August 1735 a welcoming party, complete with band, greeted her outside the prison and marched her triumphantly off. But she was incorrigible. By December she was back in gaol, remanded on suspicion of receiving stolen goods. However much Ellen Beare deserved to be charged with taking life, it was a misdemeanour that put her in the dock. This time the sentence was a year in gaol and obliged to find sureties for three more. Hutton remembered that she recovered her health, spirits and beauty and died 'in the meridian of life'.

It should be pointed out that this story, a part of Derby's folklore, often identifies the public house in question as the Old White Horse, not the Crown. The Old White Horse was first recorded in 1732 and was demolished in 1876 to make way for the new railway station in Friar Gate, being on the line of Handyside's bridge which still spans the street there. The Crown on Nuns' Green was not recorded again after 1732 and so it is possible that it was re-named the Old White Horse to escape the unfortunate association with the notorious Mrs Beare. A report only three days after the trial of 1732 certainly refers to the pub as the Crown, so the Crown it must have been, but when the story was retold over generations, perhaps the new name of the inn was used.

* * * * * *

EVEN the most cursory study of those executed for crimes other than murder would soon reveal one very obvious fact: sentences were not administered in equal terms. That inequality became more blatant as the 18th century advanced and spilled into the next. Lottery was a description heard more than occasionally. Others saw sentences not so much as impartial application of the law, rather as general warnings or timely reminders whenever concern was aroused over certain offences. What made such haphazard sentencing more reprehensible was that so many offences carried the death penalty. One county assizes might deal with four capital charges and hang all the accused; another, with the same four charges, would hang one and transport the other three. In the period reviewed here, far more were found guilty of horse stealing in Derbyshire than the luckless four whose lives were ended on Nuns' Green. The others were transported to the colonies where labour was sorely needed. Most likely they were young, strong men and the judge considered he had served the greater purpose in exercising the King's mercy.

While murder, keeping in mind its comparative rarity as well as human nature, always attracted the greatest public interest, it was transgressions against property that by far and away were the most prolific crimes. And in that category, nearly all capital offences, were found most examples of that lack of uniformity. Typical was the case of John Smith, tried in 1735. That he claimed to be a Roman Catholic gave the *Mercury* more cause for indignant comment than the all too frequent charge of burglary. Smith had stolen a silver cup from the house of a Mr Bowyer. Just before the hangman launched him into eternity on 8 August, Smith cried out, 'much to the surprise of the spectators', noted the newspaper, that 'he died at CATHOLIC'. The *Mercury* had little good to say about the victim, dismissing him as an ignorant young man who understood little of religion, 'but joined in the prayers'.

While in prison he had been visited by several people, 'one of whom passes under the character of a Popish priest'. Smith's more serious offence, the newspaper implied, was his consorting with Rome's representatives. 'So industrious it seems is the Romish Faction to make Proselytes (especially of later in these parts as well as others) that even an illiterate house-breaker whose LIFE is no Credit to any Communion, must, at last, by all means be prevailed to DIE A CATHOLIC.' Then, almost with a knowing wink, came the editorial comment, 'and what is meant by that Word is easy to understand.' Later it was learned that Smith's father had been a Catholic.

Whether Smith's offending persuasion had any bearing on his sentence is uncertain. But it is difficult to understand why he hanged when Sam Stone did not, unless it was to set at least one example of what could happen to thieves. Seventeen-year old Stone had been found guilty of stealing from the house of William Linnett of Derby, 11 guineas, six half-crowns and a handkerchief, a sizeable haul falling well within the bounds of a capital felony. Sentencing him to hang, the judge later thought a reprieve was in order and transported the young lad for 14 years.

Of those accused, the vast majority were, with rare exception, members of what was commonly referred to as 'the lower orders'. That sweeping categorisation enveloped the greater part of the England's growing population. Included were the poor, the unemployed the shiftless and unemployable, the sick, the old and unfortunate, not to mention that large army of town and rural labourers and artisans whose employment prospects seldom rose above tenuous. Also embraced, although at times designated working class, were weavers, carpenters, cabinet-makers, machine operators, all of whom were capable of earning a reasonable income in good times and by and large were honest people.

The wealthy, the landowners, the men of property and patronage, the professional classes, the Church, simply lumped everyone else together and called them the lower orders, 'the mob', or if they were unduly obnoxious, 'the scum of the people'. Polite society in general recognised no widely spread strata, circumstances, or the effects of environment, lack of opportunity, dearth of employment. Given the poverty endured by so many, the erratic levels of income, the chronic hunger of too many, the constant search for the basic food of a narrow diet, it is perhaps not so surprising that many became occasional criminals. While theft was the commonest crime, it is significant that robbery with attendant violence was comparatively rare. Put another way, the age-old fear held by the wealthier, more fortunate classes, of the lower orders revealed itself more and more in the penal code which, in effect, they controlled. What was only slowly being realised was the effect of the rapidly accelerating Industrial Revolution. The population was increasing, old towns were expanding or new towns coming into being as industry became more and more centralised. A more diverse (and divisive) class system was coming into being. The old order, much to its annoyance, was slowly being displaced.

A rare instance of someone from the higher social order being brought to trial occurred at the March 1739 assizes. James Loton of Edensor, accused of murdering a male bastard child by drowning, was found guilty and sentenced to hang. Unusually, his body was then to be hung in chains. That additional punishment must mean the circumstances of the case were particularly nasty since gib-beting did not become technically legal until 1752. Frances Coulton, the baby's mother, gave evidence against him. Charged with the same offence she turned King's Evidence and was accordingly acquitted. Strenuous efforts were made to save Loton. No fewer than six times over the following months his sentence was respited. Finally, in August, the struggle paid off when 'His Majesty's most gracious pardon' was granted and set Loton free to return to the bosom of his family. Accounts of

the trial stated that he was 'a man of good appearance', and probably more relevant, of 'considerable substance'. In those days, a man's standing was measured as much, if not more, by his income as his family.

Many hanged at Derby did so for the crime of highway robbery. Impossible to define is which villains could be cast in the popular mould of mounted highwaymen, masked and possessing elegant manners and dress, or, as more likely, the ubiquitous and, by definition, far more brutal, urban-based footpads. The technical distinction depended on the horse. An understandable desire to rise in one's chosen profession might go some way to explain all those found guilty of horse stealing. Given the paramount importance of horsepower, to steal one was a most grievous offence.

Common enough was the case of Richard Woodward, hanged on 30 March 1738. His sometimes partner in crime, a James Giddens, was executed the same day at Nottingham. As so often, particulars are lacking; nothing is learned of their road robberies. A broadsheet hawked around Nuns' Green gave the highwayman's history and his dying confession, but no copy has survived. The *Mercury* gave the barest of details. Woodward elected not only to go on foot to the scaffold but, most bizarrely, did so dressed in a coarse woollen shroud. By his side walked that busy clergyman, the Revd Lockett, who not only kept up a continuous exhortation for the highwayman to repent, but also carried Woodward's confession. That piece of paper ended up in the *Mercury* offices, authenticated by the Revd Lockett. 'For a further account, we would refer our readers thereto', the *Mercury* told its readers, meaning its own broadsheet.

Of the several appearing at the March assizes on capital offences, Woodward was the only one to suffer execution. A glance at the sentences bears out their selective nature, the policy of warning and reminding rather than equal application. John Morton, sheep stealing: reprieved; Everard Madly, sheep stealing, transported; John Sikes, horse stealing: acquitted; Joseph Lowe, burglary: acquitted; William Wragg, stealing clothing: burned in hand; Katherine Hutton, stealing cloth: transported; George Croxall, stealing various items: transported; Hannah Cater and Anne Starbuck, stealing from a house or barn at Allestree: Cater transported, Starbuck burnt in hand. 'Burnt in hand', otherwise branding with a hot iron, was administered in open court, usually by the hangman, and left a mark indicating the offence. In Starbuck's case, the probable sign was 'R' for robbery. Such stigma virtually ensured a continuing career in crime, the offender having been rendered well-nigh unemployable. First introduced in 1487, branding was replaced in 1779 by whipping or a fine.

Counterfeiting was one of the more serious of capital crimes on the statue book. Technically, the offence was high treason and prosecutions the responsibility of the Treasury Solicitor's office. So when George Ashmore found himself in the dock in St Mary's Gate in July 1740 he would have entertained little

doubt as to his fate, particularly it being the second time for the same offence. In August 1739, he had saved his skin by turning King's Evidence against fellow counterfeiter George Brentnal, a Dissenting minister. However, the evidence was insufficient and Brentnal was acquitted of filing a quantity of guineas. There were further charges not involving Ashmore: coining moidores and 36 shilling pieces. This time Brentnal was not so lucky and he must have been surprised when the noose was not to be his fate. Instead, the court declared his estate forfeit and all goods and chattels seized. Then he was sent to prison for life, a rare sentence.

Ashmore failed to heed the lesson. The 'base coiner of Ashbourne' resumed his counterfeiting activities, turning out fake guineas and crown pieces. His workshop was a cave hewn out of the rock on which stood the Royal Oak inn at the corner of King Street and Buxton Road. Above ground he cohabited with the landlady. This twin level of activity ceased abruptly when the lady concerned read a notice offering a handsome reward for Ashmore's detention. Realising that her subterranean lover was now both menace and temptation, she informed the authorities of his whereabouts. He could hardly complain at such duplicity when arrested and taken off to Derby gaol. Nuns' Green welcomed him on 29 August.

Ashmore's story becomes more compelling for what happened subsequently. After the execution, relations had come forward to claim the body and carry it away for burial in the churchyard at Sutton-on-the-Hill. The Revd Robert Holden performed the ceremony, afterwards noting in the parish burial register that George Ashmore ('the Younger') was interred on 30 August. In brackets, he added a note in Latin, *Qui pro nummi fictitii excusione suspensus fuit*; informing the learned that Ashmore had been hanged for counterfeiting coins. A day or so later the more observant among the villagers noticed that the newly-occupied grave had been disturbed. In those times that too often meant one thing, the dreaded Resurrection Men had paid a nocturnal visit. Spades were sent for and the grave opened up. As feared, George had disappeared. All that remained were the empty coffin and an earth-stained shroud. George Ashore could well prove to be the first recognised example of the body-snatching era in the country. Some studies of that grisly occupation give the earliest recorded date as 1742, following a sharp decline in numbers going to the gallows. Scaffold victims probably ended up beneath the dissecting knives of the anatomists more often than might be suspected.

Revolting though the trade of the Resurrection or 'Sack 'em up' men was, its existence was inevitable. In order to teach the intricacies of the human body and carry out research, surgeons and anatomists desperately needed fresh corpses. Henry VIII had introduced a charter authorising four murderers' bodies a year to be given for dissection and instruction. That number was inadequate from the start, which means that

grave robbing may be far older than presently accepted. An increase came in 1752, with the handing over of all murderers' remains (unless reserved for the gibbet). Still the supply was utterly inadequate; dead bodies were the source of information. Lecturers had to make-do with papier-mâché models, at best poor substitutes, or work with skeletons or the preserved remains of the innards of dogs, cats and monkeys. London and Edinburgh medical schools between them taught close on 2,000 students a year.

There were enterprising medical practitioners who either taught anatomy in local hospitals, or set up their own small teaching school. Derby had a least one example. Supply follows demand, and the highly organised trade of body-snatching thrived, succeeding the former amateur raids of surgeons and their students. Stealing corpses became a considerable industry, for medical schools were not reluctant to pay good prices for the best cadavers or 'things' as they were dubbed in the trade. Not that the anatomists dealt directly with the supply source, details were left to intermediaries. Sextons, hangmen, porters and gravediggers were the more obvious contacts. Families of victims, fighting off poverty, were not always averse to trading the dead. Legally, the depriving of a grave of its corpse was classed as only a misdemeanour. To take the coffin and the shroud was a felony, a far more serious offence; that was why Ashmore's grave still contained those two items. The era of the Resurrection Men came to an end with the passing of the

Anatomy Act of 1832, which recognised and provided for the cadaverous need of medical science.

How rife was body-snatching in Derbyshire? The answer will never be known, for Resurrectionists were careful to leave behind as little evidence as possible, since they might plan another raid on the graveyard. At High Bradfield, just across the north Derbyshire border, there is a fine example of a watch-house, built by a churchyard to accommodate those prepared to keep an eye on freshly dug graves and open for robbers. What may be a pointer is while there are accounts of bodies taken from the scaffold for burial at named churchyards, a check on church registers has failed to find any related entry. That could, of course, be a church ruling, although George Ashmore's interment was recorded.

One method of body-snatching was to steal the corpse before the grave was filled in. The collusion of the gravediggers and sexton was essential. Once the funeral service had been held, the mourners left the graveside with the coffin still exposed. Earth was then piled on a coffin that had been swiftly emptied. Given that among those who hanged, many would have been vagrants, without family or friends, nobody cared what happened to them after death. Purloining their remains for the dissecting table was a relatively simple matter.

There are at least two other grave robberies on record. In October 1825, two men carrying a large hamper were stopped on the Duffield Road at Allestree. Inside was the body of Elizabeth Deaville, wife of the innkeeper of the Red Lion at Belper. She had died a few days before and had been buried at Duffield. The two men escaped. Belief was that the body was bound for anatomists in London. The second incident was a night raid on the churchyard at Eckington in 1828. Two men, arriving in a horse and carriage, dug up the remains of Ann Allen, who had died of natural causes a day or two before. Evidence which implies that the activities of body-snatchers must be underestimated came from Nottingham in 1827. A hamper consigned to a London address was discovered to contain the bodies of an old woman and a young boy. Alarmed, the authorities carried out an immediate investigation of recent arrivals at the town's three cemeteries. No fewer than 30 graves were empty.

One man who, aided by his friends, made strenuous efforts to avoid the cart to Nuns' Green was Charles Pleasant. Sentenced to death in 1768 for forgery, the date itself was delayed several times while a reprieve was frantically sought. Pleasant displayed every confidence that he would escape the noose, although resigned to a long term of transportation. The narrowest escape came when Hinde, His Majesty's Messenger, bringing a respite from London was badly bruised when his horse fell, delaying him for a couple of hours. By the time he galloped into Derby, 'all the apparatus of death' was in place. Pleasant had put on his shroud and was sharing his cell with a handsome coffin, bearing three ornamental plates on its lid.

The forger comes across as a resourceful

man. A day or so after the last-minute arrival, Pleasant contacted the *Mercury* and dictated to its correspondent what had next transpired. He claimed that he had received a letter from the trial judge saying that he had made a favourable report in support of his application for a reprieve, and that he could now expect a term of transportation. What actually arrived was confirmation of the death sentence and a date, 4 May. That compared to executing him twice, pointed out the *Mercury*. The newspaper/Pleasant hoped that some humane gentlemen would now obtain ten days' delay to allow friends in Ireland, 'people of the first distinction', to make another application in his favour.

There was no way out. Pleasant met the hangman as arranged. His fight to escape death guaranteed that 'an incredible number of spectators' turned up. Bearing himself with great fortitude and resignation, he mounted the gallows cart, at the same time pulling off his greatcoat to reveal his shroud already in place. At his request, a special hymn by sung, the first verse of which ran:

> *O Thou that hangest on the Tree,*
> *My curse and sufferings to remove,*
> *Pity the soul that looks to thee,*
> *And save me by thy dying Love.*

Delay stalked him to the end. According to the *Mercury*, the forger took longer than usual to die. The explanation given was that he himself had arranged the rope, 'got it under his chin', with the result that he died slowly and in great agony. Many years later, research seeking a quicker end showed that death by hanging was preceded by convulsions lasting anything from five minutes to three-quarters of an hour.

Part of the hanging ritual was for the condemned to thank the gaoler and the Under-Sheriff and clergymen for their various kindnesses. This Pleasant did and he also obtained agreement that after hanging his body would be delivered to a young man standing close to the scaffold. As soon as possible, the man took the corpse and, with others, attempted to restore life. Such attempts were by no means far-fetched or unusual. There were cases of 'corpses' being revived, by wrapping in warm blankets, moving the arms vigorously or anything else that seemed appropriate. A body could be cut down when life might seem extinct (a suitable donation from friends or family to the hangman might facilitate matters) and resuscitation prove successful.

Charles Pleasant's friends' attempts failed and they had to be content with sending him to St Peter's Churchyard in some style. The grave was described as 'remarkably deep', a common practice, when affordable, to thwart the Resurrectionists. 'Genteel' was how the *Mercury* described the obsequies. Three men dressed in black cloaks followed the coffin, and mourners thought that as many watched the burial as witnessed the killing. Pleasant was laid alongside John Lowe, hanged two weeks earlier for burglary. In the same plot could have been the bones of Ann Williamson, a pickpocket executed 13 years earlier (see *Dealing With Women*). None of the three burials is recorded in the church registers.

The *Mercury*, in reporting Pleasant's painful passing, a rare departure, draws attention to something hardly ever commented on: the often quite startling changes in victims between sentencing and dying. Evidence from elsewhere shows that victims frequently aged dramatically, their faces becoming wizened and lined. Hair turned grey in a matter of hours, while severe weight loss shrivelled and weakened the body. As might be expected, suicide attempts were not unknown. The *Mercury* never reported any, but that may have been due to the authorities not wishing to have incidents highlighted. However, at least two did succeed, the brothers John and Benjamin Jones, convicted of burglary. They were found hanged at Friar Gate on 4 August 1784.

Thanks to one of their accomplices turning King's Evidence, quite a lot is known about the brothers. Ashbourne men, in 1784 they embarked on a series of robberies and burglaries. Usually working with others, they would strike at different places in Derby, Brailsford and Ashbourne. They had moved to Derby and their practice was to steal horses in the town for their country forays. Their career came to an end on 14 April when the brothers, together with the man who betrayed them, broke into the house of a Mrs Roe, who lived in the 'upper end' of St Peter's parish in Derby. The gang had disguised themselves in what seems to have been traditional manner, smock frocks and faces blackened. Once in the house, they disturbed Mrs Roe's niece and, brandishing pistols, forced her to show them where the valuables were located. The trio's haul was considerable: £38 in cash, several pieces of plate, silverware and cutlery, all of which they wrapped in a cloth brought for the purpose and made off into the night.

It was that classic clue, footsteps in the snow, that brought about the gang's downfall. Fresh snow had fallen while they were in the house and an aroused neighbourhood found little difficulty in tracking the criminals down. Despite having washed his face, John Jones had failed to clean off all the tell-tale blacking. Arrested and charged, the brothers stood trial on 3 August before Judge Ashurst. Proceedings did not take long, particularly as the brothers had no one to speak on their behalf, and the jury had little difficulty in returning a guilty verdict.

John and Benjamin Jones returned to the gaol in Friar Gate, the former in a spirit of bravado, vowing that as they had stood their trial like men they hoped they would die like men. Both were locked in the same cell. John quickly changed his tune, as the reality of the situation became apparent, becoming 'agitated to an amazing degree'. Next day both men were discovered by a turnkey, dressed only in their shirts, facing each other, and hanging from the cord used to secure their chains. A surgeon was hurriedly called to bleed them, but both were already dead. Next day, a coroner's jury brought in a verdict of *felo de se* or 'self-murder'. They were interred that same afternoon. The brothers had not cheated the gallows, for they were buried beneath it.

The Bloody Code
[1770-1830]

THE Bloody Code was the evocative name given to that period in England's penal history when it seemed that one could be hanged for virtually every offence under the sun. Executing murderers or, given the context of the times, for crimes of violence, stealing horses or sheep, or highway robbery, can be accepted. That life was also at risk for scrawling graffiti on London's Westminster Bridge, stealing turnips, wrecking fishponds and hedgerows, nowadays seems ludicrous in the extreme. Other extraordinary capital offences embraced damaging royal forests, impersonating Chelsea Pensioners, or fraternising with gypsies. With such offences having the potential to lead to a meeting with Mr Roper (gallows humour for the hangman), then the much-quoted statistic of over 200 hanging offences on the statute book at the beginning of the 19th century becomes more comprehendible.

In 1688, there were 'only' 50 capital offences. Even then, to list each one might be difficult. Scrutiny in the Code's era would show that different statutes covered practically the same offence, but for different parts of the country. For example, feloniously scribbling on Westminster Bridge meant just that. Defacing any of Derby's bridges was not a hanging matter. Other legislation was introduced to tidy up loose ends from earlier Acts whose purpose had been served. While possibly a little too simplistic, the sheer number suggests a judicial policy of 'let's sentence everyone to death and then select just a few for the hangman as examples'.

Or, as Edward Gibbon Wakefield commented in 1832, when execution reform of was getting under way:

'The power of the law consists in its terrors; if you wholly cease to hang, the common people will have nothing to fear; therefore hang one or two now and then.'

Wakefield was effectively repeating what the influential Archdeacon William Paley had

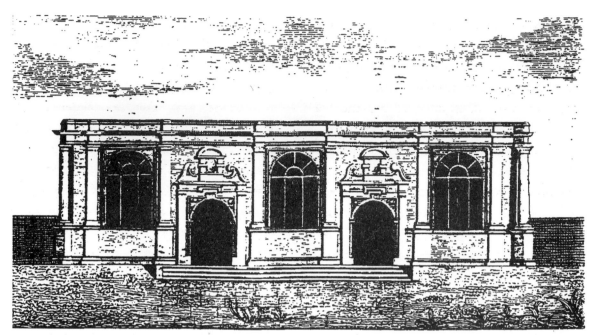

The County Hall or Courts of Justice in Derby's St Mary's Gate, as it would have appeared in 1660. Here were held the assizes and from here many went straight to the gallows on Nuns' Green. For a time the bodies of executed murderers were dissected in public in one of its rooms.

said in 1785 with his treatise *Principles of Moral and Political Philosophy*, which neatly encapsulated the Bloody Code. His thinking was that to deter crime, then as many offences as possible be made capital. However, in practice, only the hangman would be employed in 'a small proportion of each class…the general character, or peculiar aggravation of those crimes, render them fit examples of public justice'.

The churchman continued:

'The charge of cruelty is answered by observing that these laws were never meant to be carried into indiscriminate execution …it is enough to vindicate the lenity of the laws, that some instances are to be found in each class of capital crimes, which require the restraint of capital punishment…'

Researchers calculate that if all those sentenced to death had to be killed, it would have raised the problems of finding sufficient hangmen, scaffolds and time. Further calculations showed that if four had hanged every day, not including Sundays, then those difficulties would have been overcome. In reality, the highest hanging rate reached was around 50 per cent of those sentenced. This does not obscure the fact that many hundreds did die. That the Code grew and flourished under Tory administrations, then ceased almost abruptly when they surrendered power to the Whigs in the 1830s, has its modern parallel. In the 1960s a Labour administration succeeded the Conservatives and set about bringing capital punishment to an inglorious demise.

Why someone convicted of a capital offence might not hang could be down to several reasons. If the offender were young and strong, then transportation to the colonies, with their insistent demand for labour, was clearly an acceptable alternative. The judge and the jury might consider that the crime was not so dreadful as to be rewarded with such a drastic punishment. After all, you could swing for stealing five shillings as well as murder. Then again, the prisoner (could be male or female) might have children to support and the parish would have to assume responsibility if either parent was killed. That the hanging rate seldom even reached a quarter of those sentenced would signify that judges and juries were working an extempore grading system for felonies. It was all too haphazard, little better than a lottery. A prisoner might be looked on favourably if someone of substance could put in a word for him. A normally well-respected hard-working farm labourer might be saved from the gallows with a timely word from the squire or his landlord. This was the patronage system at work. That only a minority of those condemned to death would actually die was the system's principal weakness: no machinery existed to classify and grade offences. Eventually, the lack was instrumental in bringing about its fall. That and the contempt it engendered with the common people for the law and its implementation.

Two pieces of legislation paved the way for the Code's excesses and brutality. First, in 1723, came the Waltham Black Act which extended the death penalty to more offences than any other piece of legislation before or since. That era known as the Bloody Code, regarded as being from 1770 to 1830, came into being under that Act. Noted for its severity, extremely broad application and ability to absorb the latest legal judgements, the Black Act initially detailed 50 separate offences for which one could hang. At its maximum, the total had reached, in some opinions, to nearly 250. By making so many offences capital matters, terror had been deliberately introduced into the judicial system. Reference to *Appendix B* will give some idea of the variety of crimes; the perceptive layman would notice that many could easily be grouped under a single heading. The Black Act lasted over a hundred years; its spreading tentacles attained maximum reach in the early part of the 19th century and then collapsed in the 1820s, from wounds largely self-inflicted. That, and the unacceptable behaviour of the gallows-crowd.

Some explanation of the background to the 1723 Act is necessary. An accepted political concept of the day was that government best served the interest of the state by preserving and protecting the needs of the propertied classes and their property. The 17th century philosopher John Locke had crystallised that notion in his enormously influential *Second Treatise of Government* (1690) with its insistent message that the State had 'no other end but the preservation of property'. It was a mantra found most acceptable by those with property. Thereafter, everything fell into place.

A gallows scene repeated untold times. Already in his shroud, a condemned man waves farewell while the hangman makes the final adjustment to the noose. When all was ready, the cart drew away and the victim strangled to death.

The hangman and his busy noose would protect property.

Introduced as emergency legislation to combat an alarming spread of poaching, principally deer, in the royal forests (Waltham being one of the more afflicted areas), the Act was intended for:

'the more effectual punishing of wicked and evil disposed persons going around in disguise, and doing injuries and violences to the persons

and properties of His Majesty's subjects, and for the more speedy bringing the offenders to justice.'

The strictures against hunting of game meant that something like 90 per cent of the population were now forbidden on pain of death to hunt game of any sort. Other offences included cattle maiming, arson of barns and haystacks, malicious shooting at any person. Insufficient attention had been paid to drafting the Act, which made it all too easy to subsequently lump under it other offences as they arose out of legal judgements. In effect, the Black Act was a self-contained criminal code, covering far more than perhaps the original drafters intended. Initially envisaged as a three-year measure, it was first extended in 1725, and then several more times until becoming permanent in 1757.

The second Act, passed in 1752, famously shortened to The Murder Act, was 'for the better preventing the Horrid Crime of Murder'. Behind its implementation lay the realisation that with so many felonies carrying the death penalty there was no emphasising the enormous differences between offences. Equally apparent, but resolutely ignored by politicians, was that hanging was proving no deterrent. Crime figures simply did not stop rising, neither did the population, and hangmen were as busy as ever. So, to underline the singular gravity of wilfully taking life, the Act's preamble explained 'it had become necessary that some further terror and Mark of Infamy be added to the Punishment'. Torture had been ruled out, being considered

as resting uneasily with the English conscience. That belief was something of a myth, since history suggests otherwise. Only the corpse was left. That could be dissected. That there was a terror beyond hanging came with the very genuine fear, almost universal in the Christian faith, that any molestation of one's mortal remains seriously jeopardised the chances of material resurrection on Judgement Day. At his discretion, the Act authorised the judge to pass the following sentence on murderers:

'...you must be led to the place of execution and when you have come there you must be hanged by the neck until you are dead and your body be dissected and anatomised.'

Dissection should have posed a dilemma for the Church, since the practice was considered blasphemous. However, a diligent ferret among the Scriptures unearthed justification in Genesis, the passage claiming God had repented over the creation of man and sent a flood to cover the earth. A statement elastic enough to cover most eventualities. Notwithstanding its many contradictions, the Old Testament was a fruitful hunting ground.

Of course, medical schools were pleased with the latest legislation. More bodies would now come their way in the interests of teaching and research, although it was clear that the ever rising demand was still nowhere being met.

There was an alternative to the anatomist's knife: gibbeting. Again at the judge's discretion; although for murderers, highwayman had always run the risk of that fate.

Whichever horror was added, there would be no formal burial for the remains. Little enough left anyway after dissection, and what remained after years of exposure would be collected and shovelled unceremoniously into the ground around the gibbet.

If reprieves were to be sought then action had to be swift. The Murder Act further stipulated that killers would die within 48 hours, with allowance made for an intervening Sunday. Moreover, there would be no religious observances en route to the gallows. Clergyman now had just a short time to guide the condemned along the penitential road and attempt to save their souls for the afterlife; a task made more difficult with the introduction of dissection or the gibbet. With the 1752 Act came more of those disgraceful

scaffold scuffles as friends and relations tried to grab the dead body and hurry it away for a decent burial.

Dissecting had first been legislated for under Henry VIII with an allowance of four felons' bodies a year to the Company of Barber Surgeons. As medical science broadened, so did the requirements of research and the allocation proved inadequate. That was acknowledged by the 1752 Act, which raised the quota by 12 cadavers. That was nowhere sufficient and that almost uniquely British profession of body-snatching, which despite valiant efforts would never keep up with demand, became busier than ever. Since anatomists naturally preferred fresh things, their recent effluence notwithstanding, a murderer could be coming

Another woodcut popular with printers, used to illustrate street literature until the new drop executions did away with the gallows cart. The condemned man listens to the chaplain while the hangman waits his turn. Other officials are seen on the right while the javelin men on the left keep an eye on proceedings.

apart on the dissecting table little more than an hour after choking to death.

Gibbeting became legal under the Act. In fact, it had been around for centuries for cases where the crime involved was deserving of such a revolting warning. The 'infamous exposure' meant securing the felon's corpse (man or – rarely – woman) either in chains or a body-shaped iron cage and then suspended from the gibbet, a tall wooden post with a crossbeam at the top. Since there were those who might attempt to retrieve the corpse, the post would be liberally spiked with nails. Applying a coating of lead was to thwart any venture to burn it down. Traditionally, gibbets were erected near the offender's home or scene of the crime. While no time was stipulated how long a body remained displayed, in practice it was usually years. To inhibit decay, the head would first be shaved and then the entire body saturated in tar. Disintegration was then left to time, the elements and birds. Gibbets were barbaric and serve as a low water mark in the penal system. They may well be more representative of the Bloody Code's worst passages than the baying, drunken mobs at public hangings, hurling abuse or blasphemies while watching the slowly turning body of a desperate pickpocket or young woman driven to killing her baby.

As with peculiar customs associated with hangings, so too with gibbets. Skulls were much sought after. Epileptics were believed to obtain relief by drinking from them. The more practical scraped off the accumulation of moss which, when pounded into a snuff,

helped cure headaches. One Derbyshire killer's skull ended up as a sideshow exhibit. Ague sufferers could obtain some comfort relief by filling a small bag with slivers from a gibbet and hanging it round their necks.

Mounting public revulsion eventually did away with gibbeting. By 1832, the practice had all but disappeared. The Anatomy Act of that year finally forbade it. For financial reasons alone, the passing would have pleased county high sheriffs, since they were responsible for funding judges' decisions. When Anthony Lingard was hung in chains in north Derbyshire, the county's last occasion, the iron jacket alone cost £75. Other expenses added a further £85 to the bill, which did not include the £10 gaoler's fee for delivering the corpse. Dissection, too, was abolished, although attempts were made to revive it for the terrors it invoked.

Changes to hanging techniques were introduced during the Code's reign. The most important was known as the short or new drop, but effectively it brought little improvement. It was nothing more than a large scaffold on which stood a smaller platform into which a trapdoor had been let. Standing on the platform beneath the hanging beam, the victim went to his death when the hangman pulled back a bolt dropping the trapdoor. Unfortunately, the drop was only about 18 inches, nothing like that required to cause a presumed instant demise. Death was still by slow strangulation. Despite ample contradictory evidence by way of screams, kicks, and struggles, sometimes lasting many

One of the commonest woodcuts used to illustrate ballads and execution sheets. The scene represented was typical of public hangings for a great number of years until the coming of first the short drop and then the long.

minutes, the medical profession declared itself well satisfied with the new method.

'There was no pain at all in hanging for that it doth stop the circulation of the blood and so stops all sense and motion in an instance.'

With the drop's arrival, the centuries-old journey from prison to hanging tree ended. Far too large to be moved about, the scaffold when not in use presented an unpleasant sight as well as a target for vandals. So execution sites were moved from their traditional spots to the front of gaols. Except for hanging days, the scaffold's planks and beams would be stored within the prison walls. Also consigned to memory were the cart rides to the gallows.

But the public was not to be deprived of their ghastly theatre. The scaffolds, carrying the familiar uprights and hanging beam, were built on massive proportions and high enough to allow spectators a good view.

The drop's first outing was in 1760 when Tyburn's thousands watched Earl Ferrers hang for murdering his steward at Staunton Harold Hall in north Leicestershire. Unfortunately, and painfully for the Earl, the drop failed to work and his end had to be hastened by the hangman, Thomas Turlis, by the time-honoured method of pulling down on his frantic legs. Following that failure, the method was not attempted again in London until 1783 when Newgate Prison designed a scaffold with the trapdoor now incorporated into the main platform. While the new arrangement worked well enough, the drop used by executioners was still much too short to ensure a quicker death. Height remained the executioner's preoccupation, not his victim's weight. Cost of building the scaffolds was high and the new machinery took some time before it attained general use. Derby did not adopt it until 1812, nearly 30 years later after its introduction, and even then was among the earlier arrivals in the provinces. Excepting a few minor alterations, the design remained unchanged until the 1880s when the Home Office recommended a standard plan for execution sheds.

With executions taking place outside prisons, there followed some changes to the hanging day ceremonial. The wretched street theatre ambience was in no way diminished. If anything, dramatic effect had been heightened. Now the victim's arrival was quite sudden, more of an entrance as he emerged from within the prison and stepped out on to the scaffold. Possibly this sudden appearance gave rise to that whispered, rushing command, 'Hats off!' its rapid passage through the audience raising even more the atmosphere of melodrama. Other aspects remained the same. Still in attendance were the various officials to add authority and see that procedures were adhered to – and probably relieved at no longer being required to follow the cart, crowded and jostled by the vulgar mob. Unaffected were the street traders, the publicans, the ballad and broadsheet sellers, itinerant musicians, the whores, the pie-men, and those who spread the word of God. For pickpockets, it was business as usual, as they sidled through the crowds seeking 'to ease a bloke'. Commerce welcomed hanging days: trade followed the noose.

* * * * * *

SOMETHING else arose during the Bloody Code era: the first, slow movements for reform of capital punishment, aligned with the growing realisation that the whole question of judicial punishment needed examining more closely. Prison reform not only moved up the agenda but also made significant progress. England's population rose quite dramatically and it became obvious to the more perceptive that in many ways the old social order had about run its course, retreating before the Industrial Revolution. Reaction by successive Tory governments to escalating crime was not to inquire for reasons but to deter by terror and punishment; more, and more brutal. It could not and did not work. European countries had similar experiences but had sought solutions. The results were enlightened codes of punishment and a marked decrease in both crime and executions.

Over the Code's 60 years, some 35,000 were sentenced to death throughout England and Wales. Well over half that number were reprieved and mostly transported. Something like 7,000-8,000 ended up as guests of the hangman. The national execution graph suggests that in the last three decades of the

18th century the rate either slowly dipped or remained more or less constant. However, the opening three decades of the 19th century witnessed a sharp rise, and it was those years that secured the Code its evil reputation. Many factors were at play. The Tory government, deservedly named 'Old Corruption', came under fire on several fronts. The end of the Napoleonic Wars meant thousands of soldiers being discharged on a declining labour market, which meant more and more criminal activity. Reform was badly needed and stoutly resisted by those in power. Moreover, the government was haunted by recent events in France and hints of public dissatisfaction maybe manifesting itself on the streets sent politicians into a panic and turn to untoward reprisals. Execution figures rose, reprieves declined.

Derbyshire's figures fall broadly into line with the national experience. Over the Bloody Code, 51 were put to death over a range of 14 offences:

Burglary	12
Murder	9
Highway robbery	5
Horse stealing	4
Firing haystacks	4
House breaking	3
High treason	3
Robbery	2
Sheep stealing	2
Uttering forged cheques/notes	2
Rape	2
Escaping from transportation	1
Shop breaking	1
Picking pockets	1

Those figures most likely were typical of comparable assize towns. Most would seem to be nothing much out of the expected. The charge of high treason would be unusual anywhere in England. Derbyshire was not noted as somewhere harbouring particularly dangerous criminal or political activity. Luddism was not as prominent as in neighbouring Nottinghamshire or Leicestershire, while the Blanketeers had run out of steam as they approached the county border. Even though Derby's population had doubled between 1712 and 1788 (4,000 to 8,563) it still ended as the only major town with fewer than 10,000 inhabitants.

There grew an acceptance that the sheer number of capital offences was absurd. There were even rare individuals questioning the need for hanging at all, although most accepted its retention for murder. Even the most hidebound Tory had begun to realise that hanging over such a wide spectrum had failed as a deterrent. Reliable statistics began to appear after 1805 and by the 1820s were severely embarrassing politicians. Not only were they having to swallow them, but also the equally disgraceful hanging days. The excesses of the Bloody Code had turned these into events attracting enormous crowds. Executions meant to deter, but their frequency had instead bred disrespect and contempt for the law. It was inevitable, since life could be taken in revenge for the theft of so little. As the Code entered its final decade, prosecutions became more frequent. Acceleration in reprieves followed; to send for the hangman for even a quarter of the death sentences would have resulted in a rage of public hangings not experienced since Tudor times.

Oblique affirmation of the Code's ridicule came not only from the drunken, ill-behaved, bellowing mobs but also from that bulwark of the judicial system, the assize court. Juries were becoming bolder and unwilling to convict when the crimes were of stealing property or cash of no great value. Finding some poor wretch guilty of thieving they would, at times gently encouraged by the judges, place a value on the goods patently less than actual and so take the charge outside the range of capital offences. Until 1820, stealing a sum as small as five shillings, or goods to that value from a shop, could put a life in jeopardy. To be fair, the government had attempted in 1810 to reduce the offence to a non-capital status, only to be thwarted by the Church. When the Bill reached the House of Lords, the Archbishop of Canterbury and a cohort of bishops voted against the measure, thereby ensuring its failure. Ten years later came reform of a sort: the qualifying sum was raised to £15.

Also much altered by 1830, and set to change even more, was the country's prison system. In 1770, the gaols were a public disgrace, and a serious health hazard. In fact, they had been that way for centuries. Filthy, stinking places, beds of corruption and disease, mostly housed in buildings ill-suited for the task. Gaol fever, a virulent form of typhoid, laid constant siege. A national survey in 1759 discovered that each year one in four

prisoners died, in summary meaning 5,000 annually. Moreover, the majority of inmates were debtors, not criminals or those awaiting trial or sentence. As the hangmen became busier, the official mind started to listen to those voices preaching wider use of incarceration as punishment.

While Derby never showed itself in any way innovative over penal reform, it nevertheless was one the earliest towns to rid itself of a prison that had long ceased to fulfil its function properly and replace it with a building incorporating modern ideas. Even if those hanged generally had little contact with prison, just passing through in most cases, that building was the proscenium arch of the gallows theatre with its popular productions of state killings. Moreover, the coming increase in the number and size of prisons, pursuing not only a growing population and criminal element but in time a complementary decline in capital offences, means they have a place in this history.

Little is known of Derby's earliest prisons. Before 1532, felons were taken off to Nottingham, but in that year the Justices of the Peace were empowered to build a gaol to serve the needs of the county. Sited in the Cornmarket, the building straddled a brook and was described by the observant Hutton as 'being erected...in a river, as if they meant to drown the culprit before they hanged him'. Derby's historian thought it little better than an open sewer and recalled a time when the brook overflowed, drowning three inmates. There were two other prisons, serving the town itself. One was in the Market Place, beneath the Guildhall, and a smaller, equally nauseous establishment in Willow Row.

However, it is possible that some form of gaol preceded those three places. Somewhere along a boundary embankment to the east of Derby, separating it from Litchurch, was a place called Gallows Baulk. England's first recorded prison was at Winchester and known as the King's Baulk House. In Old English 'balk' means block or baulk, and prisons were sometimes referred to as blockhouses. The pairing of Gallows with Baulk, admittedly tenuous, is nonetheless suggestive. Then, maybe, some memory lingered on. In 1776, Matthew Cocklayne was gibbeted near that site, in a field called Bradshaw Hay, near the present Bradshaw Way. Some accounts called it Gallows Bank.

The call for an overhaul of the prison system saw what is regarded as England's first purpose designed gaol being built early in the 18th century, at London. While the need was much debated, no real progress was made during the rest of that century, with the seemingly notable exception at Derby. For some unexplained reason, a new gaol to serve the county was built in 1756 and its architect, William Hiorns, had incorporated the latest thinking on prison design. Erected on the edge of Nuns' Green, its impressive Palladian façade looked on to Friar Gate and in time would serve as a splendid backdrop for executions. Standing in its own grounds, accommodation had been consolidated into a single range of buildings. Within its walls lay

four separate yards, allowing plenty of fresh air to circulate (typhoid was thought to be airborne) as well as providing exercise areas. In the centre stood the keeper's quarters. Such considerations as greater visual supervision, segregation of sexes, enforcement of discipline and morality, basic classification of prisoners, had all been catered for.

Unfortunately, the new prison soon proved itself inadequate for the task. Accommodation was for 21 criminals, but rising crime rates soon nullified that figure. There were seven night cells, and rare were the times when

Drink was one of the greatest curses of the 'lower orders' and one of the commonest reasons for most crimes. Those about to hang would often warn the watching crowd to beware of the evils of alcohol.

fewer than three prisoners were housed in each; at times the figure was five or six. There was no separate cell for the condemned and modern claims for it are more than flawed. If more than one unfortunate was waiting to die, then they were locked up together. Reference to works on prison architecture does not seem to indicate that there was a cell specially designed for the condemned. In all probability, an ordinary cell, perhaps not too far from the scaffold, would be allocated the function when required. In the prison succeeding Friar Gate, the records show no specific accommodation, but the cell most convenient at the time. Some of the old evils lived on at the new gaol. Day-to-day running remained a privatised function, allowing gaolers to charge prisoners for many basic services or favours. Before long, Friar Gate slipped back into the old ways. For those about to hang, nothing had changed, even if the cart ride to Nuns' Green was now little more than just around the corner.

* * * * * *

DEEPLY conservative and stout upholder of the establishment though it was, the *Derby Mercury's* columns reasonably reflect changes of national mood over the penal system. Gradually came the questioning of punishments, the need to make them more appropriate to the crime, criticism (occasionally) of crowd behaviour, the tawdry opportunism or lack of tact of traders. In the Code's opening years, as far as the newspaper was concerned, those who died on the Nuns' Green Tree deserved to. There was no examination or questioning of the need or any extenuating circumstances. The lower orders were the lower orders, classified and disregarded. Towards the end, however, doubts were being expressed in several directions. The *Mercury* was a pedestrian newspaper, a follower not a campaigner, unlike the *Leeds Mercury* with its reporting that had such a direct bearing on Derby's most famous trial.

As with many newspapers, the *Mercury* devoted considerable space to religious matters and comment. This was not a means of filling space, that was much too valuable, but evidence of what a prominent part religious belief played in everyday life. A well-known clergyman might have columns devoted to one of his sermons, or space afforded to letters sounding off on some religious theme. Had the Church not enjoyed the enormous authority and influence it did, then it becomes questionable whether the Bloody Code, indeed much of the penal system, would have achieved anything like the acceptance it did.

As far as the churches were concerned, notably the Church of England, hanging was not only acceptable but also necessary for the well being of the State. Biblical authority could always be found whenever the penal path took a new turn. Already seen was how the bishops turned down modest capital reform. In fact, the Church of England delayed until the 1950s before coming out in favour of abolishing capital punishment.

Moreover, the Archbishop of Canterbury with 18 of his bishops took until 1969 before casting their votes in the Lords in favour of abolishment. It was little more than a gesture, for, not known at the time, England's last hanging had already taken place.

The role of the Church was pivotal in the story of hanging. Few people, excepting perhaps royalty and clergy, met their deaths with as much spiritual ministrations as the condemned. First in the cell after sentence had been passed, comforting, praying and cajoling. Priests were unremitting in their efforts to get the victim to repent, and genuinely so. To that end it was of the utmost importance that the prisoner, in admitting true and contrite penitence, accepted he would achieve life everlasting in the hereafter. On the way to the gallows, until proscribed by the 1752 Act, the clergymen continued their earnest quest. Even at the scaffold the battle for the soul continued, to the last mortal seconds. The hangman represented the final secular authority of the State, the clergyman the spiritual.

Living today in a progressively secular society, the notion of a God-fearing one is perhaps difficult to grasp. The fundamental point to understand was the conviction then of the soul's passage to heaven when the body died. Provided, of course, that the person died in a state of belief and genuinely repenting of sins committed. Had not judges and juries accepted that, then capital punishment might not have survived for as long as it did. Despatching someone to certain oblivion was a different proposition. While not denying its essential brutality, capital punishment was thought necessary to maintain society and the nation. Gilbert Burnett, Bishop of Salisbury, explained this in 1699 in his *Exposition of the XXXIX Article*: 'Therefore as capital punishments

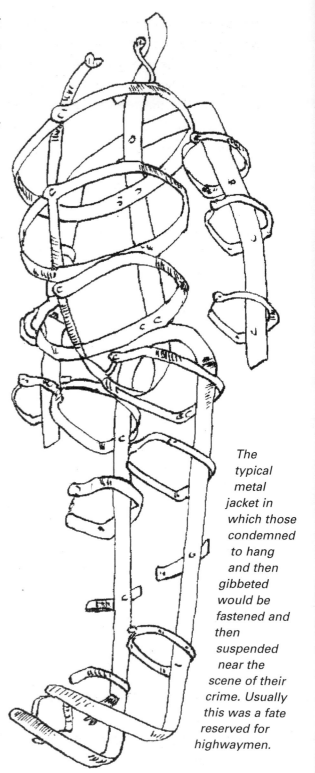

The typical metal jacket in which those condemned to hang and then gibbeted would be fastened and then suspended near the scene of their crime. Usually this was a fate reserved for highwaymen.

are necessary to human society, so they are often real blessings to those on whom they fall.' Sending the wrong man to the gallows was acknowledged as possible, countered by the logic that the unfortunate individual would be regarded as dying for their country and therefore the soul would still gain access to heaven.

What posed no difficulties was clerical support for executions in the face of Biblical disapproval. The prayer that declared, 'Almighty God who desirest not the death of a sinner, but rather that he may turn from his wickedness and live', was not seen as a challenge. St Paul in his Epistles assured the Romans that 'Vengeance is mine; I will repay, saith the Lord', but failed to convince the bishops who preferred to place more earthly reliance on the disciples of Jack Ketch. Biblical teaching was put to one side over the question of gibbeting. Deuteronomy (21: XXII/III), while accepting the death penalty, added: *'When a man hath committed a crime for which he is to be punished with death, and being condemned to die on a gibbet: His body shall not remain upon the tree, but shall be buried the same day: for he is accursed of God that hangeth on a tree: and thou shalt not defile thy land, which the Lord thy God shall give thee in possession.'*

* * * * * *

ANOTHER gradual change in perspective was over the question of policing. In the Code's closing years came begrudging acceptance that some national control was needed. However, many opposed any such moves in that direction, seeing in police forces hints of an arm of government, with the threat of secret agents and spies. European countries might tolerate them, no true-born Englishman would. More precisely, it was not so much the true-born as the echelons of upper society, the wealthy, and the propertied people, which for all intents and purpose were the law. Police forces meant loss of power. They, through the county sheriffs, the Justices of the Peace, the local squire, kept things in order, backed up by a system of parish constables, watches and local lock-ups. Local communities were quite self-reliant. Because an offender did not end up in court could mean that he had been dealt with summarily and properly in local acceptance. Strangers were noticed and watched; a criminal on the run did not have the easy passage we might like to think, conditioned as we are by today's communication technology.

What does not stand up to too rigorous inquiry is the popular image of parish constables and watchmen being mostly old, lazy and incompetent, often drunkards. Naturally some were, and campaigners for a more organised, uniformed police system helped to nurture further that impression. Guardians were paid out of funds provided by the wealthy and they demanded value for money. Nor were parishes organised in isolation. That there was a need for proper, more widespread control and monitoring because of mounting population – and consequently more crime and criminals – was recognised. One result was the formation towards the end of the 18th century of the Association for the Prosecution of Felons. A loosely knit, quasi-insurance organisation, it concerned itself with disseminating information about crimes and criminals, warnings of outbreaks of crime and published Wanted and Reward notices. To modern eyes, England lacked any but the poorest form of communication. The horse was the fastest way of spreading news, the roads were poor and the arrival of canals did not speed matters up any. However, the Association worked, and worked well (extraordinarily, a Derby branch, at Chaddesden, was not disbanded until the 1930s). Its efficiency was well exampled by the case of the murderer Matthew Cocklayne, who killed in Derby, was arrested in Ireland and was returned for trial (see *The Last of Nuns' Green*).

However unpopular the notion of a properly established and funded police system might have been, the changing structure of England demanded it. Disappearing was the wholly rural environment, submerged in places by the factory towns and concentrated communities of the Industrial Revolution. Sir Robert Peel, as Home Secretary, recognised the need and the start came in 1829 with the formation of London's Metropolitan Police Force. Despite stubborn rearguard actions by unresponsive councils against the various Acts of Parliament, all over the country men gradually began to don police uniforms.

* * * * * *

BUT what of those who ended their lives dancing to death upon the air or, in the slang of the day, as gallows apples? If one judges from the number of capital offences, the calendars of assizes, the hundreds hanged, the thousands transported, then surely England must have been a most violent society. True, there were periodic outbreaks of rioting: over food shortages, much needed reform or machinery breaking by the Luddites. But they were local happenings, sometimes regional, hardly on a national scale. Except for relatively short-lived periods, Derbyshire was never a restless place. Derby witnessed violent Reform riots in 1831, but nothing on the scale suffered by Nottingham or Bristol. Nor did anyone hang, as in those places. Quite why the county town should have erupted so invites more research than hitherto. There were food riots but on a minor scale, while King Ludd's banner never rallied followers in the same numbers as in other counties. The importance of the Pentrich Rising (see *Rising at Pentrich*) lay in its background, not the hopeless, nocturnal raggle-taggle reality.

That the vast majority of those executed came from the lower orders was demographically inevitable, since they formed by far the greater majority. Nor can the fact that the greatest number of crimes involved theft, which must surely obtain anywhere, any time. If there was one overall cause for much of the wrongdoing, it was being poor. It might be argued that there is no such thing as poverty, only exploitation. Poverty, others claim, can only be created. Oliver Goldsmith, the poet, observed: 'Laws grind the poor, and rich men rule the law.' That eminent social historian, E.

P. Thompson, sought to explain the condition when he wrote: 'The greatest offence against property was to have none.' And lowest common denominator of the lower orders was a glaring lack of property. On the other side of the coin, in his much-quoted *Essay on the Principle of Population* (1798), the Revd Thomas Malthus was quite definite about the lower orders. They were to blame for much of society's ills, a thought that gave solace to the comfortable. That the ill-considered masses had little or no say in that society and yet be blamed for its faults was surely illogical. Malthus also saw war, famine, and disease as necessary checks on population growth.

Poverty apart, there were other almost chronic conditions: uncertainty of employment; unemployment; the constant quest for sufficient food, whatever the quality; exploitation; squalid housing; the evils of inadequate if not altogether absent sanitation. Education, if any, was of the most basic. Such considerations, accepted nowadays as part of society's tapestry, were not taken into account when considering ever rising crime rates. You and you alone were responsible for the condition you were in. There remained the ancient fear of the lower orders, the masses, or whatever, held by those higher up the scale. Governments regarded them as a permanent threat, so did the Church. The criminal classes were perceived as coming from there; for many the descriptions were synonymous. Of course there were hardened criminals, as in any society, but in that vast army of the lower orders were many who drifted in and out of

lawless activity as the needs arose. And the greatest of those needs was food. Food could be stolen. To kill and carry off a sheep was a hanging matter. Or one could steal things that could be transmuted into cash, and so purchase food. In the ragged army that trooped through the dock in St Mary's Gate, most were there for stealing articles easily turned into cash. The money came from the numerous pawnbrokers or the 'dolly-shops', more downmarket, and illegal establishments. Food was a necessity, drink a curse. Dedicated imbibing was a feature at all society levels. For the poor it meant only more misery. But so drab were their lives that drink was the only means of obtaining relief, albeit temporary, from the daily grind. Public houses, little better than the hovel most customers lived in, were havens with a little light, warmth and companionship, a place to exchange views or maybe meet a chance of employment. Once behind the inn door the coldness and misery of the outside world disappeared, but that same door was also an exit. And, if the ballads and broadsheets are to be accepted, all too often Mr Roper lurked in the outside shadows.

Two examples will help explain how commercial considerations could have a direct bearing on the lives of those in the poverty trap. Harvests, once gathered in, were at times deliberately held back, by either farmers, millers or merchants, to force up prices. So, too, was moving corn from one area to another to depress or inflate the market. Bread, generally of the poorest quality, formed the staple diet of the poor, and its price often the victim of market manipulation. Corn was a sensitive issue and its deliberate burning, whether out of revenge or protest (was there any other motive?), was a capital offence. On the industrial front, the introduction of new machinery into weaving mills or workshops had an obvious effect on employment prospects. Not so apparent was the ploy of some mill owners *not* to introduce the latest machinery. Always there was a surplus of hungry labour and, with the inevitable grinding down of wages, the temptation to delay investment was plain.

Those influences would be recognised today. The period under discussion did not, or only very few saw the problems for what they were. Politicians and clergy were convinced as with all members of polite society, that there really was a huge criminal class, born and bred. It possessed marked inbred peculiarities, passed down from one generation to the next. Phrenology, now thoroughly discredited, was accepted as confirmation of that viewpoint. The basic flaw of that 'science' – how did the original criminal arrive? – was ignored.

* * * * * *

SINCE transportation was massively substituted for hanging, a brief description would be appropriate. First established in 1615, mostly to the developing Americas, particularly Virginia, Jamaica and Barbados, it continued until almost ceasing in 1776 with the American War of Independence. Those sentenced went for periods varying from seven years to leaving 'this country never to return', in other words, life. Demand for labour meant an enforced escape route for many an able-bodied person otherwise destined for the gallows.

There were those who dreamed of escaping back to England, something not so far-fetched as it may sound. With the build up of the colonies, the increased trade and population, vessels regularly sailed to and from the homeland. The more determined did make their way back, knowing that if caught the executioner might get them this time. Such a fate befell Thomas Hulley, found guilty at Derby assizes in March 1754 for breaking into a shop at Baslow and making off with several pieces of dressed leather. Where he was transported to is not known, nor for what term. However, he escaped and eventually arrived back in his native Derbyshire, where he was soon arrested. Hulley stood trial at the March 1757 assizes, charged with returning from transportation 'before his time limited'. Sentenced to die, he requested to be allowed to walk with a clergyman to Nuns' Green and further that 'a coffin be provided for him, as he did not have it in his power to buy one'. His wish was granted and he was accompanied by the Revd Blackwell who later reported that the condemned man had little to say on the way. Hulley's escape could have been his second. As a rule, first-time escapees were sent back; second timers were not dealt with so leniently. William Bradbury, transported for seven years in 1805 for felony, managed to escape and remained at large until 1811. Arrested in Derby, he was tried and sent back.

America's War of Independence posed many problems, the most pressing as far as the courts were concerned being what to do with those who would have been routinely transported. Numbers were growing at an alarming rate, for transportation did not apply just to capital offences. Part of the solution was to hang more, but clearly there would have to be something else. That turned out to be prison hulks, former warships located in different waters around England's coastline. Those dank, haggard vessels were yet another disgraceful episode in penal history. Disease-ridden, timbers rotting, filthy, overcrowded and nursing every vice and perversion, an accompanying high death rate was assured. They were hopelessly inadequate for the task envisaged. So transportation was re-introduced, this time to Australia where the first convict shipment arrived in 1787. Stephen Glover, a 19th-century Derby historian and compiler of useful statistics, noted that between 1827 and 1832, 42 males and eight females were despatched to the Antipodes to serve varying sentences. For the period 1843-1849 he was more detailed: sentences of seven years, 45; ten years, 81; 14 years, 12; 15 years, 48; 21 years, two; and life, 21; total 209 felons, male and female. How many were originally charged with capital offences Glover did not elaborate.

In some ways, transportation to the southern hemisphere could be regarded as something of a blessing, with reservations. Those sent might enjoy a lifestyle that was an improvement on what they had known, not necessarily that difficult. Usually there was plenty of work, adequate living accommodation, the possibility of becoming a free man and an opportunity to create a new life in a young country. The hardest part of transportation was the separation from one's country, home and loved ones, the caress of the familiar; that was always the real punishment.

Transportation ceased in 1868, coincidentally the same year as public executions. By then 162,000 men and women had sailed to Australia, now claimed as the greatest number of forced exiles until the exceedingly far more ambitious and more sinister regimes of Stalin and Hitler.

Dealing with Women

HOW women were treated as regards capital punishment is a subject in itself. On the surface, there would seem no reason why they should have been treated any differently than men in matters of criminal culpability. They were hanged, gibbeted, whipped, humiliated in the stocks or pillory, imprisoned and transported. There were exceptions, however. Burning at the stake, after first being strangled, was exclusively for females when the crime involved was treason, murder, or coining. While the end result was the same, a woman who killed her husband or master (meaning employer) was charged not with murder, but petty treason. In England, the last woman died at the stake in 1789 for the offence of coining, and in the following year the punishment was abolished.

In Derbyshire, comparatively few women are known to have been executed. Joan Waste has already been discussed. Nothing is known about the one gibbeted in 1341 on Ashover Moor, nor the one hanged at Tapton Bridge in 1608, or the unfortunate female pressed to death in 1665. A probable charge of petty treason saw another burned at the stake at Derby in 1601, for murdering her husband. A second case of petty treason occurred in 1693, with a farm girl from Swanwick going to the stake for slaying her employer, the last reported death by incineration in the county.

Some maintain it was man's ancient fear or mistrust of women that saw a terrible departure from what could be termed the evenness of application of punishment. The crime concerned was witchcraft. While male witches were not unknown, they were rare and in essence the offence was seen as exclusively a female transgression.

Witchcraft and its followers reach back into history and most likely prehistory. For a long time witches were viewed with suspicion, occasionally tinged with fear, suffering ostracism and humiliation. Mostly they were old women, bent by age and its attendant afflictions, sometimes victims of dementia that gave rise to bouts of hallucinations. Many would have knowledge of the ways of Nature and could prescribe herbal cures. They knew that henbane possessed aphrodisiac qualities. Known also as Devil's Weed, users often imagined they could fly. Witches were the ideal scapegoats for when things went wrong, such as a harvest failure, cows not giving milk, poor weather or hens refusing to lay. Superstition held sway over reason and observation.

Despite such a reputation, those unfortunate women were not hunted down or run the risk of execution; suspicious toleration was their usual lot. That sufferance withered before a murderous pogrom that spread across Europe and into Britain when the Church identified witches as being responsible for much of Man's ills. From 1400 to 1716 it is estimated that approaching 30,000 women were hanged for witchcraft. In 1231 Pope Gregory founded the Inquisition, an organisation that found sorceresses wherever it chose to look.

Matters worsened in 1486 when Pope Innocent VIII issued a Bull to serve as preface to a document written by two Dominican monks, *Malleus Maleficarum* (The Witches' Hammer). A dreadful publication, it unleashed a minor Holocaust lasting until well into the 17th century. It was nothing short of a hysterical diatribe against witches, that detailed their evil supernatural powers, their diabolical association and grotesque sexual practices (a recurrent, much considered theme in witch-phobia). Women's sexuality disturbed the authors, the monks claiming:

The notorious Malleus Maleficarum (The Witches' Hammer). The work of Dominican monks, and with Papal approval, it provided the authority for the fatal persecution of untold thousands of women believed to be witches.

'All witchcraft comes from carnal lust, which is in woman insatiable.' The monks explained how to recognise a witch, how to torture them into confessing and then detailed various ways by which they could be done to death. How many tens of thousands of women died because of that document is impossible to calculate. Strangely enough, no one ever seemed to question why witches did not draw on their supernatural power to spirit themselves out of harm's way. Even more curious was that in denouncing women as witches, it was women, more than men, who pointed the finger.

England did not persecute witches as much as on the Continent. In 1563, Elizabeth I laid down that any who

'shall use, practise, or exercise any Witchcraft, Enchantment, Charm or Sorcery, whereby any person shall happen to be killed or destroyed…shall suffer pains of death'.

The interesting thing here is that witches were only to be executed where it was believed they had brought about death. However, matters worsened when King James I, a most superstitious monarch, wrote his *Demonologie*, in essentials little more than an update of *Malleus Maleficarum*. Ascending the throne in 1603, James issued precise terms how witches were to be disposed of. England, unlike Scotland, never burned witches, judging hanging quite sufficient.

That Derbyshire has little recorded history of witches does not in itself signify much. That could be due to lack of research or documentation, or, indeed, activity. Other areas of England are similarly unremarkable, while in some places they were seemingly everywhere. While there are localised whispers and traditions, only three accounts of women condemned to death have survived the centuries. Impossible to date is the story of the Duke of Rutland's two sons said to be victims of sorcery at Haddon Hall. They died after long illnesses and doctors in attendance declared that since they were unable to

establish cause of death, then it could only have been witchcraft. For motives unknown, but presumably torture, two sisters living in the locality confessed to being sorceresses and causing the brothers' death. Both were tried, found guilty and executed. Their mother had also fallen under suspicion and felt sufficiently moved to tell the questioners that if her daughters were in any way implicated, then she hoped to drop dead. No sooner had she spoken than she did just that.

Documentary evidence in some detail has survived to preserve the unhappy tale of Alice Gooderidge, the Witch of Stapenhill, whose death in the miasma of Derby's pestilential gaol deprived the hangman of a victim. This tragic event amply demonstrates the most extraordinary stories that judges and others were quite prepared to accept as evidence when confronted by tales of magic. In February 1596, 14-year-old Thomas Darling of Burton upon Trent, 'the Boy of Burton', had enjoyed a day out with an uncle catching rabbits. Walking back home through the woods near Winshill, he met up with a woman known by everyone as the Witch of Stapenhill. She was Alice Gooderidge, although her mother, Elizabeth Wright, was sometimes styled by that same title. Alice conformed to the accepted mould. Getting on in years, her face disfigured by three ugly warts, she wore a long grey dress complemented by a broad brimmed hat. Darling and Alice got into an argument, ignited by a young boy full of idle mischief.

Back home, Thomas complained to his father and mother of feeling unwell. A while later he suffered a series of fits and swore he had seen visions of a green cat and green angels. There were others, among them a man emerging from a chamber pot, the flames of Hell and the heavens opening. Suspicious that their son had been bewitched, the parents read out passages from the Gospel of St John. His condition only worsened. A doctor was sent for, but could diagnose nothing more serious than worms. Over the next three months young Thomas suffered more periodic fits. Finally, he told the story of having met a witch. Alice Gooderidge was brought to the Darlings' house and when Thomas saw her he promptly threw another fit and deliberately scratched her face, drawing blood. Known as 'scoring over breath', the attack was an attempt to break the spell. It was common belief that by wounding a witch, the demon in the bewitched's body would have to emerge to suck clean the injury.

Two days later, Alice and her mother were arrested. Both were questioned closely and subjected to intimate examinations. Telltale 'witch's marks' were found on their bodies, probably warts. While her mother was released, Alice was packed off to Derby and in prison there confessed to placing a spell on Thomas, because of his rudeness when their paths crossed in Winshill woods. She further admitted there was a familiar spirit, a red and white dog called Minny, which she had despatched after the Boy of Burton to torment every part of his body. This extraordinary admission was forced out of Alice by sitting her close to a hot fire, making her put on a

pair of new shoes until 'being thoroughly heated desired a release, and she would disclose all'. Still the authorities had not finished with the Witch of Stapenhill. She was taken to Burton Hall for more questioning. Once again she was confronted by Thomas Darling who, running true to form, had 37 successive fits. By way of a response, Alice herself had a choking fit and, when recovered, declined to say anything further. Satisfied there was enough evidence anyway, the inquisitors returned Alice to Derby gaol to await trial on a charge of witchcraft.

She was arraigned before Sir Edward Anderson, a learned judge with quite definite views on witches:

'Their malice is great, their practices devilish, and if we shall not convict them, without their own confession or direct proofs, they will in a short time overrun the whole land.'

Alice was found guilty and returned to prison to await the hangman. There she died, a few days before the date set. Maybe the harsh treatment gave her merciful release, although local opinion held that an evil spirit had hastened her death to prevent more disclosures.

Alice Gooderidge may have been in trouble before. An Act of 1604 (James I was on the throne) laid down that hanging would be the penalty for the first offence of bewitchment; presumably before then the first occasion drew a lesser punishment. The ultimate tragedy of Alice's story came a year or so later when Thomas Darling confessed that the entire story was untrue. 'I did it all, either of ignorance, or to get myself a glory thereby,' was his pathetic explanation. By then his family had enlisted the aid of John Darrell, an exorcist and ordained preacher, to cast out the devil in their son. Darrell was to be accused later of trickery with his practices and cures.

However incredible to modern eyes is the Gooderidge case, it pales dramatically against the judicial killing of the Witches of Bakewell and just what people were prepared to believe. Although contemporary sources are lacking, the details passed down over many years have proved reasonably consistent. The two women, who hanged in 1608, were victims of the fever generated by James I and his *Demonologie.* William Hutton, recording the year it happened, made the comment, 'Nor is it a wonder that innocence should suffer, under that weak and witch-ridden monarch.' That would appear to be the oldest reference available. The *Mercury* never listed the Bakewell incident.

There are two, quite similar stories, both remarkable even by the standards accepted by the courts as evidence. In 1608, a Mrs Stafford kept a boarding house in Bakewell in addition to running a millinery business. A Scotsman lodging with her was awakened early one morning by a bright light in his bedroom, coming through a crack in the floorboards. Curious, he peered down and in the room below saw his landlady and another female dressed as if for a journey. As he watched, Mrs Stafford uttered some strange words:

> *Over thick, over thin,*
> *Now, devil, to the cellar in Lunnun**
> *(*London)*

Immediately, the room plunged into darkness, and the Scotsman somehow knew that the women had disappeared. Intrigued, he repeated the words, but made a mistake:

> *Through thick, through thin,*
> *Now, devil, to the cellar in Lunnun.*

Before he realised what was happening, and still in night attire, he was sucked up by a mighty wind from nowhere. After a few frightening moments the lodger landed in a cellar lit only by a dim lamp. Already present were Mrs Stafford and her companion, busily tying up parcels of silk and other items. Instinctively, the Scotsman knew the goods not only were stolen, but that the women were witches. Realising his presence, they offered him wine. Accepting it gratefully, the man fell into a deep sleep and when he woke, found himself alone in the cellar. Shortly after, the Scotsman was arrested by a watchman and brought before a magistrate. The charge was that of being found in an unoccupied house with felonious intent. Asked to clarify his half-dressed appearance, the man explained that his clothes were actually still in Bakewell, and related his extraordinary tale. The magistrate accepted the testimony, seeing the whole episode as an example of the power of witches. Statements were taken and despatched to the proper authority in Derbyshire. Mrs Stafford and her friend were arrested, tried and sentenced to death.

In the second version, the Scotsman fell into arrears with his rent. Mrs Stafford threw him out, keeping some of his clothes to be returned when the debt was settled.

Gravitating to London, the man plotted his revenge. Finding an empty cellar, he stripped off most of his clothes and then attracted the attention of a watchman. Taken before a magistrate to explain himself, he told the story of his nocturnal adventures. Whether or not the unfortunate women were tried at Derby is not certain, for in 1608 one of the year's two assizes was transferred to Chesterfield because of plague in the county town.

Although Biblical authority for the execution of witches was available, 'Thou shalt not suffer a witch to live,' (Exodus XII.18), the persecution of witches gradually faded away in the face of common sense. England's last trial for witchcraft was in 1712, while the last execution had been more than 25 years before. However, the old fears died hard and in 1735 a modified Witch Act was introduced. Bizarre though it may seem, that Act was last used in 1944 at the Old Bailey, when a spiritualist was charged. Seven years later it was repealed.

* * * * * *

WHILE comparatively few women were hanged, there was one capital offence theirs almost exclusively. That was the killing of newborn or very young babies. There were rare cases of men being charged, but almost invariably were in some way involved with the mother. The reasons why any woman is driven to killing her child are numerous and complex. How prevalent was the crime would be almost impossible to compute. A Victorian doctor claimed that in 1866 alone, 16,000 women murdered their babies, but that might

have been an exceptional year. Suffice it to say, far fewer women were charged than committed the offence. Over the years, the columns of the *Mercury* reported more findings of babies killed than mothers charged.

Accepting that earlier times were harsher, more robust and lacked sensitivity, nonetheless there was realisation that mothers could suffer from physical and mental strains that might lead them to kill. Women did hang for the offence, but for most the courts looked on their sad circumstances with a degree understanding, or at least forbearance. An Act of 1624 was the relevant legislation, although it did specify unmarried mothers, a reflection of society's moralistic attitude to illegitimacy. Seen as 'harsh and cruel', that Act had been ameliorated by the middle of the 18th century. Infanticide was still to be dealt with as murder, but grounds for acquittal now included the mother making suitable preparations for the birth. If murder could not be proved, then a verdict of 'concealment of birth' could mean a two years' maximum prison sentence. Infanticide ceased to be a capital offence in 1922.

Elizabeth Jones killed her youngest child, just five months into life, at Duffield on 7 November 1817. Her story was not the more usual one of a man taking advantage of a young, innocent girl. A native of Nantwich, she had travelled up to Derby from Birmingham bringing with her two of her eight children. The father of those two – evidence suggests an itinerant tinker – had abandoned her following a quarrel. Learning

A fine woodcut heading from a ballad sheet printed by Ordoyno, a Nottingham printer, being the lamentation of Elizabeth Jones as she awaits trial for the murder of her infant at Duffield. As was often the case, the picture illustrates the type of crime but does not depict the circumstances.

In Derby gaol, long time I've been
Confined within a cell,
The grief that overwhelmed my soul
No one on earth can tell.

But soon the time will surely come
When judged I must be,
Then to receive my fatal doom
Be hanged from a tree.

What's more alarming to my view
Or dreadful to my ear,
Before a just and righteous judge
I quickly must appear.

that he had set off for Derby, Elizabeth followed. Whether she found him we are not told, but arriving at Duffield she reached her nadir of despair. Life was proving too much. The two children were being more than bothersome. In a barn she killed the smallest by pushing it under some straw and sitting on it until life had ceased. A few hours later the tiny body was found hidden between two hayricks. At the inquest Elizabeth Jones confessed to the killing and Charnell Bateman, the coroner, returned a verdict of wilful murder. Taken to Derby gaol, she remained there for five months awaiting trial.

A local printer lost little time in getting out a ballad sheet. Clearly a stock composition, easily altered to suit circumstances, a few sample verses are quite sufficient:

The printer anticipated too much. In the end, Elizabeth Jones never appeared before the assizes. Evidence against her was looked at by the Grand Jury, found wanting and she was released. Doubtless they thought little would be served in sending her to trial and possible hanging. There were seven other children to be considered, and they would become a liability on some parish. How she fared subsequently is lost but predictable: a continuing descent into her personal abyss.

A rare case of a man hanging for murdering a baby was that of Charles Kirkman, on 24 March 1759. In late January, the body of a newborn baby girl was fished out of Derby's Gaol Brook. Inquiries were initiated and within a few days Sarah Hall, the mother, was arrested. She implicated Kirkman, saying that it was he who delivered the baby. Sarah agreed to give evidence against Kirkman, thus escaping a charge. After a trial lasting several hours, he was found guilty and sentenced to death. While admitting leading an almost mandatory 'wicked and debauched life', he maintained to the end that he had nothing to do with the killing. Kirkman's case in some ways parallels that of James Loton (see *Towards the Bloody Code*) and could serve as an illustration of the selectivity of hanging. On the face of it, the only difference between Kirkman and Loton was the latter's greater social acceptability.

Lack of evidence allowed Elizabeth Townsend to walk free from the July 1763 assizes over a charge of suspicion of murdering her bastard female infant. Freed with her were Ann Saint and Ellen Elliott, acquitted of charges of assisting in concealment of a birth and murder. For a great number of years the bearing of illegitimate children was an offence and severely dealt with. Henrietta Sowter discovered how much when, in 1815 (a time of comparative leniency), she was charged with secreting the birth of a male child. Fined one shilling, she was also sent to prison for two years and, to keep her occupied, that time to be spent on hard labour.

There were those who objected to the tendency of courts to deal leniently with women, especially over deaths of babies. Churchmen were among those asserting they should be treated equally before the law. Those favouring retention of public executions when moves were being made against them, were raising those same objections. Apart from an inborn reluctance by juries to hang women, the givers of life, there was another aspect. In addition to its rarity, the public hanging of a woman attracted those titillated by the prospect of exposure of the female body. Kicking and struggling against the tightening noose could be too revealing. Tying the women's dresses at the knees usually thwarted the voyeurs

Surviving records show only 15 women executed in Derbyshire, including the one pressed to death in 1665. Rosamond Ollerenshaw, in 1732, was the first about whom anything much is known. Two years later the *Mercury* listed an unnamed female executed for rick burning, an offence to be met with again in more detail. Then in 1754 orders were issued for a new gallows to be built on Nuns' Green. The former one, last used in 1741 when the law had George Bowler stretched for dangerously wounding, had been dismantled. After such a long break, never to be repeated before abolition, the 'vast crowds' of 29 March were inevitable, more so because the hangman was to execute a female.

Little is known about Mary Dilkes. The *Mercury* bemoaned the fact that the wretched woman had given several different versions of how she murdered her 'bastard child', a little girl. So many that the newspaper, maybe lamenting more the loss of broadsheet sales, told its readers:

'Publishing what is commonly called a confession on such occasions, could not have given that satisfaction to the public, as might have been expected from one in her unhappy circumstances, 'twas therefore thought most prudent to decline to publish anything of that kind.'

The trial, before Mr Justice Birch, lasted

three hours. She became a small footnote of local history after being found guilty. As well as hanging, she was to be dissected; Derby's first victim 'agreeable to the late Act of Parliament', as the *Mercury* put it, referring to the 1752 Murder Act. She made the ritual cart journey to Nuns' Green and there spent some time in religious devotions before the white cap was fitted and the noose put in place. After an hour, her body was trundled back to the County Hall. There, in a special room, Mary Dilkes' mortal remains were sliced up and 'the Parts explained to the young Gentlemen of the Faculty by Mr Meynell, Surgeon of this place'. Meynell may have established his own small medical school in Derby, or was perhaps one of those surgeons who taught anatomy in the local hospital.

The next judicial killing of a woman came the following year, on 1 August. Once again vast crowds poured on to Nuns' Green. Ann Williamson was a pickpocket and thought to be a member of a gang of notorious gamblers. She always refuted that, but it was a fact that her mother and father and another person were simultaneously languishing in Leicester gaol, awaiting trial for stealing greatcoats at Melton Fair. Ann had been charged with picking the pocket of George White at Ashbourne Fair, a regular venue for itinerant pickpockets, relieving him of six guineas and a 36-shilling piece. Lodged in Derby gaol, she escaped on 21 February. Out went the warning notices, salted with a ten guinea reward for her recapture, offered by John Greatorex, the Derby gaoler.

Rarely do we have a meaningful description of a criminal, but here one has survived. Speaking with a Yorkshire dialect and sometimes using the alias of Sparrow, Ann Williamson came across as rather attractive; but 'looks sharp' warned the notice.

'A handsome faced young woman aged about 24 years with dark brown hazel eyes, with light, silver-coloured hair parted in the middle and of middle height.'

That she was soon apprehended must have been down to the very full dress description.

'In a dark brown gown, black tuned hat, black quilted petticoat, pink coloured stockings, a pair of large silver buckles, a gold ring on one of her fingers and a long red cloak reaching below her hips.'

Back in gaol, Ann behaved 'with great decency while awaiting execution, confessed to the crime, but denied she was a member of any gang of gamblers or sharpers'. At the scaffold, she 'did not say much, asked for the prayers of the crowd and asked that all young persons take warning by her'. Then she was sent to eternity. Her body was taken off to the Debtor's Gaol to await burial in St Peter's churchyard. No entry occurs in the parish registers.

More fortunate was Susannah Moreton, a 24-year-old mother, reprieved on the morning of execution, 17 March 1796, after being sentenced to death and dissection for murdering her male bastard child. Not so lucky was 70-year-old James Preston. Although charged with the same offence, there was no reprieve from the executioner and the anatomist. This seems a little unfortunate, for he appears to have acted out of compassion for the girl. Preston lived with his wife just outside Derby, at Mickleover, sharing the house with Sarah and her mother. Sarah was not, as sometimes supposed, Preston's daughter. A witness at the trial testified that a baby had been born at the house and the body concealed in a chamber pot. To add confusion to the story, Sarah claimed (quite naturally, under the circumstances) that the child was stillborn. Preston's honesty sealed his own fate, admitting that the infant had been alive.

Over 60 years passed before another woman hanged. This time the charge was murder and the accused the youngest victim on record. Despite her age, 16, Hannah Bocking never came across as a sympathetic character and the manner she disposed of her friend was vicious and calculated. That the crime took place in view of the gibbet bearing by the bones of Anthony Lingard (to be discussed later) did little to endear her to the jury at the March 1819 assizes.

Lingard and Bocking must have murdered their victims near the north Derbyshire village of Litton, at sites within yards of each other. For some curious reason, the Lingard case remains one of the best known and surely most recounted. Bocking's on the other hand is hardly ever recalled. (When the author visited Litton he could find no one who knew of the case.) This seems odd, for the murder of Jane Grant was carefully planned, coldly executed and the killer showed little if any remorse. The method used was poison, a means that can only mean premeditation.

Apart from Hannah Hewitt in 1732, it is the only killing in this history that falls outside those committed in drunken rages, rising tempers or panics. (William Webster in 1807 was an example of someone in a violent hurry.) Within its morbid category, the Bocking case is a minor classic.

Hannah, a creature of 'unamiable temper and disposition', and Jane Grant, around the same age, were both in service with the Brammer family at Litton. Hannah had lost her position in the household and replaced by Jane. Demotion rankled and Hannah determined to regain the ground lost. Taking her time, she started by making overtures of friendship. Ten weeks before the murder, poison (most probably arsenic) was purchased and later mixed in a cake baked by Hannah. Then one day the two girls, by now firm friends, were told to move some cattle out of a field. That was Hannah's opportunity. On the way, and in full view of Lingard's gibbet and the Brammer house, she offered Jane some of the cake. Her death, the jury was later informed, was excruciating. Hannah was charged with the murder on 19 September 1818. Her subsequent demeanour shocked the *Mercury*. Never once displaying any real emotion, she kept her feelings under firm control and to the outside world appeared reserved, almost withdrawn. In the early days following her arrest and imprisonment at Derby, she attempted to implicate not only several friends at Litton but also her sister. The latter suffered delicate health and the vicious accusation, not surprisingly, had an adverse affect on her.

Hannah remained unshaken right through the long remand, the trial and passing of the death sentence. Commenting, the *Mercury* remarked on the lack of change in countenance and deportment. The agonies suffered by her trusting victim 'seemed to awaken no remorse in the guilty mind of the wretch who had caused them'. Finally, as the gallows drew nearer, Hannah confessed, admitting that she alone was responsible for the trusting Jane's agonising demise. While there was some softening in her manner, she remained controlled as ever. That coldness communicated itself to the crowds spilling around the gallows and there was little display of the usual sympathy. Public executions were now being carried out before the county gaol in Friar Gate. On her last night on earth, Hannah Bocking slept soundly. On rising and after making the last preparations for when, as the *Mercury* somewhat poetically put it, 'the light of heaven was to be withdrawn from her eyes', she quit her cell and with a steady step ascended the scaffold. Inscrutable and unemotional as ever, she delayed little with the attendant clergyman before allowing the hangman to put the white cap and noose in place and then pull the lever. As the body plunged through the trapdoor, a shudder passed through the watching crowd, which, though appalled at her crime, nonetheless felt shocked that one so young should have been so guilty and yet so insensible. Nonetheless, Hannah Bocking was among the wickedest to die on the Derby gallows.

Friends attempted to have the body given to them for burial, but its destination was the anatomist's table. The *Mercury* was in no doubt that the correct thing had been done:

'*...but it should be remembered that in proportion as the present judgement of the law in cases of murder is dreaded by survivors, it is necessary to preserve this distinction in capital punishments; and in cases of the dreadful crime for which she suffered, nothing short of torture to the criminal should be omitted which can protect society from their commission.*'

The newspaper went on with a comment which threw an interesting light on urban/rural perceptions of the day:

'*The criminal resided in a remote and retired part of Derbyshire, and nearly all of those who have suffered for many years past on account of violent and outrageous offences have lived in similar situations. However this may be explained the fact is certain. The civilisation of the towns seems more favourable to the virtue of their inhabitants in these points of view than even the villages of our county, however unfriendly they may be to morals in other respects. Will not the same observation be found true of all large associations of individuals, excepting perhaps the metropolis of the kingdom and a very few of our overgrown manufacturing towns?*

Given the inclination of courts to deal sympathetically with mothers who had killed their newborn babies, it did not extend to Hannah Halley. At the March 1822 assizes no fewer than 12 people were tried on capital offences and found guilty. She, however, was

A somewhat stylistic illustration for an 18th-century broadsheet, showing a woman being burned to death for the crime of coining.

the only one to die, a decision not difficult to understand.

From Mayfield in Staffordshire, Hannah, 31 years old, was just one in an anonymous army of mill girls. Coming to Derbyshire for work, she found employment at a Darley Abbey cotton mill. Home was a cheap lodging house in Derby's Brook Street. One day in August 1821, she returned there complaining of feeling unwell and retired to her room. A noticeable recent increase in size had been passed off as dropsy. Later, a baby's cries were heard. Other women lodging in the house went to her room and claimed she had given birth. Hannah denied the accusation. The same day someone looked under her bed and pulled out a large jar covered with coarse cloth. In it was a newborn baby. Subsequent examination showed that the infant had been badly scalded, probably by being placed in boiling water. Incredibly, the child lived a few days before succumbing to such frightful treatment.

On being charged she claimed 'it was the

devil that caused her to do it' – the almost standard explanation in such sad and all too frequent cases. Hannah Halley had married seven weeks before the birth and somehow contrived to keep her condition from her husband, who was not the father. It was also learned that she had given birth five years earlier. Tried and found guilty, she spent much of the time before dying in devotional periods with the gaol chaplain. She became increasingly listless and weak, but on 25 March walked with a purposeful step to the scaffold. Remaining passive in front of an enormous crowd, she said a last prayer with the chaplain and, stated the *Mercury*, died with scarcely a struggle.

Hannah Halley was the last woman executed in Derbyshire and the last victim to fall prey to the anatomist's knife. The first had also been a female, and for the same crime.

The Last of Nuns' Green

THE last 20 years or so of executions on Nuns' Green saw a steady rise in the numbers hanged. The reason was the Bloody Code. While its genesis lay in the Black Act of 1732, it was not until 1770 that the death rate became more pronounced. From that year on, until 1830, England's gallows were extremely busy. Nuns' Green proved no exception. The criminals concerned were nothing extraordinary, although two or three stood out in the drab parade. One was a highwayman who went some way to fitting the derring-do of romantic legend. Another a murderer who, had he succeeded in carrying out his desperate intentions, would assuredly have won a prime spot in the nation's gallery of famous poisoners.

The name of Matthew Cocklayne is chiefly remembered for being the last person gibbeted in Derby, and the grisly tales told of his withered remains. His arrest and return to Derby for a savage murder is an illustration of how effective communications could be in an era which we, with today's technology, might glibly suppose were somewhat lacking. Moreover, the *Mercury* was now publishing more details of public executions. In Cocklayne's case, the prison chaplain, the Revd Henry, who accompanied the killer to the Green, delivered his confession to the newspaper's office. To establish that it possessed the only true document, being alert to bogus admissions, the paper warned that 'if any other is published (not signed by the said printer) it is false and spurious'.

In December 1774, Cocklayne, with a man called George Foster, broke into the home of Mrs Mary Vickars in Derby's Tenant Street. The pair rushed up the stairs, Cocklayne intent on finding money which a former maid of Mrs Vickars had told him about. That lady, aroused by the noise, was knocked to the floor by an iron bar wielded by Cocklayne. Foster pinned her down while Cocklayne broke open the lid of the chest where the money was, over £300. Grabbing it, he ran into the new maid coming to investigate the noise. With threats to kill her echoing in her ears, the terrified girl fled back upstairs. To add to the confusion, the Waits or Town Music came past the house (Derby was a well-known centre for these musical groups, diluted descendants of long-gone minstrels). Cocklayne, in his confession, said he thought Foster prevented Mrs Vickars from crying out by stuffing a handkerchief in her mouth. Rushing from the house, the two burglars made their way along Full Street, through All Saints' Churchyard and on to Nuns' Green. There they agreed to go their separate ways and meet up at a tavern in Liverpool.

Reaching the port, Cocklayne found the tavern where he listened to a wanted notice being read out. Mrs Vickars had died. Now he was wanted for murder as well as robbery. Foster duly arrived and Cocklayne told him the dreadful news only to be interrupted by his partner who not only knew already but who was also aware that he had removed the gold rings from their victim's fingers. Thoroughly alarmed, the murderers made their way to the docks and boarded a ferry to Dublin.

In Ireland, the pair resumed the criminal life. Their freedom ended when they held up a post-chaise carrying two gentlemen, who stoutly resisted. Foster was shot in the head and died three days later. Cocklayne was captured, discovered as being wanted in Derby and was returned to stand trial. His execution attracted an 'amazing number of spectators' to watch him swing on 21 March

1776 on Nuns' Green Tree (the *Mercury* favoured the capital 'T'). He took 90 minutes over his religious devotions. Before being turned off, he cried out that his fate was fully deserved and begged that no reflections might be cast on his wife. That unfortunate woman had never been privy to his criminal activities; indeed, she had always warned him against keeping bad company. Quite composed, Cocklayne helped the executioner in putting on the white cap and fixed the noose himself. Then, 'launched into boundless Eternity'.

Sir Henry Ashurst, the judge, had added dissection to the sentence. However, the anatomists at St Mary's Gate were denied their cadaver. While under the 1752 Act, dissection of murderers' bodies was the more usual rider, friends or relatives of the victim could alter it to gibbeting on suitable application to the judge. This happened in Mrs Vickars case and her killer's remains were suspended at Bradshaw Hay, somewhere near the present-day Bradshaw Way. Tradition, a sometimes fickle guide, significantly claims two gibbet sites in Derby, while Cocklayne is the only documented example we have. One was in the grounds of the present Derbyshire Royal Infirmary (almost certainly where Cocklayne hung), the other near the junction of Loudon Street and Normanton Road.

Fifteen years later, the weather-beaten carcass was still on display. In August 1791, a lad walked into Derby carrying the yellow, grinning skull. A high wind had shaken Cocklayne 'from his exalted situation the previous night', explained the *Mercury*.

Despite the passing years, the murderer's skin, hair and most of his bones were in 'high preservation,' testimony to the skill of unknown hands that applied the preserving tar. The gibbet had become something of a local meeting place, where those '…who had often stood in melancholy gaze repaired to the gibbet and returned the various parts of his remains'.

While documented at other places, the practice of juries and occasionally judges at times lowering the value of goods and even money in order to avoid the gallows, was not notable at Derby assizes. Perhaps they were not usually reported. One who did benefit from such leniency was William Gray, who stood accused at the Crown bar at the Lent 1777 assizes. He had broken into a confectionery shop and stolen 16 pence and three farthings. After a short hearing, the judge, Sir George Nares, addressed the jury and, following his direction, they decided the cash value was only ten pence. That reduced the offence to non-capital petty larceny. Doubtless very thankful, Gray was sent to have his back bared and soundly whipped at the next market day.

Many were found guilty of highway robbery. How many were self-styled Knights of the Road, or the High Toby (from the Gaelic *tobar*, meaning road), is impossible to establish. From other regions, the indications are that generally it was the dashing highwayman of romance, the mounted and masked robbers, who might end up being gibbeted. Accepting that criterion (for what it is worth), then those who preyed on Derbyshire's roads were the far more common footpads, since there is no evidence of any mounted robber being dressed in an iron jacket. Against the supposition, is the fact the footpads, violent in surprise, generally operated in towns where escape down darkened streets was more accessible. Of course, there are rumours of mounted thieves. Folklore claims one in Belper, with the gibbet being burned to the ground by friends and the corpse spirited away for burial.

However, there would have been a few mounted robbers haunting the county's lonely roads. After all, the notorious Bracy gang had been active in Derbyshire in the 17th century about the same time as was John Nevison ('Swift Nicks'), the highwayman who actually rode from London to York. The stagecoaches rumbling over the lonely highway to Manchester would have been an irresistible temptation. And a horse would have been essential, not only to reach the hold-up spot but to leave it as quickly as possible. Two can be identified as highwaymen with some certainty, and both hanged for their crimes in 1780.

First was James Meadows whose arrival at the gallows on 31 March caused many to shed tears. His offence had been to relieve Peter Featherstone, a traveller on the highway, of £40. He was a cut above the usual run of the Tree's victims, this being assumed from the *Mercury's* observation that 'his behaviour since his condemnation has been very suitable to his circumstances'. That Meadows left Friar Gate gaol in a mourning coach would have set him apart from that mournful procession which travelled by the less exalted and comfortless cart. Meadows was accompanied by the Revd Henry, a person almost as familiar to the gallows' rabble as the hangman. Heavy rain fell as they drew up at the Tree, and Henry was obliged to stay with the highwayman in the coach to say the last prayers. However, Meadows did not altogether avoid the ignominy of the gallows cart, being obliged to scramble into it to allow the executioner to perform his duty. He was joined by a Methodist minister who, ignoring the downpour, remained until the rope had snared its victim. After that it was burial in St Werburgh's churchyard, with no entry made in the register.

His wife, who had desperately campaigned to win him a reprieve, was not reported as being present at Nuns' Green. She had written from their home at Soho, near Birmingham, a few days before, asking if he wanted her to make the journey. If so, 'I will immediately set out for Derby, to bid an everlasting farewell, as every means to obtain your pardon has been already used'. She had endeavoured to speak to gentlemen of influence named by her husband, only to discover 'most...you mention are from home, which happens most unfortunately'. Among them was the engineer Matthew Boulton, who had strong commercial links with Derby.

William Buxton was definitely a Knight of the High Toby. In fact, he was something of all-round rogue. Not only did he carry a brace of pistols, but rode a black horse. Moreover, he was a handsome young man of 25, son a respectable farming family from the 'upper country' beyond Hartington. Although capable of earning an honest living, the criminal life held more and easier attractions for him. Of his earlier life, little is known although he did return to Derbyshire well versed in crime. A spell in the Army ended when he deserted. In 1778, he was a convict when he escaped from a Thames ballast lighter, sent there by an Old Bailey judge, for some unspecified transgression. Arrested on his wedding day for forging his employer's signature, it was only that gentleman's compassion that saved him. Clearly, a Derbyshire lad destined for the gallows.

Succumbing to the lure of the open road, Buxton became the terror of the vital but temptingly wild and lonely stretch between Ashbourne and Manchester. While no account survives of his career, a description of his last robbery and capture has. It was a July day in 1780 and Buxton, genteelly if shabbily dressed, had a good horse under him and was well armed with a brace of pistols and ample powder and ball. First, he held up a post-chaise but the spoils were scanty. His next target was the Ashbourne to Manchester stagecoach near Newhaven. On board was John German Kennedy, whom he relieved of six golden guineas and some silver.

Satisfied with this haul, the highwayman fired off a pistol to frighten the horses into moving off. They failed to respond, but the shot alerted two haymakers working in a nearby field who rushed over to the stagecoach to see what was amiss. Learning of the robbery, the pair got themselves horses, and galloped off in pursuit of the fleeing Buxton. He was heading for Ashbourne and three miles from that town reined in at a public house. He either was aware of being followed, or had spotted the two-man posse at a distance as he dismounted. Whichever, he tethered his horse, entered the building and walked straight through, to slip out a rear door and continue the lengthening escape on foot.

Buxton might have thought himself safe as he reached Ashbourne and sought the shelter of another hostelry (one account identifies the Anchor Inn). He reckoned without the farm workers' persistence. Having been tricked at the first public house, they too abandoned their mounts and continued on foot. At Low Top, the pair stripped to their shirts, borrowed a couple of scythes and thus disguised continued the pursuit into Ashbourne. Newhaven was now some dozen or so miles behind them. The pair's doggedness was rewarded. They found their quarry still in the tavern, captured him and handed him over to the grateful authorities.

Found guilty at the summer assizes, Buxton was sentenced to die on 25 August. There were those who plotted his escape, however. A day or two later and chained in his cell, he received a visitor who thoughtfully left some tools behind. Unfortunately for the prisoner, the friend underwent a sudden fit of conscience, sought out Blyth Simpson, the gaoler, and confessed all. A man of simple decision, Simpson promptly arrested the friend and then confiscated the tools. Buxton went by cart to Nuns' Green while his wife travelled behind and more comfortably, in a post-chaise. She had come down by stagecoach to Derby, an expensive business but at least safer now her husband was removed from the theatre of operations. She created quite an impression. 'Genteel', was the *Mercury's* verdict, seeing an attractive woman of 24, handsomely dressed in mourning. Her husband stood up in the cart, joined in the prayers 'with great fervour', admitted his guilt and then the executioner sent him on his last journey.

On the other hand, John Shaw did escape, but his freedom was a short lived thing. There were doubts about his age; he claimed 17 but on his coffin was given as 21. Either way it was young to die, but then the national average age of the hanged was 19. A red-headed Wirksworth lad, Shaw was one of life's unfortunates. Arraigned at the March 1782 assizes, he was sent for transportation to labour on the coast of Africa, to remain there for the rest of his life. In fact, that harsh sentence was a reprieve, for he had been condemned to die for breaking into the house of Anthony Goodwin of Wirksworth.

Africa held no appeal for Shaw. He broke out of Friar Gate, only to be recaptured soon after, roaming the streets. Another death sentence was his lot, handed down at the August assizes. This time there was no reprieve. Nuns' Green's yelling, boisterous crowd greeted Shaw on 2 August. Apparently saying nothing, although the hangman later confirmed that he had admitted his guilt, Shaw was turned off. An hour later his body went by cart to Wirksworth in a coffin provided by his mother, 'agreeable to Shaw's particular request'. Reporting the event, the *Mercury* thought the victim's behaviour had been 'rather stupid and thoughtless'. Quite what was expected of someone forced for the first and last time to peer through John Roper's window, argot for the noose, the newspaper declined to enlighten.

Spectators at Derby's killing field occasionally were entertained in a style more in keeping with the great processions, the heckling and bantering between victims and watchers at Tyburn and later Newgate. Forced gaiety generously underpinned with drink and encouraged by the rabble determined to get full value, there were those who put on a frantic show of bravado and a willingness to enter a next world they could then hardly avoid. Most went to pieces when confronted by the hangman carrying the white cap and testing the rope. A few maintained a brave front until the tightening noose jerked them into the wild and grotesque rhythms of the death dance. James Williams, sometimes preferring to be known as John Green or George Holmes, adopted the brisk, cheerful approach when he died on 28 March 1782, having thieved a gelding that was not his, valued at 25 guineas. With commendable alacrity, he leapt into the waiting gallows cart. Given the traditional orange to suck, he threw the peel among the watching people, a gesture

familiar at executions. At the Tree, he shouted to the crowd: 'God bless you all, and I don't doubt but he will bless and guide me.' With that, he let the executioner complete the formalities. Reports said he died without struggle. For once they may be correct, for Williams was a very stout man and that should have quickened his exit.

Thomas Greensmith did not share Williams' bravado. Arriving at the Tree on 8 April 1784, he made a sad, despairing attempt to thwart death. As the cart moved off from the gallows, he raised an arm, seized the rope and bore his own weight. For several minutes, he clutched on to life, but the contest proved unequal. Too exhausted to hold himself up any longer, Greensmith released his grip and dropped to his death. Such vain attempts would have been more common than the absence of reports might suggest. An extant broadside makes no mention of Greensmith's despairing act. Which is not too surprising, since reading it shows nothing that could not have been printed hours before – and surely was. Describing the final scene, the sheet told its buyers: '...upon a Signal given, the Cart was drawn away, and he was launched into a boundless Eternity.'

Greensmith, a labourer and widower with two children, had broken into a watchmaker's premises at Walton-on-Trent and stolen a variety of goods. According to the broadside, the judge, Sir James Eyre,

'...*on pronouncing the Sentence of the Law, urged the Culprit to make Preparation for his approaching Dissolution, as his Offences were of* such a Nature as to exclude him from entertaining the least Hopes of Pardon; he begged him to endeavour to make his Peace with God, by proper and suitable Behaviour, during the short Time he had to live in this World.'

Reported words, or assumption by the broadside? Quite likely the latter. Printers were anxious to be 'first on the street', for competition was fierce. Hanging day habitués would have been well aware of the hawkers and higglers keeping just out of sight until the cart moved away, their arms clutching sheets reporting what had just happened.

In his cell, Greensmith, a Roman Catholic, began preparation for the next world by asking for religious instruction. There were several visits by a 'Romish Priest', augmented by those from the Revd Henry, the gaol chaplain, who as well as praying with the doomed man also endeavoured to convert him to the Anglican persuasion.

As a rule, hanging days at Derby had only the one candidate for the gallows. Occasions when two or more arrived in the carts were rare. The Easter Fair on 1 April 1785, traditionally held on the Green, attracted far bigger crowds than normal, for there was the added enticement of a triple hanging. The *Mercury* did not make much comment beyond saying that 60 years had passed since there were so many. Two brothers, William and George Grooby, with James Peat (or Pitts) were to die and their crime, burglary. William, the elder brother, faced his last hours with a cheerful fatalism. As the turnkey opened the cell door, William remarked that 'it was a fatal morning,

but he hoped it would be a joyful afternoon'. Peat seemed similarly at ease in his mind, chalking on a prison door:

> *Calm and compos'd, my Sold a Journey takes,*
> *No Guilt that troubles, nor a Heart that akes.* (sic)

Friends had delivered Peat's coffin and he sat on it as the tumbril bore him to the Green. Also supplied was a woollen shroud, which he insisted on wearing for the journey. Help was at hand when he admitted being at a loss as to how to put it on.

Of all those who came to grief on the Derby gallows, few had a tale more tragic than John Porson. Nineteen years old, he remains only the second pickpocket known to have been executed (the other being Ann Williamson, 32 years before). He died on 9 April 1787, ending a journey through a life that only ever had that awful destination. The night before a friend had sat with him, giving what comfort he might to a prisoner who spent much of the dark hours in prayer and acts of devotion. Next day, just before noon, he left the prison in a composed frame of mind, received the last sacrament and, shroud donned and accompanied by the Revd Henry, went to the Green. At the scaffold, more prayers followed. A special hymn had been requested, with the opening line: 'Come let us join our cheerful songs.'

Maybe somewhat inappropriate. But then, when facing death, a buoyant, cheerful sound with the message of better things might not be entirely unsuitable to usher out one's last mortal moments. Others had made the same request.

In thieves' jargon, Porson's crime was 'to ease a bloke'. At Ashbourne fair he dipped the pocket of John Johnson, a farmer, extracting a purse containing eight guineas and some silver. However, he had not been deft enough. Johnson immediately missed the purse and set off in pursuit of the fleeing thief. Catching him, an altercation broke out during which Porson managed to lean against the farmer and by sleight of hand replace the purse. But again he was not quick enough. An onlooker had spotted the move, and it was his evidence that sent the thief to the gallows. Johnson assured the court that it was Porson who had picked his pocket 12 months before. Porson easily refuted that allegation; he was in Manchester gaol at the time.

John Porson's life was a litany of petty crime. Born at Retford in Nottinghamshire, his father had set up as doctor on the strength of having assisted the regimental surgeon when in the Army. His mother sold confectionery at markets and fairs. Apprenticed to a pot seller and tending his horses, John thought himself badly treated and ran away, scrounging a living from begging. At Snaith in Yorkshire, he opened a gate for a passing horseman in the hope of a few pennies. To his surprise, the rider was none other than his father going to a patient. Shocked at seeing his son again and in such circumstances, Porson persuaded him to return home.

Unfortunately, the young man could not settle and before long fell among thieves. In partnership with an older man, he stole a silver tankard and a cloak, and was caught. In view of his tender years Porson was not prosecuted but ordered into the Navy. That he was refused entry into a service that would virtually enlist anyone breathing surely implied he was a particularly unhealthy specimen. The life of a vagrant was the next career move. From then on, it was travelling about the country, often with a gang, picking pockets at fairs, market days and race meetings, anywhere where there were crowds. At Bury he broke into a shop and stole some ribbon. Apprehended, the punishment was two sessions of public whipping, followed by a month in the house of correction.

Back out of prison, it was a return to the old ways. Derby saw him 1785, stealing from a market stall and then 18 yards of cotton from a mercer's shop opposite the butter market. On another occasion, at Wakefield, he was with a gang that robbed a butcher of £100. Porson should have paid more attention to those he worked with. 'Being then only a boy, my companions put me off with one guinea as my share.' For his last outing, he had travelled from Birmingham to Ashbourne with other thieves, Matthew Gordon, and two women. After farmer Johnson was robbed, all four were apprehended. The other three were released since nothing could be proved against them. Porson went to the gallows and later St Peter's Churchyard, where his burial went unrecorded.

John Porson, the Grooby brothers, and James Peat before, all hanged for crimes that were commonplace. Theft in all its variations was by far the greatest supplier to the hangman's noose. Their hangings provide typical examples of the selectivity of the Bloody Code. It is no exaggeration to suggest that had they appeared at a different assizes in Derby, let alone another town, they may have been reprieved and despatched to the hulks, or alternatively a public whipping and a spell in gaol. Death was a lottery, to be applied as the judge thought fit. And his thinking would be guided by how prevalent a particular felony was; had there been more than usual? Had Derby been targeted by itinerant gangs of thieves? No doubt, the sheriff's office briefed him, or he listened to representations from people of good standing, willing to speak up for particular prisoners.

Forty-three were judicially slaughtered over the 18th century and of those only seven were for murder. When the hangman stretched Thomas Grundy on 22 March 1788, guilty of poisoning his brother, John, he was the first killer the Nuns' Green commoners had seen for 12 years. The Grundy family lived in the Dale Abbey area and from the *Mercury's* report of a trial lasting nearly six hours, John may not have been the only one to die under questionable circumstances. Admitting to murdering John, Thomas tried to put some of the blame on the 'base woman' he had been involved with. She turned out to be John's wife and, according to Thomas, had killed (by poison?) her own father and child. Grundy warned those gathered to witness his death dance, to 'avoid lewd, false women'. More must have been said, for after his corpse disappeared under the anatomist's knife, the authorities detained his sister-in-law, Mrs Mary Grundy. Mr F. N. C. Mundy, a leading magistrate, questioned her and 20 or so others from Dale Abbey. After a 'most thorough examination', he concluded that Mrs Grundy was totally innocent of any ill-doing.

Apart from providing this book's title, William Rider's execution on 1 April 1791 provides an instance of the Code at its sternest. A handsome-looking Yorkshireman from Leeds, 22 years of age, with a tolerably good education, his offence was to rob Mary Barton of threepence or, as the *Mercury* put it, 'three pennyworth of halfpence'. Rider attacked her at the Makeney toll-bar, near the present day Holly Bush Inn. In a statement, he admitted the robbery while very drunk, but claimed he had returned the money. Initially, he was accused of ravishing as well as robbery. On the direction of the judge, Sir Nathan Grose, the jury dealt only with the robbery indictment. They returned a guilty verdict and as 'the evidence was of the clearest', his Lordship 'thought it proper to have him hanged'.

Rider was well embarked on a life of crime. Among earlier charges was a pickpocketing offence. When he attacked Mary Barton, he was travelling back to Leeds after a spell in the Derby house of correction. That was not his first experience, already having suffered similar accommodation at Tideswell. In his

The Life, Trial, and Behaviour, of

W I L L I A M R I D E R,

Who was executed at DERBY, on Friday the 1st of April, 1791, for robbing MARY BARTON, on the Highway near Makeney Toll Bar, on Tuesday Evening the 28th of December last.

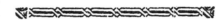

ILLIAM RIDER, the unfortunate malefactor, we are told was born at Leeds in Yorkshire, and was about 22 years of age; his friends are in the cloth-weaving branch, to which he (when of proper age) was also put; though his parents gave him a tolerable education, and it is said, intended him for the excise, but being of a roving unsettled disposition, he left home, and connected himself with a set of loose disorderly persons, who attended at fairs, &c. picking pockets, and committing various frauds; and also frequently attending different assizes, following the Judges for the same purpose. Rider said, that at our late assizes he saw one of the gang in the felon yard, but did not choose to own him.

At the last Buxton Races he attempted to pick a gentleman's pocket, but was detected, and very roughly handled by the populace; for which crime he was committed to the House of Correction at Tideswell. He was afterwards removed to Chesterfield for trial at the Sessions held there in October last.——(His friends at Leeds had not heard of him for a considerable time, until they were informed of his being in this situation).—No specific charge, however, being brought against him at the sessions for picking pockets, he was committed by the Court, to the House of Correction at Derby, to be confined for three months, and kept to hard labour as a rogue and vagabond.

Having served his term of three months in the House of Correction, agreeable to his sentence, he was liberated; and from the road he took, appeared to be returning home; but meeting, at a short distance from Makeney toll-bar, with a poor woman named Mary Barton, he took from her three penny-worth of halfpence, abused her very much, and according to her declaration, ravish'd her.— She had made a very stout defence, as her eyes were nearly swelled up by his ill treatment;——the keeper of Makeney toll-bar, hearing her cries, pursued, and very soon apprehended him, at a publick house where he was drinking, and finding blood upon his cloaths, it confirmed his suspicion, that he was the person who had committed this atrocious offence; he was therefore conveyed before a Magistrate, when the woman having sworn to his person, he was committed to the county gaol to take his trial for the said offences of robbery and ravishment.

At the assizes held for this county, March 22, before the Hon. Judge Grose, he was indicted only for the robbery, that is, taking from the said Mary Barton, on the King's highway, the sum of three penny-worth of halfpence, of which offence, after a trial which lasted some time, being clearly convicted, the learned Judge passed the dreadful Sentence of the Law upon him, in the usual form.

After his condemnation, he behaved, in general, with decency, and said, that if his life had been spared, he feared he should have returned to his old courses; that when he was liberated from the House of Correction, he went out of the same with a full resolution of committing some daring robbery; and that he had been drinking much before he met the unhappy woman, Mary Barton, on the highway, where he so much abused her.—He owned the fact in general, but says he gave her the halfpence again, though he acknowledges he was so drunk that he scarce knew what he did.—— He has been properly attended by the Rev. Mr. Henry, chaplain to the gaol, who exhorted him to make a public confession of the crimes he had been guilty of, but this he said he did not chuse to do.

He was visited by several other persons, who generally attend such unhappy men, with whom he joined in prayer, &c. complaining of the hardness of his heart, and wishing he could have been a greater penitent; he acknowledged that he thought it might be as well that his career was not lengthened, as he should certainly have committed some more audacious crimes.

On Sunday evening previous to his suffering, he was locked down in his cell, and a prisoner lay along with him, notwithstanding which, he made an attempt to break out; and for which purpose he had artfully procured a light; and by the help of a large stone and a piece of a brick, he broke one of the links of his irons, and thereby disengaged himself from the heavy chain by which he was locked down to the boards, and by some means he had ingeniously cleared one of his legs from the basil to which his fetters were rivetted. He then fell to work upon the wall of his cell, but had made very little progress, when the turnkey (who lies in a room adjoining the cells) going to bed nearly an hour sooner than usual, called to know if all were safe, but was some time in obtaining an answer; at last, however, the man that lay with Rider, had courage enough to call to the turnkey, telling him that Rider was breaking out. Upon this alarm he was properly secured, and appeared much terrified; he said that he intended not to have been hanged so soon, but as it was he must submit—or words to that effect.

On the solemn morning of his execution, several persons visited him, to take their last farewell. As usual the sacrament was administered to him, and other religious services performed by the Minister, &c. After which, on the arrival of the Under-Sheriff, and the Javelin-men, he was put into a cart, and carried through the streets, amidst a great concourse of spectators, exhibiting an awful lesson to Youth in particular, and Mankind in general, and proving the truth of that old proverb—*Honesty is the best Policy*—as well as that often inculcated and equally true lesson——*That misery is the certain consequence of vice, in a greater or less degree; and that dissipation when ripe, is frequently cut down in woe and ignominy!*—— After the usual prayers, &c. at the place of execution, the cap being drawn over his face, he was launched into eternity!!

The execution sheet of William Rider who was hanged for stealing three pennies. Convicted of highway robbery, he was hanged at Derby on 1 April 1791.

cell, he behaved 'with sulleness and inattention', to the religious exhortations. On the eve of his execution, Rider tried to escape, managing to slip off the chains securing him to the wall. However, his frantic hammering alerted the guards who hurried along and fastened him more securely.

Rider did not die easily. When taken from the cell he was in a state of near collapse and had to be half-carried by turnkeys to the cart. At the gallows his behaviour became 'extremely agitated', talking excitedly, almost hysterically to the spectators, 'earnestly entreating for mercy at the hands of God'. There was nothing original about his admitted downfall, ascribing it to Sabbath-breaking and drunkenness; loose women were not mentioned. As the hangman drew on the white cap, Rider begged him to stop for a moment. 'In this posture his addresses to the throne of mercy were exceedingly fervent, and he seemed under the most dreadful apprehensions about his fate.' Onlookers were shocked. 'Many of the spectators, and those unaccustomed to weep, were in tears, who described it as one of the most affecting scenes they ever saw!'

Scrutiny of capital charges during the Bloody Code show that relatively few of those sentenced to death actually met the hangman. At the March 1801 assizes there were 11 such charges, covering felonies such as burglary, horse and sheep stealing, and, inevitably, highway robbery. All were commuted to either gaol terms, whipping or transportation. In Derbyshire, as elsewhere, those who stole sheep seldom paid the ultimate penalty, it being generally accepted that it was a crime driven by starvation. During the Code's span, 56 were sentenced to death for that felony and yet only two were executed, John Evans of Duffield and John Dent of Coleorton in August 1801.

Reported without comment was the bungled stringing up of William Wells on 19 March 1803. From different parts of the country there exists so much evidence of incompetent killings that it is safe to accept matters were not conducted any more efficiently at the Green. Little is known about Wells, beyond that he was sentenced to die for murdering a 70-year-old man, George Bingham, at Barlborough. The hangman failed to secure the noose properly with the dreadful result that Wells fell to the ground as the cart drew away. He was hauled to his feet and put back on the cart. This time the hangman gave more attention to the task in hand and the Barlborough killer died as required by law. Whereas the *Mercury* might comment on a victim's unacceptable behaviour, almost as if it were a solecism, incompetence on the part of the executioner was disregarded. Perhaps it was not that unusual as to excite observation. As customary, his name was not divulged. Maybe he was a local man, as indeed might have most. High Sheriffs not only had the duty of hiring a hangman; they also had the power to appoint one. Strictly speaking, if a sheriff failed to find someone, then by law it was his personal obligation to carry out the duties.

There was never the slightest danger of that happening; volunteers were never in short supply.

Had William Webster paid more attention to what he was about, then he might have gone down not only as the last murderer to die on Nuns' Green but also the county's sole mass killer. He hanged on 20 March 1807, having slain two and gone close to making the total eight, which would have created a noticeable dip in the population of Hartington.

Webster's *modus operandi* was poison, a method popular in the 18th and 19th centuries. Because of its subtlety and, if planned well enough, lack of the killer's presence at the critical moment, it traditionally has been seen as a woman's weapon. While such a premise is common, men were not averse to using it. In fact, most of Derbyshire's known murders by poison were committed by them (excepting Hannah Bocking, the almost certain exception of the notorious Ellen Beare and, possibly, Rosamond Ollerenshaw). It could mean, of course, that women were far more careful. Without any doubt, some murders went undetected. There were those sudden deaths having the whiff of suspicion about them, but lacked sufficient evidence. Infant and child mortality rates were high and the temptation to insure their lives and then murderously cash in proved irresistible to some. Peter Bradbury was charged in 1816 with poisoning his four children at New Mills, but the grand jury considered the evidence insufficient.

As his duties took him around the Midland Circuit, Judge Sir Robert Graham must have listened to some extraordinary cases. However, it is doubtful if he heard many quite as daring as Webster's attempts to rid himself of debt. That amounted to something in the region of £600, a substantial sum for the times. He owed the money to Thomas Dakin of Hartington, who foolishly neglected to obtain any sureties. Repayment was pursued. Webster responded by obtaining (or forging) letters from other people, confirming that they owed money to him. Once that money was received, Webster assured Dakin, then the liability would be settled. At the same time he convinced himself that if Dakin died, then the debt would be cancelled, there being no security.

On 11 February, at the inn of John Sims, Webster mixed what was described in court as a corrosive sublimate into Dakin's glass of ale. It was too strong and Dakin, nauseated but unsuspecting, declined to finish the drink. Next day Webster tried again. At breakfast with the Dakin family, he accepted some posset, a hot milk drink mixed with wine or spice. After drinking a little, he surreptitiously added arsenic to the remainder and returned it to the breakfast table. All the Dakin family drank some. Fortunately, the mixture this time was not lethal enough and no ill effects were felt.

Four days later a frantic Webster made his third attempt. Again, the plan misfired, but this time with tragic results. Showing utter disregard for the consequences, he put arsenic into the Dakin family teapot. Yet again, Thomas Dakin escaped, although falling seriously ill. His wife, Elizabeth, and her sister, Mary Roe, died. Four of the Dakin children were violently sick, as was a servant, Jane Fern.

Webster pleaded not guilty at a trial lasting 11 hours. The jury learned he 'told many gross falsehoods', particularly to Thomas Dakin from whom he extracted the money under false pretences. Throughout the hearing, Webster continued to protest his innocence. He persisted right until the morning of his execution, when he made a clean breast to a clergyman and afterwards received the sacrament of the Last Supper. The noose took his life and the surgeons took his corpse.

Not quite three weeks later a huge, boisterous, noisy mob, many half-drunk, again invaded Nuns' Green, displaying the sort of unruly, appalling behaviour that did so much to bring about the end of public hangings. Time would reveal that when the cart left Joseph West kicking and screaming his life away on 8 April 1807, the Green had seen its last judicial slaughter. No one will ever know how many died there, nor over what time span. Nor is the gallows site known; contemporary maps are silent.

West's story is one of the more interesting. For a change, the background moves from the parochial and also serves as an example of the circumstances that set so many more of the working class-cum-lower orders on the (sometimes occasional) criminal path. By trade, he was a shoemaker. Indeed quite a good one and put his skills to good use while

awaiting trial. By birth a Yorkshireman, he moved to London to find work. To protect his livelihood, West joined a union, the Journeymen Boot and Shoemakers (Motto: 'May the Manufactures of the Sons of Crispin be trod upon by All the World'). Under the Combination Acts of 1799 and 1800, unions were proscribed, although several managed to function covertly. Specifically, workers as a body were not allowed to negotiate wage increases.

In 1805, the Shoemakers went on strike. Their aim was twofold: higher wages and some protection against shoddy, under-cutting practitioners, whose activities at times were encouraged by the shoemasters. There was as well the spectre of rising competition from newly-created centres in Northamptonshire and Staffordshire. It was a scenario only too recognisable in often overcrowded trades of the day. Equally familiar was the response of the masters. The Combination Acts, effectively if not in original intent, were only ever used against employees, not employers. Warrants were taken out against many of the striking shoemakers, whose response was to quit the capital and scatter. Joseph West was among them. Cut off from employment, several turned to crime, often the passing of forged bank notes. That was what landed West in Derby gaol.

He had come to Derby from Birmingham the previous September, accompanied by two companions. All three were passing counterfeit notes to local tradesman. The other two moved on, to be later arrested in

Lancashire and ending up in Lancaster Castle, a prison with perhaps the most evil, and well deserved reputation outside London. What made West's offence the more serious was that when apprehended he was carrying not only a bundle of forgeries in his pockets but a loaded pistol besides.

'Peculiarly interesting' was how a broadside described West, a man in the prime of life – he was 29 – with pleasing deportment and behaviour that excited the pity of everyone. For reasons unexplained, his journey to the Green was by coach, not the usual open cart. He had already made a confession. In the admission expected of him, West hoped that his situation would be a warning to all young men having the means to earn an honest living, not to indulge a restless and dissatisfied temper and turn to dishonest ways to 'supply the expenses of pride and intemperance'. After sentencing, he asked that neither his real name nor place of birth be disclosed so that the news of his disgrace might not reach the ears of his mother. His plea was ignored.

Five years passed before the next gallows' theatre. By then, the Tree on Nuns' Green had disappeared and the era of the short drop arrived. The Green had been the scene of the Bloody Code at its most rampant. While the Code lasted from 1770 to 1830, proportionately the first 30 years saw more people executed. This was true both nationally and for Derbyshire. Thirty-eight were charged with 11 capital offences over the period 1770 to 1784. Seven, or 18.5 per cent, were executed. 14, or 26 per cent, died from 1785 to 1810, out of 54 charged with 12 offences (see *Appendices B and C*). A startling figure, for it was higher than London's and Middlesex's at 23 per cent, the accepted leaders in the execution numbers league. As will be seen, the next 30 years set off at the same high rate, and then fell sharply in the final decade.

Death in Friar Gate

Hark to the clinking of hammers
Hark to the driving of nails;
The men are erecting a gallows,
In one of Her Majesty's gaols!
A life – a human life's to be taken,
Which the crowd and the hangman hails;
For the men are erecting a scaffold,
In one of Her Majesty's gaols.
'Tis midnight: without its deep silence –
The doom'd wretch in agony moans,
But the clattering still of the hammers
Is drowning the poor victim's groans.
The Chaplain now earnestly prayeth,
To the God of all mercy – for him;
But his mind on his misery strayeth –
For his cup is full to the brim.
(The Song of the Scaffold)

SEVERAL influences lay behind the shift of the execution site from Nuns' Green to the main entrance of the county gaol in Friar Gate. Primarily it was to facilitate the new drop, an innovation first seen at Tyburn nearly 30 years before and adopted at Newgate in 1783. Another was that the congestion created by surging, at times unruly crowds at public hangings might be better controlled. In addition, people generally were getting more sensitive and the fairground ambience surrounding the killings was disturbing. Such considerations meant that Derby introduced the new drop quite early on in its reign. Commenting on the slow adoption of the system outside London, mainly on grounds of cost, the historian V. A. C. Gatrell cites Northampton as introducing one as early as 1818. Derby first saw the new death machine six years earlier.

Then there was the gradual development of the Green itself. Derby was expanding under the continuing influence of the Industrial Revolution and space to do so was much sought after. There was much pressure on available land, particularly where there flowed streams and rivers whose power could be harnessed to that icon of the Revolution, the textile mill. More housing was needed, both the salubrious and the cut-price squalid.

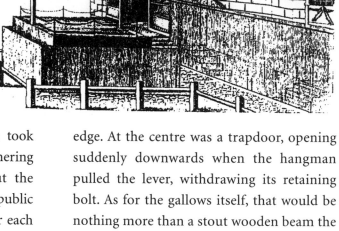

The new drop at London's Old Bailey in 1783. The one used at Derby's Friar Gate prison would have been very similar in appearance.

Nuns' Green was a most obvious target and the commonage had been much whittled down when the fatal Tree finally disappeared.

From now on, the scaffold would be erected when needed; otherwise it would be stored within the gaol. The structure was solid and its timbers heavy. Building took many hours and the workmen's hammering and attendant clatter would beat out the message up and down Friar Gate that a public killing was imminent. None would hear each hammer blow more acutely than the condemned within the prison walls. The drop was generally about 18 inches and even with the sudden weight of a now falling body, still nowhere sufficient to cause death other than by slow strangulation. Predictable, if not recorded, would have been the thoughts of the widows of impoverished clergymen, living in the almshouses directly opposite the gaol. For 13 years, those gentle ladies could enjoy, if they so chose, a grandstand view of the busiest era of the scaffold.

No description has survived of what the new machinery looked like, though it is unlikely to have differed much from the others beginning to appear up and down the country. A large wooden platform, or scaffold, some six feet or more above ground, with a wooden rail guarding its edge. At the centre was a trapdoor, opening suddenly downwards when the hangman pulled the lever, withdrawing its retaining bolt. As for the gallows itself, that would be nothing more than a stout wooden beam the width of the platform and supported by two wooden uprights. Access was by a set of steps, reached by a passage leading from the prison.

By 1822, for the hanging of Hannah Halley (see *Dealing With Women*), the *Mercury* was able to inform its readers that a new gallows had since been put in place. Moreover, its replacement brought with it 'a consequent diminution of expense on every execution, and decreased annoyance to the neighbourhood'. Friar Gate was becoming residential and respectable. Designed by a smith named Bamford, the new construction, while retaining the standard appearance, was built principally of wrought iron. Its weight was less than its wooden predecessor's and with it went the great advantage of ease of erection, taking just 20 minutes to assemble and demolish. There is no reason to suppose it achieved its ultimate purpose any quicker.

Despite the advantages, the *Mercury* hinted that the excesses of the Code were now causing growing concern:

'*...it would be infinitely more consonant to our feelings to report such improved arrangements in prison discipline, and such modifications of the existing criminal code as should render the use of this dreadful instrument of death less familiar to the public mind.*'

Over the 13 years that Friar Gate hosted public hangings, there would be signs of several shifts in thinking over judicial punishment. There was the emergence of a national prison building programme, based on Robert Peel's Gaols Act of 1823. More and more would question the necessity for so many capital offences. That England manifestly lagged behind much of Europe in dealing with serious crime was causing embarrassment. And, very slowly, almost muted at times, would be more radical calls, these for the abolition of hanging altogether. Others, while agreeing there were too many capital offences, nevertheless thought some should retain the death penalty. Some argued that executions should no longer be occasions for grotesque public spectacle. Moreover, realisation was dawning that hanging was not a deterrent, feelings confirmed by the introduction in 1805 of reliable statistics and returns. In another direction, Peel, as Home Secretary, started floating ideas about police forces.

Calls for reform were not confined just to the judicial and penal systems. On several fronts, the government was coming under pressure. Demand for parliamentary reform, stoutly resisted by Westminster, was gathering momentum. Bouts of food shortages led to regional rioting. In the East Midlands, unhappy textile workers, mainly from the dominant stocking industry, had launched the Luddite movement around 1811-1813. Derbyshire experienced some of their machine-breaking forays and intimidatory tactics. There were demands for trades unions. Even though the wars with Napoleon were over, there was a feeling of restlessness in England, as trade and employment slumped, and the old ways were finally superseded. Farmers, feeling the pinch, pressed for that time-honoured measure to maintain the price of grain, the Corn Laws. Passed in 1815, the Act saw the price was kept unduly high, which meant the poor, consequently hungrier, shouldered the burden. The Tory administration sought, unsuccessfully, to scrap the Poor Laws, which did nothing to redeem the government's poor reputation.

The Industrial Revolution had spawned the growth of urban populations, introduced new towns. Politicians agonised over the comparative ease by which subversive meetings and agitation might be organised, and kept away from prying eyes. Whether the Tories were getting attacks of the jitters or, as others thought, used the unease to reassert their authority by introducing severe measures, has long been debated. One restriction of personal freedom was to suspend *habeas corpus*.

Another was the marked rise in executions. From 1770, the catch-all legislation under which the Code multiplied, grew in severity for the next two decades. Thereafter actual executions fell, despite the continuing rise in capital convictions. The more were condemned, the more were reprieved; the law was being made to look ridiculous. Had all those sentenced hanged, then the ensuing slaughter rate would have challenged the Tudor mayhem. After a virtually unbroken 60 years tenure, the Tory administration was replaced in November 1830 by a Whig government. The Bloody Code collapsed.

* * * * * *

GIVEN that theft was the commonest capital felony, it is no surprise that the first to demonstrate the short drop in Friar Gate were two burglars, Percival Cooke and James Tomlinson (alias Fruz) on 10 April 1812. Tomlinson, aged 27, was a frame worker from Belton in Leicester. Cooke, 26, another frame worker, came from Dale Abbey. Both were deserters from the Army. On the scaffold, each insisted on facing the prison wall and not the crowd. Their crime was breaking into the homes of Samuel Hunt of Ockbrook Mill and John Brentnall of Locko Grange. With them at the Crown bar had been Thomas Draper, but he agreed to give evidence for the prosecution and so saved his skin. At the same assizes, Tomlinson's brother, William, had been transported for 14 years for forging bank notes.

Apart from remarking that the executions were carried out 'on a new drop erected in front of the county gaol', the *Mercury* had nothing to add about the new death machine. Nor was it any more forthcoming when, a year later, on 9 April, three more burglars dropped to their deaths. Five executions in a year was excessive for Derby. For the next few years, a regular diet was forthcoming for those who

The old County Prison in Derby's Friar Gate. From 1812 until 1825 it formed the background for public executions, including those of the Pentrich rebels and of Hannah Halley, the last woman to hang in Derbyshire.

THE

CONFESSION

OF

Percival Cooke

AND

James Tomlinson,

WHO WERE EXECUTED ON FRIDAY, APRIL
10, 1812, ON A DROP NEWLY ERECTED
IN THE FRONT OF DERBY GAOL,

For Robbing the Houses of Mr. S. Hunt, of
Ockbrook-Mill, and Mr. J. Brentnall of
Locko-Grange, in the County of Derby.

————

NOTTINGHAM:

PRINTED AND SOLD BY C. SUTTON.

The confession of Cooke and Tomlinson, the first men to be executed in front of the Friar Gate gaol using the new, or short, drop.

liked watching people die. There were more capital prosecutions. No fewer than 14 prisoners were found guilty of capital offences at the March assizes, but only three danced beneath the gallows beam. Paul Mason, Richard Hibbert and Peter Henshaw were members of a large gang that ransacked the home of John Drinkwater at Bugsworth. Two others had their sentences reduced to transportation, while nine more were acquitted. This hanging of some and transportation of others provides yet again a perfect example of the 'heads or tails' selection that hallmarked the Code. What sets this crime apart a little is that the gang claimed to be Luddites. Now that may well have been true, for it was not unknown for King Lud's followers to break into premises for motives other than machine wrecking. On the other hand, thoroughgoing villains were at times inclined to make that assertion when caught, as if somehow it lent some credibility to their violation.

When a military escort delivered the remains of Anthony Lingard to Litton, the villagers made sure that such a momentous event in an otherwise too predictable yearly calendar was celebrated in style. A fair was held, and folk from neighbouring parishes flocked in. There were pedlars and hawkers, ballad sellers, tinkers, musicians, and much noise and gaiety. John Longden, a noted local Methodist, turned up and preached to a congregation far greater than customary. He should have spoken at Tideswell chapel but when he arrived there, most of the flock had strayed over to Litton. Like a good shepherd, he went to seek them out. One who found the whole occasion utterly revolting was William Newton, the 'Minstrel of the Peak'. The poet's mind was not so much on the ribaldry, the drunkenness, the shouts, the itinerant traders bawling out their shoddy wares, but the reason for the holiday atmosphere. That was not difficult to find. Presiding over the hustle and bustle of Litton Fields was the tarred body of Lingard, locked in a frame of iron, swinging from a newly-erected gibbet post.

A Tideswell man by birth, Lingard's story has remained popular in local history. Perhaps because he was the last person to be gibbeted in the county. Full details of his killing of Hannah Oliver in January 1815, the trial and execution are, for once, readily available. The off-stage information makes the tale that much more interesting. Such as a toast rack fashioned from part of the cage, or the gibbet's upright later incorporated into the cellar of a Litton house. That his grisly bird-pecked visage gazed down on the poisoner Hannah Bocking, despatching the trusting Jane Grant, lends a further macabre touch. Moreover, the remains were still creaking in the wind 11 years later and witnessed William Lingard, his brother, together with William Bennett, assault and rob travellers on the nearby road. Both were sentenced to death, but reprieved. Still around is a copy of the warrant for Lingard's arrest, as well as the handcuffs fastened at his capture and a shoe-maker's measure used on Hannah Oliver's feet. When the gibbet was dismantled, the skull was sent to Belle Vue in Manchester for public display. The relic is now displayed in a small museum in Friar Gate, not many yards from where Lingard originally hanged. The rest of his bones were buried in the gibbet field at Litton.

Hannah Oliver, probably a widow, was the toll-keeper at Wardlow Mires turnpike, a mile or two north of Litton. Her death was discovered when a stagecoach's warning bugle failed to attract her attention. A maidservant from the inn opposite, hearing the commotion, hurried across and discovered Mrs Oliver's body lying in the doorway of her cottage. She had been strangled. Suspicion soon focused on Lingard and it was the discovery of a pair of red shoes that led to his arrest and eventual execution.

Lingard, a young man of 21, filled the role of local rake. His girl friend, also from Tideswell, had become pregnant and he desperate. Quite what he had in mind when he went to visit Mrs Oliver, with whom it was rumoured he had once enjoyed a liaison, is not certain. Whatever it was, a furious row broke out and ended up with her death. Lingard stole what money he could find and also took a new pair of red shoes. Returning to Tideswell, he gave them to his girl friend and offered the stolen money provided she would swear that the coming baby was not his. When the news spread about Hannah Oliver's death, the girl became alarmed and returned the shoes. Lingard swore he had got them in exchange for a pair of stockings, but the girl was not impressed. Lingard first hid them in a haystack near his home in Litton (still pointed out) and later, foolishly, recovered them. When his house was searched, the shoes were found and he was arrested. Samuel Marsden, a shoemaker from Stoney Middleton, had made the all-important footwear for Mrs Oliver. After examining them, he assured the investigators that they were his work. Pulling them apart, the cobbler exposed some packing bearing the warning, 'Commit no crime.'

Lingard hanged on 28 March. For some reason, the trial judge ruled that his body would not be dissected, as generally the case,

With the opening of the new County Prison in Vernon Street, the old prison in Friar Gate was used as the Derby Borough Prison and House of Correction.

but gibbeted, specifying in view of the toll-house. Maybe a salutary warning was thought more appropriate. All the arrangements and preparations had to be undertaken in Derby and when finished Lingard's corpse was loaded into a cart and transported to Litton.

The minutiae surrounding the Lingard narrative extends to the history of the gibbet. Its exact location is not certain, although tradition puts it in a field between the main road and Peter's Stone, an impressive limestone outcrop. For 11 years, Lingard's remains hung and slowly rotted within their metal jacket. On 10 April 1826, on the orders of a magistrate, the gibbet was dismantled. Years later a local man, Thomas Platt, would reminisce that as a boy he learned that a 'cow doctor' from Tideswell had assisted a medical

man from Wheaton Hall in collecting the murderer's remnants and burying them.

A persistent tale is that Lingard was the last person in England to be gibbeted. That is true for Derbyshire, but there were several others elsewhere and much later. For the record, the last to suffer the infamous exposure was James Cook of Leicester in 1832, who hung in chains on a post 33ft high. The belief that the touch of a hanged man's hand could cure blemishes was still very much alive. After they took down Cook's body, several people entered the room where his remains lay and with his cold hands stroked their wens and warts.

Another story associated with Lingard's gibbet is that William Newton, the poet who had been so disgusted by the festive scenes, was instrumental through one of his compositions in having gibbeting abolished. That could be an example of misplaced parochial pride. In fact, the gibbeting that led directly to abolishment also occurred in 1832, at Jarrow. Demand to see the revolting spectacle was so great that local boat owners made small fortunes ferrying sightseers across the Tyne, their enterprise only stopped when the victim's friends stole the corpse.

Newton began to write *The supposed Soliloquy of a Father under the Gibbet of his Son, upon one of the Peak Mountains* not long after the Lingard episode but did not immediately publish it. That came in 1819, following the execution and dissection of Hannah Bocking. While the Litton gibbet may have finally persuaded him, Newton's original inspiration came from an incident over 20 years earlier.

In 1792 Spence Broughton, a grazier educated above his position in life, was hanged and then gibbeted on Attercliffe Common near Sheffield, for the crime of highway robbery. From York Castle prison, he wrote to his wife, Eliza, mother of his three children, and it was that final letter which fired Newton's imagination. Dated 14 April, an extract read:

'One part of my awful sentence – a sentence aggravated by being merited, chills me with horror. When I reflect that my poor remains, the tokens of mortality, must not sleep in peace, but be buffeted about by the storms of heaven, or parched by the summer's sun; and every passenger shrinks with terror and disgust. This consideration freezes my blood. This cell – this awful gloom – this death is not so grievous. Why will the laws continue to sport frowns with the wretched after life is at an end?'

So the Minstrel of the Peak responded with his feelings:

TIME, – MIDNIGHT. SCENE, – A STORM
Art thou my Son suspended here on high?
Ah! what a sight to meet a Father's eye!
To see what I most prize, what I most loved,
What most I cherish'd, – and once most approved,-
Hung in mid air to feast the nauseous worm,
And waving horrid in the midnight storm!

Let me be calm: down, down my swelling soul;
Ye winds be still, ye thunders cease to roll;
No! ye fierce winds in all you fury rage;
Ye thunders roll; ye elements engage;
O'er me be all your mutual terrors spread,
And tear the thin hairs from my frenzied head:
Bring all your wrathful stores from either pole,
And strike your arrows through my burning soul,
I feel not, – fear not, – care not, – shrink not, – when
I know, – believe, – and feel, – ye are not men!
Storms but fulfil the high decrees of God,
But man usurps His sceptre and His rod,
Tears from His hand the ensigns of His power,
To be the petty Tyrant of an hour.

Broughton's remains were on the gibbet for 35 years; a lane in Sheffield named after him passes the site.

* * * * * *

THE move from Nuns' Green to Friar Gate

brought no improvement in the crowd's behaviour. At least that was what the *Mercury* hinted. Rarely did that newspaper comment on how the lower orders conducted themselves, especially at public killings. What prompted the departure was the hanging of Joseph Wheeldon on 9 August 1816. He had murdered two children, his niece and nephew, but no one seemed clear as to motive, if any. Wheeldon's character singularly failed to impress the *Mercury*'s correspondent, whose conclusions, in view of the awfulness of the crime, may not have been far off the mark:

'The truth is, that his mind was of the lowest possible order not to be marked by idiocy; he had not received cultivation sufficient to rank him much above the condition of human savage; and his total insensibility to the infliction of pain or the value of life may probably be referred to the mean condition of his intellectual powers, and the want of the restraining influence of religious views.'

Sensing the growing abhorrence of public executions, the *Mercury* enlarged its theme. While not denying the gravity of Wheeldon's behaviour, the newspaper entertained doubts that the thousands gathered in Friar Gate that August morning had heeded the message supposedly contained in the manner of his death. The mob's indifference or inability to grasp what the age-old ritual was intended to convey, compelled the *Mercury* to comment further:

'It is one of the unfortunate tendencies of frequent executions to blunt the feelings of spectators; this may probably account in part for the levity and unconcern which we observed in too many of those who were present on Friday last. But let us hope that others derived from the frightful scene motives to circumspection and to holiness; and that in particular the young thus seeing what vice in its excesses would resolve to shun its first enticements.'

While the *Mercury* was reporting public killings more fully, there still remained (today's) frustrating lack of background and courtroom detail. Nowhere is that more felt with a multiple hanging on 15 August 1817 when no fewer than four arsonists walked down the prison passage and climbed the steps to meet their hangman. Their crime was to burn hay and corn stacks, a matter considered so serious that the judge had warned: 'The heinous nature of their offence precluded all hopes of mercy.' What records there are suggest that no one had been executed for that offence since an unnamed woman in 1734, and that an incident lacking supporting evidence.

To understand fully the judge's remark, it has to be borne in mind that burning corn was an extremely serious offence. That crop was a very viable as well as emotive commodity, as any study of the contentious Corn Laws would show. Apart from its obvious function, grain could be used most effectively to manipulate the market. Farmers could delay harvesting to help force up prices, or they may store the yield with the same aim in mind. They, or the corn merchants, might move it about the country to create a demand and so again increase profits. Millers had their own ploys in market manipulation. Such moves would inevitably hike the price of bread. That sustenance was for many, if not the staple diet, then an important part of it. It was the poor and unemployed who suffered the most.

To destroy corn was a tactic employed by farm labourers with a grievance, or tenants wanting to score off a landlord, perhaps a protest against church tithes, or to exact revenge for some perceived wrong. In 1817, it could have been a protest against the imposition of the much-hated Corn Law of 1815, or the proposals to abolish the Poor Law. There could be no profit motive. What made these executions that more noteworthy is that the county, like most of England and indeed Europe, had suffered appalling harvests in 1816, the 'year without a summer'. The weather had been so dreadful that for many farmers, harvests were not garnered until very late or in some cases not at all. (Incredibly, the dreadful conditions were due to widespread dust thrown up by an enormous volcanic explosion in Indonesia in 1815). That natural disaster had come hard on the heels of the slump in farming (and other industries) following the end of the Napoleonic Wars.

No specific reason, among the many available, is known as to why, in February 1817, a small band of men set fire to corn and hay stored at the farmyard of Colonel Winfield Halton of South Wingfield. Owner of Wingfield Manor and a magistrate, Halton was also Colonel of the Derbyshire Regiment of Militia and later that year would be prominent in the hunting down of the Pentrich Revolution

rebels. Clearly he was a man of much local influence, and moreover with an ear to the ground over pernicious rumours of revolutionary stirrings in the neighbourhood.

There is the inescapable feeling that somehow the arson attack was enmeshed with the forthcoming rising. William Jeffrey Lockett, the Derby solicitor responsible for preparing the Pentrich prosecution papers, entertained no doubts about the characters of the fire raisers. Shortly after their conviction he percipiently noted:

'*These miscreants are part of the Pentrich political society and if they had not been in gaol would have been active parties in the insurrection of June 9.*'

Those planning the rising had talked of reprisals against Colonel Halton over the holding in gaol of the arsonists. Presumably, he had initiated the prosecutions. At a meeting in the White Horse inn at Pentrich, William Turner, who would be executed for his involvement, moved that Halton be killed. He proposed that they 'draw the badger' by lighting a bundle of straw in front of the Colonel's home and shooting him when he came out to investigate. The suggestion was not acted upon.

A broadsheet printed by Wilkins of Derby told how a group of men on the night of 9-10 February went out to South Wingfield. Concealed beneath a hat, the men carried a burning length of thick rope. Two stands of hay and one of corn were set alight. Five men were arrested. One of them, Thomas Hopkinson, an 18-year-old weaver from Woolley

Moor, earned his acquittal by turning King's evidence at a trial lasting 11 hours. According to the *Mercury*, Hopkinson became suspicious that one of the gang, John King of Matlock, was preparing to betray his companions and decided to get there first. The remaining three were John Brown of Nottingham, George Booth from Chesterfield and Thomas Jackson of Woolley Moor, the latter a partner of long standing in many crimes with Hopkinson.

Just before 1pm on execution day, the arrival of the four beneath the gallows beam was witnessed by a gathering of several thousand. Preliminaries to the noose included the singing of the ritual hymn. As the voices rose on the air, a heavy shower of rain fell. Two of the condemned sought the shelter of a handy umbrella, while another protected himself in a nearby prison doorway. 'The inconvenience of being wet was felt and avoided by men who knew that they had not five minutes longer to live!' exclaimed an astonished *Mercury* reporter, adding:

'The whole of the scene now recorded was one of great horror, increased by the conduct of the criminals themselves. The many thousands of spectators behaved with great decorum, but retired from the spectacle apparently little impressed with sympathy towards men who had evinced so much insensibility to the real nature of their own unhappy condition.'

The broadside, referring to the many hangings in Derby, spoke of their futility:

'We are sorry to find that they have not had the long-term wished for effect, by deterring men from committing these crimes.'

One man standing close to the scaffold behaved with due decorum, when otherwise would not have been surprising. Passively he watched Thomas Jackson expend his last mortal moments fighting for breath. When it was all over, he returned home to Woolley Moor, burning with anger and revenge over Hopkinson's role in his son's death.

After remaining suspended for the usual time, the corpses were carted away. George Booth was buried in Pentrich graveyard on 17 August. As insisted by law, there was no burial service. However, the Revd Hugh Wolstenholme, curate at St Matthew's Church and a noted reform advocate, took the opportunity to deliver a sermon during which he claimed that Booth had been murdered. In the parish register he wrote: 'George, son of Miles Booth of Wessington, who suffered at Derby on the 15th inst, aged 21, with John Brown, aged 38, Thomas Jackson, aged 20, and John King, aged 24, for setting fire to the corn and haystacks of W. Halton, Esq, of South Wingfield. No ceremony performed.'

Lockett, the solicitor, nursed a strong antipathy towards the curate and strove unsuccessfully to have him removed from office. Member of a Yorkshire family prominent in agitating for reform, the clergyman, probably with every justification, was viewed with great suspicion. In Lockett's opinion, he was 'of the lowest order of clergyman – uneducated, of vulgar habits – and low connections.' In fact, Wolstenholme was a Cambridge graduate.

Hopkinson failed to heed the lesson of his

narrow escape. Two years later Friar Gate claimed him. Born in Ashover, he was 14 when his family moved to Woolley Moor. There he fell in with bad company, chiefly Thomas Jackson, a lad two years older. Jackson was described as a bad lot, the 'son of an abandoned father'. The two became firm friends and Hopkinson was introduced to the delights of poaching, a capital risk. From then on, it was just a matter of time before the pair graduated to sheep and horse stealing, highway robbery and housebreaking. What money they obtained was quickly squandered in some distant town, usually Sheffield, 'in the company of lewd women and in every indulgence of riot and debauchery'.

After Jackson's execution, Hopkinson went back to the old ways with redoubled zeal. For two years he robbed at will until February 1819 when he was arrested for highway robbery, a crime for which he hanged on 2 April. Immediately after his capture, he was placed in Chesterfield gaol. Questioned there by Mr W. A. Lord, a Justice of the Peace, he confessed to numerous other crimes. Hopkinson's litany of hauls takes some believing, not so much for what was stolen but the precise detail:

Breaking into one house, one shop, one pantry, two corn mills, and one turnpike house, and stealing thereout flour, meal, meat, &c, &c.

Robbing gardens of cabbage plants and other vegetables, fruit, &c, 27 times.

Stealing at 95 different times, 209 fowls, 21 geese, 9 ducks and 4 turkeys.

Stealing at 20 different times, 72 rabbits.

Stealing at 20 different times, 18 sheep and 3 lambs, and skinning one alive.

There was a great deal more.

In prison, Hopkinson continually protested his innocence, although there were occasions when he changed tack and admitted his crimes. An insistence on breaking into bawdy songs as the mood took him drew sharp criticism from the *Mercury*. Twice did his bravado falter, once when his father visited him and he broke down and cried. The other was when he became acutely aware of his own situation, seeing the poisoner Hannah Bocking an hour before she hanged. She was seated in the condemned pew of the prison chapel.

Hopkinson himself went to the scaffold with the usual rituals, time spent with the chaplain, forgiving all his enemies and sending out the message to all young people that to avoid his fate they must avoid bad company. Then the walk along the short passage to the scaffold, to be 'dismissed to that dread tribunal, where no disguise can avail'. For once, the *Mercury* reported that death came neither quickly nor painlessly. 'He was much convulsed after the drop fell; he seemed to suffer more than is usual on such occasions.' This could mean an incompetent hangman. As always, the name was withheld. It might have been James Botting, then England's principle executioner, but there were others. There is a strong possibility that it was Thomas Jackson's father, surely an act of poetic justice. That man had watched his son

The condemned man makes his final confession – a highly unlikely although oft-used illustration for execution sheets. Most of those sentenced to hang were unable to write and their 'confessions' were more likely the handiwork of the prison chaplain or ordinary, who at times had agreements with local printers.

hang and when Hopkinson, whose evidence had condemned him, was sentenced to death, he volunteered to kill him. Whether the offer was accepted is not made clear by the *Mercury's* somewhat ambiguous comment:

'*...the same wretch applied for permission to be his executioner. Human nature recoils with horror from such a monster, and rejoices to hope that his may be a solitary instance of such depravity.*'

Volunteer hangmen were not that rare; nearly two centuries before, Derby's John Crosland had made a lengthy career for himself. There was at least one other Derby

volunteer, possibly not many years after Jackson's offer. Unfortunately, a sensitive censoring hand in the archives, not wishing to upset anyone, made certain deletions; otherwise the application is as written:

For the Town Clarke solicitor, Stafford, December 13.

Sir,
I write to you to no whether any one his enquired for the Place of Smith to hang at Stafford, as i ham at your Sarvice at any time i shall be obliged if you will to Place in office of Smith i will come down and see you any day for infamason — Derect to Mr — Boot and Sho Maker — Lane, Derby.

The only other available information available is that Smith was known as the Burton murderer. Whether the offer was accepted is a matter for others to inquire, but the applicant was in a trade followed by several of the hanging brotherhood.

Friar Gate prison staged just one more public hanging. On 8 April 1825 George Batty of Norton Woodseats swung for rape. His victim, curiously described by the *Mercury* as 'an interesting young lady', had been Martha Hawkesley, aged 16 of Beauchief.

Rising at Pentrich

'…there is too much reason to suspect that the rising in Derbyshire, which cost the lives of three men upon the scaffold and the transportation of many more, was stimulated, if not produced, by the artifices of Oliver, a spy employed by the government of the day.'

(Lord Melbourne, Home Secretary)

AMONG the thousands who watched Colonel Edward Despard and six fellow conspirators die so horribly in February 1803 was a young, swarthy, unemployed framework knitter from Nottinghamshire. Quite why he was there outside Surrey's Horsemonger Lane prison has never been established; possibly while visiting his sister in Brighton. Despard had been found guilty of treason, plotting to assassinate the King and the Cabinet. His failed enterprise was just one page among many in the agitation for parliamentary reform.

Sentenced to death by hanging, drawing and quartering (later amended to hanging and beheading), the colonel and his companions were tied to hurdles and dragged by horses to the scaffold. After the hanging, their bodies were cut down and a surgeon commenced cutting off their heads. Coming to Despard, he either demonstrated lack of skill or nervousness, for he botched the job. It was left to the executioner to grasp the resisting head between his hands and by twisting and turning, wrest it from the trunk. Then, as ritual required, the grisly, dripping object was held up high to allow the crowds to gaze on the head of a traitor.

What the young man could not possibly have realised was that he had just witnessed nothing less than a preview of his own violent exit, 14 years later. Jeremiah Brandreth was his name, leader of the ill-fated Pentrich Revolution.

* * * * * *

NOTHING else in Derbyshire's recital of capital punishment compares with the so-called Pentrich Revolution. There is no disputing that the rising itself was a miserable failure. Ill-equipped, badly organised, lacking

Report

OF THE WHOLE OF THE

PROCEEDINGS

UNDER THE

Special Commission,

HELD IN THE COUNTY HALL, AT DERBY,

In the Month of October, 1817,

INCLUDING

THE TRIALS

OF

JEREMIAH BRANDRETH,

ALIAS JOHN COKE,

Alias the Nottingham Captain;

WILLIAM TURNER,

ISAAC LUDLAM, THE ELDER,

AND

GEORGE WEIGHTMAN,

FOR

HIGH TREASON;

WITH THE

Speeches of the Counsel,

AND OTHER

INTERESTING PARTICULARS.

NOTTINGHAM:
PRINTED BY SUTTON AND SON,

Where a trial attracted enormous interest, publishers, in addition to ballads and execution sheets, would produce factual accounts of the proceedings. This one deals with the Special Commission set up to try the Pentrich rebels.

government had long since infiltrated their ranks with spies and could have put a stop to the movement at any time. That it chose not to do so goes some way to substantiating a belief widely held that the authorities were determined to hand out a severe lesson, to quieten restlessness for reform. Events overseas such as the revolution in America, then the cataclysmic happenings in France had made the Tories apprehensive. They feared the next rising might be in England itself. There was sufficient evidence that already there were strong pockets of discontent. Like a cauldron of near boiling water, angry bubbles were disturbing the surface.

The real fascination of the Pentrich affair lies in its background. Derbyshire in 1817 was in a bad way, as indeed was much of England. The disastrous harvest of 1816 loomed large over everything, adding to the slump that followed the ending of the war with France. The year before, the Corn Law had been re-enacted. Government contracts dried up. Farming went into decline. So did the textile industry and the iron works at Butterley. Unemployment rocketed. The consequent strain on the poor rates was countered by the Tories' idea to abolish the Poor Law. Bread prices doubled and potatoes soared beyond the reach of those most dependent on them.

The ending of the war years saw a growing polarisation of society. Class differences were becoming more defined, adding to the government's growing unease. The old order

realistic planning with nothing more than a vague notion of somehow throwing over the government, meant the revolutionaries were doomed before even setting off in pouring rain on the night of 9 June 1817. The was changing. On one side of the fence sat the squire, the landowner, the propertied and the clergy, their authority of patronage and protection earning obedience, whittling away. On the other were grouped the lower orders, the labourers, the factory workers, the skilled and semi-skilled, all more aware of their status, their class, the bonds and practices that kept them in place. Many historians have seen these few years as giving specific birth to the working class. A third element was now more potent, the industrial entrepreneur whose economic hand was not yet fully matched by political power.

Discontent led to demonstrations and riots all over the country. The Luddites were not long gone over the horizon, and Lord Liverpool's government needed no reminding that it had never really got to grips with an organisation that had its origins in the East Midlands. The leaders were never brought to book. Agitation, localised upheavals, physical manifestations of discontent were something that 'The Old Corruption', as the government was known, could contend with. More worrying were those pressing for reform who chose appeals to the mind as their weapons. Tom Paine, with his *Rights of Man*, or the writings of William Cobbett, the Radical and former Tory, were influences that the Tories could not easily frustrate. Their thoughts, together with political pamphlets and newspapers, were now available in the Hampden Clubs springing up all over the place, and to which the working class could subscribe for a few pence. As far as Locket the

solicitor was concerned, the Hampden Clubs in Derbyshire and elsewhere in the Midlands were merely the Luddites regrouped, but with a broader and more political agenda. On the political front, reformers such as the Radical MP Sir Francis Burdett of Foremark Hall in South Derbyshire, were stirring matters up. Burdett knew that the way forward was through correction of parliamentary and electoral procedures. His appeal to the Pentrich movement was plain.

Riots at Spa Fields in December 1816, the march of the Blanketeers in early 1817 (some may have reached Derby), the petition movement for reform based on the Hampden Clubs, the general surliness and discontent, prompted a nervous government to act. Fearing insurrection, it suspended *habeas corpus* in March 1817 while meetings of more than 50 people had to first obtain magisterial approval. In addition, Committees of Secrecy were set up to garner reports on the mood of the country; their particular target was the Hampden Clubs. For their part, the clubs were careful to distance themselves from anything that might suggest subversion and behaved with the greatest circumspection.

To gather information, the Committees had to employ spies, a species that had been a hidden arm of government since Tudor times, but about which the English apparently remained largely in ignorance. Such creatures were the employees of foreign government. That the Pentrich rising led to the embarrassing exposure of Oliver the Spy, one of the more famous and successful of the breed, lent the incident far more importance than it might otherwise have merited. Reports prepared by the Committees gave an exaggerated impression: unrest was rife, subversive incidents everywhere. There was a whiff of treason in the air.

Pentrich was in fact just one section of a planned national uprising to overthrow the government. Its prominence stems from being the only one, apart from a minor flourish at Huddersfield, which actually set out to march on London. Those 200 or so who tramped through the rain believed that great numbers were involved in the grand enterprise. Thousands, they had been told, were marching down from the North and they would all meet up at Nottingham. From there, something like 100,00 rebels would cross the Trent and advance on the capital, where yet more thousands awaited their coming. Once London had been reached the hated government would be deposed and a new one, based on the United States model, installed. Sir Francis Burdett would head the new administration. Even a flag had been agreed, a tricolour of red, white and green.

It was an enterprise that never had the remotest chance of succeeding. Activities of government spies apart, the leaders lacked the enormous organisational skills, the intellectual scope, the political reality called for. Certainly, it would have held no attraction for those of ability and influence who recognised the urgent need for reform. For them, the path to success lay in more subtle and patient means. Burdett, while understanding what the revolutionaries were about, would have had nothing to do with them. The movement had leaders and schemers of parochial ability, but lacked an upper stratum of operational guidance. That, quite simply, was never available.

The man leading the Pentrich 'army' into the wet June night was Jeremiah Brandreth. Thirty-one years old, from Sutton-in-Ashfield, he was a compelling figure. His elevation to leading the Pentrich rebels was due mainly to elementary military skills acquired through militia service. Dark and swarthy, with unruly black hair, comparison at his trial with Conrad, Byron's *Corsair*, affords an unusual pen picture:

There breathe but few whose aspect might defy
The full encounter of his searching eye;
There was a laughing devil in his sneer,
That raised emotions both of rage and fear…

Known as the Nottingham Captain, he had been despatched to organise the march from Pentrich, linking up with the promised thousands from the north. A forceful man, his driving personality alone kept the Derbyshire men moving, despite the growing realisation that nothing was going to plan, if indeed there was a plan.

While Brandreth's role is understandable, that of the other principle leader is more difficult to evaluate. Thomas Bacon, a 64-year-old Pentrich man, was clearly higher in the echelons of the movement. A framework knitter, he had earlier worked at the iron works in Butterley. A disciple of Tom Paine, a Jacobin and well-known as a reform agitator, it is sensible to assume that he would have been involved in Luddism, as was generally presumed. It is difficult to see him not being. An intelligent man, educated and travelled (he visited the United States on three occasions) he was active in the Hampden Clubs. There was a branch at nearby Ripley. Bacon travelled frequently between Derbyshire, Nottinghamshire and Yorkshire, helping in the planning of the rising. That he was one of the main instigators of the whole business cannot be disputed, indeed he was regarded as such by the Crown. This only serves to heighten the puzzle as to why Bacon was not executed along with Brandreth and two other principals.

While Brandreth and Bacon were leading figures, it was the clandestine activities of Oliver the Spy that dominated the Pentrich story. As with all successful spies – and he remains a classic example – his precise role still defies precision. Was he just very good at his job, reporting on the revolutionaries' plans, or were there deeper motives? Some claimed him an *agent provocateur* and present a good case. Others saw him as a man anxious to earn money, goading the rebels on. Then again, the government was suspected of needing something or someone to make a fearful example of, and Oliver turned up the necessary evidence. With all the information emanating from him, the government could have stopped the so-called revolution at any time; that it chose not to has to be significant.

As with any good spy, confusion over identity is essential. William Oliver may have been his real name, but he was also known as W. J. Richards, an identity some think more likely. On occasions, he introduced himself as Hollis. A tall, handsome man in his late 30s he was blessed with an engaging disposition. He was also a bigamist, a former sergeant in a grenadier company of Volunteers and amassed sufficient debts to have him thrown in London's Fleet Prison.

When the government recruited Oliver, he was handed the task of insinuating himself with agitators suspected of planning some form of uprising. Posing as a delegate from the revolutionaries' London base, Oliver soon ingratiated himself with the plotters. Their main centres of activity were Nottingham, Derby and Leicester as well as cells in Birmingham, Yorkshire and Lancashire. Oliver made two principal tours of the various planning committees, establishing himself as a man of ideas, proposals, and provider of intelligence about what was happening at the other centres. He became a conduit of information, a fulcrum around which so much happened. Just how far he coaxed and cajoled the rebels in their aims, to what degree if any he was responsible for the Pentrich marchers taking to the field has never been agreed. Nonetheless, it was he who talked about the tens of thousands who were preparing to advance on London, and that Burdett would head the coming provisional government. On the other hand, his reports were accurate when describing the insurrectionists' plans as 'weak and impractical'. Among the plotters there were those who suspected Oliver's true motives and some muttered that he should be killed.

Oliver arrived by coach in Derby on 26 April en route to Sheffield and, while horses were being changed, held discussions with a leading plotter. Although never identified, this person may have been Bacon. The spy was back again on 26 May, having left London three days earlier and returned to the capital on 7 June, two days before Pentrich. Originally the rising had been planned for 23 May, but the decision was taken to move it to 9 June, when the insurgents would have the advantage of a moonless night. Whichever date, the government was ready, with troops and magistrates alerted. Lord Sidmouth, the Home Secretary, had two weeks' warning of the revised date. For various reasons, only two of the many centres actually moved into action. On 8 June, around 200 textile workers advanced on Huddersfield. Quickly suppressed after a skirmish with the military, some were later charged with burglary. Those charged were acquitted.

On the same day, the final briefing was held in the White Horse inn at Pentrich. The next night, at about 10pm, what has been styled as England's last revolution set off from Hunt's Barn at South Wingfield. So well had Oliver done his job that the Town Clerk of Nottingham was already 'on the look-out near Pentridge'. When Brandreth marched his men towards Nottingham and promised glory on 9 June, there was one notable gap in the straggling ranks. Missing was Thomas Bacon. Why remains a mystery, the usual explanation being that he had learned of a warrant out for his arrest and decided to make himself scarce. Quite why the authorities would issue such a document when they had a marvellous opportunity to arrest such a prominent figure under such damming circumstances is not easily explained.

Apart from Pentrich itself, Brandreth attracted recruits from South Wingfield, Swanwick and Ripley and other villages. Estimates of how many were armed with anything from guns to pitchforks, vary from less than a hundred to around 400. Not all were volunteers. There were pressed men, who took the opportunity presented by pouring rain and a dark night to slip away into the shadows. Convinced of success, Brandreth had a few lines of verse that he would quote to his followers:

> *Every man his skill must try,*
> *He must turn out and not deny;*
> *No blood soldier must he dread,*
> *He must turn out and fight for bread.*
> *The time is come you plainly see*
> *The government opposed must be.*

The only fatality happened early on. When the marchers reached the home of Mrs Mary Hepworth at Wingfield Park, a window was broken and a single shot from a gun killed Robert Walters, a servant, who was indoors tying up his bootlaces. Although he never spoke about the incident, most believed

Brandreth fired the shot, more as an act of bravado than intent. No charges were ever preferred.

Reaching Butterley Iron Works, the rebels demanded recruits. None were forthcoming, and without too much trouble, George Goodwin, the works manager, persuaded Brandreth and his troops to move on. By then, it was 3am. More and more deserted. In twos and threes, they escaped under cover of darkness and made their way back home. Langley Mill was reached. The men crossed from Derbyshire into Nottinghamshire and when they climbed up to Eastwood, there were even fewer going to capture London. On towards Kimberley and then, in a tanyard at Giltbrook, the whole sad enterprise fizzled out. News arrived that a detachment of soldiers from the 15th Regiment of Light Dragoons, led by Captain Frederick Phillipson, was coming their way. There was no battle. Before the soldiers arrived, the rebels had fled. Throwing away their few weapons, they scrambled and fell over hedges, waded through ditches, only too anxious to put as much ground as possible between them and retribution. Around 40 were captured, and more were rounded up over the next few days.

Among the first ringleaders to be taken was William Turner. Eluding the military, he managed to stay free until approaching Codnor. From South Wingfield he was, at 46, among the older marchers. A stonemason, he was a former soldier of 16 years who had seen real action in Egypt. Another leader was Isaac Ludlam, aged 52, part owner of a stone quarry near Pentrich and noted as a Methodist preacher. For several weeks he remained at large, eventually being taken at Uttoxeter. George Weightman, a big man of 26 and a sawyer by trade, whose mother kept the White Horse inn at Pentrich, was on the run for five weeks before being hunted down at Eccleston, near Sheffield.

As for Thomas Bacon, he avoided arrest for many weeks. He was finally apprehended at St Ives in Huntingdonshire on 15 August, the very day the South Wingfield arsonists were executed. Henry Newton, 'our active police officer' praised the *Mercury*, never gave up the chase and was rewarded not with just Thomas Bacon but John, his younger brother.

Brandreth, with a reward on his head, and no doubt well aware of his fate if taken, made strenuous efforts to escape. First, he headed for Brighton (where his sister lived), and then cut across country to Bristol. There he twice attempted to board a ship bound for America, but was recognised and had to keep running. Out of luck, he made his way back to Nottinghamshire where his wife and children were, and was finally arrested at Bulwell.

Inept though the rising was, its repercussions were enormous. At Westminster, Sir Francis Burdett was on his feet questioning Lord Castlereagh, the Foreign Secretary. Burdett understood that Oliver had told the insurgents that it was he who would head their provisional government. Had the spy been authorised by the government to use his name in such a fashion? The question would have been expected. Castlereagh was active in thwarting any movement for reform; Burdett was one of the leading lights for it. Sir Francis was assured no such authority had been given.

Back in Derbyshire, action was being taken against those who might have been involved. Among the first to suffer was Mrs Ann Weightman, licensee of the White Horse. She was hardly in a position to complain when her licence was revoked, for allowing seditious meetings on the premises. Pentrich was part of the Duke of Devonshire's huge Chatsworth Estate. He was travelling in Russia when the rising took place, and it fell to his agent to deal with matters. While not essential to this history, the village's appearance today owes much to what followed.

The *Mercury's* long report on the momentous events gave more than a hint of what was to come:

'*We hear with great pleasure that strict inquiry will be made into the conduct of the Duke of Devonshire's peasantry in Pentridge; and that no man will be permitted to remain on His Grace's rental who has in any manner aided, or has been in the least degree concerned in the late insurrection.*'

Friar Gate's cells were bursting at the iron bars as the marchers were rounded up and brought in. Overcrowding was not the only problem. There was too little to eat, mainly bread and water. It took a letter of protest to the Home Office before a more substantial diet was permitted. No matter how great was the excitement in Derby, how triumphantly the *Mercury* told the story of how the rebellion ended, nor the buzz of conjecture over the forthcoming trials for treason, all faded before the revelations published by the *Leeds Mercury.* What Edward Baines, its Whig editor and proprietor, had to tell shocked the nation and severely embarrassed the government. Derby's own pedestrian *Mercury*, unknowingly at the centre of things, must have been equally mortified.

Baines had exposed Oliver the Spy. He had been spotted on one of his lightning visits, which hardened speculation that his role was not quite what it seemed. That a British government actually employed spies and informers came as a shock to the vast majority of people. The idea of such characters going about smacked of a State police force, acceptable and expected of Continental countries but anathema to the average Englishman. Suggestions were already being made that some form of national policing would have to be considered, bearing in mind the changing conditions of the country. It is of interest, and still little known, that there already existed a form of national police force, in fact two. Formed around the 1730s, the Press Messengers had the responsibility of seeking out and suppressing subversive and seditious literature. The second body, the King's Messengers, was created to combat dissident movements; Oliver may well have been associated with the latter.

Embarrassed though the government was, its discomfiture increased with the line taken by Baines in the *Leeds Mercury.* That was to suggest Oliver was more than a spy, but the driving force and principal schemer behind the events of 9 June. Chasing that argument, it could only mean the Tories wanted the rising to go ahead, and thus give them an opportunity to administer a crushing blow against national unrest. Or, as Baines succinctly explained it, the whole affair was 'a diabolical conspiracy, not of the people, but against the people'. He was a remarkable man. A Lancashireman, he had owned the *Leeds Mercury* since 1801, and over the years built the newspaper first into one of the finest in Yorkshire and then into one of the leading provincial publications.

Baines' revelations forced an embarrassed Lord Liverpool into conceding in a House of Lords' debate that Oliver's role was indeed as a government spy, a duty he embraced with enthusiasm:

'Spies and informers have at all times been employed by all governments and ever must be. And this being granted it would and must sometimes happen that such persons from zeal in their business would sometimes go further than they ought.'

With the unmasking of Oliver, the government became most concerned that his activities were not subjected to more public scrutiny. Should he give evidence at the insurgents' trial, then the politicians would certainly have to face an even more awkward situation. In the end, Oliver did not appear in court. Thomas Bacon did not hang, notwithstanding the fact that the Crown regarded him as among the leading conspirators. The Pentrich man had dealings with Oliver, probably more than any other. The inference that some sort of deal was done cannot be dismissed lightly.

Thirty-five accused stood at the Crown bar in July 1817, to be remanded to a special commission set for October. One reason for the delay was that most of the jurymen were farmers and it was of the utmost urgency that the harvest was safely gathered in. Bearing in mind the disasters of 1816, the delay would seem acceptable, albeit underlying the narrow strata from which juries were selected and operation of justice existed. In addition, the trial would be a long business (prosecution witnesses alone totalled 268) and in view of its importance, a special sitting was not inappropriate. It also allowed the defence more time to prepare its case.

For their defence, the accused had to rely on just two barristers. One was John Cross, who quickly unfurled his true colours by refusing to even enter St Mary's Gate until his £100 fee had been paid. The second was a Thomas Denman, whose family had Derbyshire connections. His masterly presentation was one of the stepping stones to a distinguished career in law. A compassionate man, he was totally opposed to slavery and campaigned ceaselessly for a reduction in the number of capital offences. Fifteen years later he became Lord Chief Justice. Raising money for their defence presented enormous problems for the accused. Not only had they to find their lawyers' fees, but also fund their witnesses' appearances in court. Their families were obliged to sell everything and anything they possessed. Sympathisers sent contributions, while a wire worker in London formed a defence committee.

On 15 October, the trial began and lasted

ten days. Leading the ten-strong prosecution team was Sir Samuel Shepherd, the Attorney General, a post to which Denman succeeded a few years later. Presiding judge was Sir Richard Richards, Chief Baron of the Court of the Exchequer. For once Derby was the focus of national attention. St Mary's Gate was thronged; ballad sellers were already doing a roaring trade, so too the publicans and traders, the prostitutes and pickpockets.

Oliver the Spy was also in town, but in hiding. Scrawled around Derby was the message, 'Jurymen, remember Oliver,' and repeated on the walls of All Saints' Church where the ritual services preceding law court sittings were held. Not that the prosecution needed any reminding; it was determined to keep the spy out of the proceedings. Denman had his own thoughts about the 'respectable Mr Oliver', and expressed curiosity as to his precise role. Visiting newspaper correspondents learned of his hidden presence with the result that the government agent had to be hurriedly smuggled out. As the newspaper at the heart of activities, the *Derby Mercury* did not compare at all favourably with its out-of-town contemporaries, most of which provided far more comprehensive coverage.

Of the 35 charged with high treason, the prosecution offered no evidence against 12, and they were freed. Gaol sentences ranging from six months, to one and two years was the lot of six more. Transportation for 14 years was the fate of three others. Eleven more were sent for life. Included in that last group were Thomas and John Bacon. Sentenced to death were Brandreth, Isaac Ludlam, William Turner and George Weightman; the latter was later to be reprieved and transported for life. The killing of Robert Walters was not pursued by the prosecution.

Twelve landowners and farmers made up a jury that would have entertained little doubt of the verdict expected of them. Oliver's role in the rising was never discussed in court; indeed his name was never mentioned. By then, he was the most exposed spy in the country; everyone must surely have been waiting to hear him on the witness stand. From a tactical point of view, the prosecution had enough evidence without Oliver's to bring in the required verdict. Not to call upon the spy would spare the government further embarrassment. As for Denman, his reluctance could have been because of the risk that, if called, Oliver's evidence might well uncover many of the insurgents as being more deeply implicated than would be productive for their defence. Thomas Bacon would surely have hanged if Oliver gave evidence; the Pentrichman would be spared if the spy did not. The speculative permutations are endless. The prosecution pursuing Brandreth and two or three more leading lights to the gallows would satisfy a government anxious to send out a salutary warning.

When asked why the sentence of death should not be passed on him, Brandreth replied:

'I would ask for mercy, if mercy can be extended to me. Let me address you in the words of Our Saviour: "If it be possible, let this cup pass from me, but not my will but your Lordship's be done."'

The Nottingham Captain, Isaac Ludlam, William Turner and George Weightman heard a sentence that had not been passed at a Derby assizes for 229 years:

'That you and each of you be taken hence to the gaol from whence you came, from whence you must be drawn on a hurdle to the place of execution, and there severally hanged by the neck until you are dead; your heads must then be severed from your bodies, which are to be divided into four quarters, and to be at his Majesty's disposal.'

In the end, there was to be little of the horrors suffered by the Padley Martyrs. The decision was taken that the sentence would be reduced to hanging until dead and then beheading. There was no drawing and burning of intestines, nor public display of butchered remains.

Back in gaol, Brandreth wrote to his wife, Ann, at Sutton-in-Ashfield. A touching letter, entreating that 'you will act a motherly part to the poor fatherless children and bring them up in the fear of God', it concluded:

Jeremiah Brandreth in chains at Friar Gate gaol.

'My dear, you may suppose my feelings are not easily described. My dear wife, it would give me great consolation if I could see you before I depart this life, but my dear, if you are enceinte I would have you advise with your poor distressed mother-in-law, whether it would be proper or not; and if she thinks it would not be of serious consequences, I should be very glad, but let it be well considered before you come to me, and if you do not come, let your father (if he thinks it would not be more than he could bear, as I know he is of a timorous turn) but if neither come, I shall write again, if God permit me. So my beloved wife, I hope you will excuse my short letter at this time. You may inform all friends that God gave me great fortitude to bear up my spirits on trial. So I hope the blessings of God be with you all, and most especially with you and our little babes.
Your most affectionate husband,
Jeremiah Brandreth'

Ann Brandreth replied. It has been claimed that her husband

never saw the letter, it being redirected to the Home Office. Maybe that was because she wrote, *inter alia*:

'*...and if you have (as is the general opinion) been drawn by that wretch Oliver forgive him and leave him to God and his own conscience.*'

The sad response finished:

'*O that I could atone for all and save your life. Praying that God will be with you to strengthen and comfort you (and should you suffer) bring you through Christ to Eternal Glory which is the prayer of your unhappy wife,*
Ann Brandreth.'

Ann Brandreth, nearly six months pregnant, did visit her husband. She walked to Derby and after speaking with him, walked back, all in the same day. Brandreth and the gaoler's wife, Mrs Eaton, gave her some money to pay the return coach fare and, whatever was left over, to provide something for the children, Elizabeth and Timothy. That Ann Brandreth ignored the coach to have more money for her family identifies an unusual woman of rare quality.

On 2 November came confirmation of the sentences for Brandreth, Turner and Ludlam, and the date was fixed for Friday, 7 November. Weightman would have an agonising time, waiting to learn his fate.

Despite escaping the noose, Bacon could not submerge his natural instincts. Back in Friar Gate gaol, while the prisoners pondered their various destinations, he kept reminding them they were 'not tried by their Peers but by men of property'. This, of course, was quite correct. Few standing accused at the Crown bar were ever tried by their peers.

With the date now set, the condemned three were kept apart and, with Weightman, only allowed into the exercise yard when restrained by chains. Turner, the former soldier, decided to petition for mercy, and wrote to the Duke of York, under whose command he had once fought. In 1797 he had enlisted in the Derby Militia and later volunteered for the 20th Regiment of Foot, with which he saw active service in Holland and then Egypt. After the 1802 Treaty of Amiens, he was discharged and returned home to South Wingfield. Unfortunately, a creditable military career failed to promote any ducal sympathy for his plight.

Early on the Friday morning, workmen began erecting the scaffold. Already waiting the great event were those anxious to obtain a good view of proceedings. An early arrival was the horse to draw the hurdle on which the condemned were to be pulled around the prison yard. Because of the prison layout, the hurdle could not deliver them directly to the scaffold so once having served that part of their sentence, the prisoners would then walk down a passage to reach the scaffold steps. There are several detailed descriptions of the executions, but none say very much about the executioner and his assistant. The latter, presumably, was the 'muscular Derbyshire miner' mentioned in some reports. Given the importance of the occasion, James Botting, recently appointed principle hangman for London and Middlesex, could have been hired to take charge of matters.

Two axes, copies of an execution axe retained in the Tower of London, had been fashioned by Bamford, the Derby smith. He also manufactured two large knives as further aids to chopping off the prisoners' heads. The harsh, silver glitter of the newly-shaped metal contrasted oddly with the blackness of their handles. A beheading block had especially built by a Mr Firmy, described as the 'town-joiner'. A contemporary account said it was 'a long piece of timber supported at each end by pieces a foot high, a small log of wood being fixed across the upper end of it, on which the neck of the body was to be placed for the purpose of decollation'. It is presently stored in Derby Museum.

Before the three men went to the prison chapel to receive their last Communion, Brandreth penned a final letter to Ann. He had arranged to have his few possessions sent to her: a workbag, two balls of worsted and one of cotton, a handkerchief, an old pair of stockings and a shirt. There was also a small sum of money. His last paragraph read:

'*These I suppose will be sent by parcel to you by some means. My beloved wife this is the last correspondence I can have with you so you will make yourself as easy as you possibly can and I hope God will bless you and comfort you as he has to me. So my blessing attend you and the children and the blessing of God be with you all now and evermore, adieu adieu to all for ever. Your most affectionate husband, Jeremiah Brandreth*'

Following the service, the three went out into the prison yard. Other prisoners, standing by, were visibly affected by what they were witnessing. Thomas Bacon 'seemed disposed to keep out of sight as much as possible'. Bamford came on the scene, and exchanged their irons for ones that were fastened by lock and key. This was to facilitate removal after death, and had the advantage that their weight would help hasten things. After that, each prisoner took a turn at being dragged round the yard on the hurdle, Brandreth first, then Turner and finally Ludlam. At midday, they were led along the passage to the scaffold. At the same time Mr J. B. Simpson, the Under-Sheriff, arrived at the prison gates to set the final act into motion, demanding of Mr Eaton, the gaoler, that:

'*In the name of the High Sheriff of the County of Derby as his Under-Sheriff, I command you to bring forth upon the scaffold the bodies of Jeremiah Brandreth, William Turner, and Isaac Ludlam, the elder, that their several sentences of death, for the High Treasons of which they have been convicted may be executed forthwith.*'

Simpson had not come alone. With him was 'the usual retinue' for executions, together with 200 special constables each carrying a white wand, some of whom would form a close guard on the scaffold. Bringing up the rear were mounted javelin men. In position for the last two hours was a detachment of the Enniskillen Dragoons, charged with the duty of keeping carriages from passing along Friar Gate until after the slaughter. The soldiers were to maintain a discreet distance, to be summoned should matters get out of hand. The presence of regular soldiers reflected the gravity of the occasion. Normally, authority eschewed the employment of professional soldiers for such occasions, preferring to use members of the local militia if thought necessary. Estimates of the crowds jamming Friar Gate were well over 6,000. Many spectators were from rural areas, having made the journey in an almost endless caravan of coaches and carts.

First to mount the scaffold was Brandreth in company with the Revd George Pickering, the prison chaplain. Then came Turner and Ludlam. By custom, those about to die were permitted a few words and usually little restriction was exercised. Brandreth exclaimed: 'God be with you all, and Lord Castlereagh.' To say the least, that was most unlikely. Castlereagh, while a brilliant Foreign Secretary, was becoming one of the government's most detested ministers. An ardent opponent of any measure of parliamentary or democratic reform, he was generally felt to be responsible for the Peterloo Massacre outrage of 1819. Shelley castigated him with the lines:

> *I met Murder in the way –*
> *He had a mask like Castlereagh*

It made sense for Brandreth to have actually said 'and all but Lord Castlereagh', as other witnesses averred.

Ludlam's last words were: 'I pray God bless you all – and the King upon his Throne.' It was left to Turner to make the most controversial statement, 'This is the work of the government and Oliver.' He had touched a sore spot and officials were furious. Any chance of Oliver's name and role to be allowed to fade from the scene was dashed. There were those who would assert that the Revd Pickering then positioned himself in such a way that any further remarks were either frustrated or silenced. Afterwards, the chaplain would deny any such motive. So charged was the atmosphere, that simple gestures or overheard remarks could be translated several ways, depending on one's viewpoint.

All the preliminaries were out of the way; the time had come for the executioner and his assistant to bring down the final curtain. The three ropes were dangling, each noose yawning for its victim. Stacked on one side were three coffins, with names chalked on. When the nooses had been placed around the trio's necks, the Revd Pickering led them in the Lord's Prayer and then retired from the scene. Next to the fore came the executioner to put on the white caps and as he did so each victim cried out: 'Into Thy hands, O God, I commit my spirit.'

The clock showed just after 12.30pm when the hangman drew back the bolt, the trapdoor opened with its stunning clatter, and so died the leaders of the Pentrich Revolution. Lockett, who witnessed the hanging, later reported that they died apparently without a struggle. Others swore that Ludlam had been repeatedly convulsed. It is difficult to accept that all three died immediately; even one doing so was a rarity.

The bodies remained suspended for somewhat less than the customary hour, twisting and turning in the charged atmosphere. Still grasped in Brandreth's hands was a black silk handkerchief, there since the chapel service. After death was certain, ropes were tied to the legs of each corpse so they could be hauled to a horizontal position, and then secured to the scaffold rails. The trapdoor was closed and the scaffold platform spread with sawdust, to absorb the coming blood. After the leg irons were unlocked, the bodies were forced into a kneeling position, waiting for the chopping block.

Brandreth was the first to be beheaded. Either the executioner failed to use enough force, or the axe was not sharp enough, but the blow failed to cleave the head. 'A groan of disapprobation and horror' rose from the crowd. Taking up one of the knives, the assistant executioner completed the task. Blood flowed as the head fell into the waiting basket. Immediately the executioner seized the bloody object and holding it by the long, black hair, stalked around the platform, calling out: 'Behold the head of a traitor, Jeremiah Brandreth.' Some women in the crowd could take no more and fled. Hisses, groans and catcalls rose on the Friar Gate air 'and these unusual sounds added to the terror of those who had previously begun to retreat'. For a

How an artist depicted the head of Jeremiah Brandreth, the 'Nottingham Captain', displayed by the executioner for all to see outside Friar Gate gaol.

few moments, it was feared there might be mass panic. Rumour whispered through the crowd that the dragoons were about to charge. More of the crowd decided to leave the terrible place and scurried off in all directions. Fortunately, there were no casualties. Brandreth's dripping head and trunk were loosely reunited in their designated coffin. Ludlam and Turner's bodies suffered the same awful ritual.

The drama was over, the last formality something of an anticlimax. A wagon carried the three coffins to St Werburgh's churchyard, at the end of Friar Gate. There, a single deep hole, dug no doubt to deter grave robbers received the remains of the Pentrich rebels. No marker was erected, nor any entry made in the parish register. George Weightman, who listened with mounting terror and unnamed horrors to the noise and bustle of the triple killings, learned the following Monday that his sentence had been commuted. He was transported to Australia for the term of his natural life.

Over the years, a belief has grown that Shelley had been among the spectators in Friar Gate. The idea took root with the publication of his political polemic, *An address to the People on the Death of Princess Charlotte*, appearing under the pseudonym, the 'Hermit of Marlow.' At the time, the poet was living in lodgings in London's Euston Road and the capital's newspapers carried detailed reports of the happenings at Derby. It was not necessary to make the journey north, and biographies have not claimed he did. A few days before the three revolutionaries were executed, Princess Charlotte, the Prince Regent's only daughter, died in childbirth. That sad event precipitated a highly charged outbreak of national grief. Shelley, like several of his contemporaries, an advocate for reform, contrasted the royal demise with the killing of the Pentrich leaders. His comparison drew on a comment made by Tom Paine in his *Rights of Man*: 'We pity the plumage, but forget the dying bird.' The government was the bird.

What direction Oliver's life took afterwards remains in the realms of speculation. He was by then too well known and, in any event, Turner's dying words ensured he was of little further use. Under the name William Oliver Jones, he emigrated to South Africa where he died in August 1827. Oliver's exposure did nothing to stop the government using secret agents to infiltrate what were perceived as subversive organisations. His shadowy mantle was donned by George Edwards, 'Edwards the Spy', who unmasked the Cato Street conspiracy of 1820. As with Pentrich, Lord Sidmouth, still Home Secretary, knew every move the plotters made from intelligence supplied by Edwards. And, as with Pentrich, the Cato Street leaders were hanged and beheaded for high treason, the final occasion such a dreadful sentence was carried out.

With the ending of the trials in Derby, Locket had ridden out to Pentrich, to ascertain how the lower orders were reacting. He must have been well pleased 'with a visible alteration in the manners of the people and several of the young men who were discharged are now at work'. His visit was made too early. Pentrich's population declined. Of those transported or sent to gaol, their families, unable to pay the rent, quit their homes and moved to parts well away from Derbyshire. Locally, it has been claimed that the Duke of Devonshire's agent either evicted or raised rents of those known to have been sympathetic to the revolution. Some of their houses were pulled down. There is a belief that those who gave evidence for the prosecution later acquired some of the land of those evicted. Today it is probable that no descendants of those in the revolution are living in the Pentrich area.

Beyond dispute is that the population of Pentrich fell from 726 to 508, with inhabited houses declining from 122 to 82. In the *Census Abstract of Answers and Returns* for 1821, there is a note that Pentrich township had decreased by a third since 1811,

'which is said to be owing to the insurrection which took place there in 1817, in consequence of which the Duke of Devonshire's agent destroyed many of the houses'.

* * * * * *

THE final note, almost inevitably, involves the enigmatic Oliver the Spy and a curious parallel. A century after the Pentrich Revolution, while World War One raged in

A Brief Narrative of the

Jeremiah Brandreth,

Isaac

Lives and Execution of

William Turner, and

Ludlam,

Who this day, (Nov 7th, 1817;) Suffered the Sentence of the Law, at **DERBY**, *for* **HIGH TREASON**, *on the Scaffold erected for the purpose, in front of the County Gaol*

The trial of the Pentrich rebels would surely have seen a large number of ballad and execution sheets, and yet few seem to have survived. This heading was for a publication that lacked detail and was clearly aimed to be 'one of the first on the streets'.

Europe, there was a sensational trial at London's Old Bailey in March 1917. In the dock stood Alice Wheeldon of Derby, who, with three others, was charged with conspiring to assassinate the Prime Minister, Lloyd George, and one other. There have always been doubts as to who was doing the conspiring. Was it Mrs Wheeldon, or the government of the day in an attempt to discredit and at the same time hand out a sharp lesson to conscientious objectors? The prosecution, led by the Attorney General, claimed that the scheme was hatched in Derby. Much of its case was based on information supplied by an MI5 spy named Alex Gordon, who had infiltrated the conspirators' ranks. Something of a man of mystery, his role aroused controversy, especially as he was never called to give evidence. His conduct seemed more that of an *agent provocateur*. After prison sentences were handed down, Gordon disappeared from view. However, such was the odium attached to his name that an embarrassed government thought it better if he was moved overseas. Like Oliver before him, Alex Gordon ended up in South Africa, and there he, too, lived out the remainder of his days.

The End of the Bloody Code

THE final decade of the Bloody Code, 1821-1830, proved something of a paradox. Victims of crimes were more prepared to initiate prosecutions, with the result that more capital offences than ever before were tried by the assizes. The consequence was not more executions, but significantly less, a result of judges and juries preferring in some cases not to sentence to death but inflict a non-capital punishment. Often, a sentence of death was recorded, only to have a non-capital one substituted. In Derby's case, there were only two hangings, for murder and rape, from 120 offences. In the previous decade, 1811-1820, there were 16 hangings from 90 prosecutions.

The fall is emphasised even further with a look at the opening decade of the century, when just over a quarter of those sentenced mounted the scaffold. Extraordinary though it may seem, proportionately more were hanged at Derby during the period 1785 to 1810 than in London and Middlesex combined, a period when the Code raged at its most virulent. The Code's unlamented demise, following the ousting of the Tory administration, becomes more startling when looking at the 1830s, even bearing in mind the fewer capital offences. In England and Wales, 96 per cent of death sentences were commuted. In Derbyshire, the only one to die was the tragic John Leedham, whose death was possibly more the result of the judge's personal distaste rather than judicial disapproval.

So, why this extraordinary *volte-face*? There was no single answer. The incoming Whig administration's introduction of much needed reforms, particularly the more appropriate grading of felonies, goes some way to an explanation. The sheer task of killing everyone sentenced to death simply could not be undertaken, lack of gallows and hangmen would have been just two of many problems. Even in the Code's bloodiest passage, sentences commuted were well above the halfway figure. As already pointed out, judges and juries were sometimes inclined to downgrade the severity of some charges (not murder) to place it outside the frame of a capital offence. That disposition became more pronounced, casting the Code into further ridicule.

There were other factors. People were becoming increasingly sensitive. Compared to their European neighbours, England's treatment of felons, the harshness of sentences (whipping was popular), the comparative sheer number of executions, did little to enhance its vaunted claim of a just and law abiding society. Other countries had achieved that status without resorting to the gallows and lesser brutalities. As late as 1830, despite the drop in executions and some much-needed reform of capital offences, Sir Robert Peel still felt constrained to admit:

'It is impossible to conceal from ourselves that capital punishments are more frequent and the criminal law more severe on the whole in this country than in any country in the world.'

Moreover, capital punishment was not the only matter causing disquiet. The need for some sort of deterrent other than hanging was self-evident. Peel was pressing not only for the establishment of a police force, but also looking to prison reform as part of easing the embarrassment. Up to then, prisons were places that principally housed debtors; convicted felons were restrained for relatively short periods. Three years was an unusually long time to spend behind bars. Before his

untimely death in 1818, Sir Samuel Romilly, the former Solicitor General, had done much. He had effected many improvements in criminal law and questioned the efficacy of capital punishment as it stood. Consciences were being aroused. Not only were there those questioning the scope of capital punishment, but others wondered if it should not be abolished altogether. In between lay calls for fewer capital crimes, with demands that executions ceased to be public spectacles.

On the face of it, Peel had done much to rationalise some of the worst aspects of the 1723 Act. With a series of measures known as the 'Peel Acts', he consolidated some 90 statutes relating to larceny and allied offences, and repealed obsolete statutes. With regard to malicious injuries to property, he condensed a further 50 statutes, with a similar number relating to offences to the person. All this activity was not so much reform as tidying up the chaos and confusion generated by the Black Act, which was then abolished. The effect was a drop in capital offences, although the path to the gallows was still too easily trod. While as Home Secretary, Peel did much to rationalise the criminal law and push through legislation to establish a police force in London, he did not show himself any more compassionate than his predecessors. There was no significant lessening of the notation 'The law to takes its course,' on the appeals against death sentences arriving on his desk.

In November 1830, the detested Tory government, 'Old Corruption', came to the end of its long reign, to be succeeded by a

Whig administration under Earl Grey. Over the ensuing ten years or so, the new government did much to ameliorate capital punishment. Among offences reduced to non-capital status were returning from transportation, letter stealing, coining and forgery, burglary and theft from dwelling houses and rape. By the end of the 1830s the only hanging offence effectively was murder (intent to murder remained on the book for a few more years), although that punishment was retained for piracy with violence, arson in His Majesty's shipyards, and treason.

Peel's best-remembered political act was the introduction of England's first recognised police force. Appointed Home Secretary in 1822, he immediately started on his campaign. In 1829, it came to fruition with the formation of the Metropolitan Police, which served the capital. Resistance outside London was considerable. For many, it represented a loss of power as well as resentment at what was regarded as creeping centralisation of control. It was one of the last nails in the coffin of the old social order. Under the Whigs, Peel's work was continued. In 1835 came the Municipal Corporation Act, which enabled provincial boroughs to set up their own forces. Derby made an application in 1836. Under the Royal Constabulary Act of 1839, counties were to establish their own forces. The County and Borough Police Act of 1856 made it obligatory for all counties and county boroughs to establish police forces. Those early forces were seen by the upper classes as a device for keeping the dreaded

lower orders in order. Regional control was largely exercised through the landed and gentry classes. Recruiting was confined almost exclusively to the working classes; the rationale being who better to apprehend criminals who sprang only from those strata, than their compatriots.

The last two decades of the Tory government saw the start of a major prison building programme in England. For many centuries such places were regarded not so much as a means of punishing criminals as for somewhere to keep them pending trial, transportation or hanging. Vagrants and those sentenced to hard labour went into the local house of correction, or bridewell. The notion of incarceration as a punishment began to emerge towards the end of the 18th century. Growing distaste over public punishment such as whippings, the stocks and pillory helped turn thoughts in that direction. An even more pressing for reason for reform was the condition of the country's gaols, most totally inadequate for their roles. They were disgraceful places and an embarrassment, not to mention a hazard to health for those within as well as passing by. The philanthropist John Howard with his monumental work, *State of the Prisons in England and Wales*, published in 1777 had already aroused public awareness and anger. Further disquieting evidence came in 1819 when another philanthropist, Elizabeth Fry, with her brother Joseph Gurney, published an influential report on prison reform.

England's new prisons were designed with

several objectives. They were to be places of discipline and confinement, and that meant away from the public gaze. Visitors were to be discouraged. The teachings of the Bible were to be emphasised, and prisoners' compulsory subjection to the chaplains' lengthy sermons formed a prominent part of the weekly routine. To keep inmates busy, boring, often mindless labour occupied a large part of the daily round. The classic example was the treadmill; it did little for a prisoner's rehabilitation. Administrators were much taken up with the classification of prisoners (the ridiculous 'science' of phrenology was widely endorsed), with nominated blocks of cells, termed wards, neatly annotated on maps.

The new buildings were a constant source for implementing penal theories beloved of planners and zealous reformers. Indeed, they were in many ways almost classic examples of the architectural mantra, form follows function. Behind the forbidding walls, there grew a regime of harsh discipline, a world silent and grey, a community ruled by a monotonous, soul-destroying timetable regulated by clock and bell. While a great improvement on what had gone before, the age-old problem of gaol fever or typhoid remained unsolved. Still believed to be airborne, the designers paid much attention to ventilation and incorporated big yards for exercise.

It was not so much reforming zeal as the threat of financial retribution that finally forced Derby into building its new county prison to replace the one in Friar Gate. The latter had come in for some fierce criticism. In 1817, a prison architect had described it as 'insecure and insufficient; wrong and defective in construction'. The Pentrich Rising had exposed its limitations. His recommendation was simple: pull it down and build another one. Three years later a judge expressed surprise that so little had been done towards a new prison. He left town with the warning that 'if, upon his next coming to Derby, he had cause to complain again, he would impose a heavy fine upon the County'. By 1823 still nothing had been done. At a meeting of the General Quarter Sessions of the Peace, the gaol was reported as a building in a 'deplorable state' that had been 'little altered or improved' since construction. Built to accommodate 21 offenders, overcrowding in the seven cells was inevitable. Seldom accommodating less than three each, there were times when five or six had to be locked in. Another drawback – and one which refutes claims for it in an attempt to promote a tourist attraction – was the lack of a condemned cell. 'There are not any cells for prisoners under sentence of death nor any means of keeping them apart when more than one.' Something had to be done.

Despite the procrastination, Derby's new gaol at the bottom of Vernon Street was nevertheless among the earlier of the new prisons envisaged in the government's programme. Designed by Francis Goodwin, it was completed in 1826 and opened for business the following year. With seven wings radiating from a central hub, in this case the governor's quarters and chapel, the layout followed the much favoured wheel concept. Originally, there were 185 cells, later increased to 228. In the original plans, there was again no provision for a specific cell for the condemned. Nor is there any indication that there ever was one. At times a cell in the hospital block was used, as was another in the debtors' wing.

Surrounding the complex were 25ft-high curtain walls, with the top 15 courses made up of loose bricks to thwart escape attempts. Dominant feature was the massive entrance gates, doubtless designed to emphasise the prison's role of separating the criminal element from decent society. Strong towers either side of the wooden gates were enhanced by handsome-looking walls, their strength accentuated by great stone blocks. That was the front of the prison. The remaining walls, mostly out of sight to the passing public, were of utilitarian plain red brick.

This barren world drew from one chaplain the mournful, almost Wildean comment: 'There is so much routine that the history of a week is the history of a year.' Following the Reform riots of 1831, Martello towers (of which two remain) were added for extra defence and firearms stored there. Public health was not alleviated any by the discharging of prison waste into the nearby Bramble Brook, where it joined that jettisoned by a tannery and chemical works.

Derby's prison gateway found enthusiastic aesthetic approval with the historian, Glover.

In his eyes, 'the front of this model prison may be classed amongst the finest specimens of Doric architecture of the kingdom', with 'a truly classical portico.' Equally entranced was the architect who saw in it 'a façade of primitive Levantine massing through classical Greek in detail'. Additional to its primary role, the portal also served as the execution area. Within the gateway was the drop room in which the broken-down scaffold and gallows were kept. Another room was where the hangmen would pinion their victims and fasten leg irons. Still to be seen, high up in the wall of the left-hand tower, a metal grilled door guards a small doorway. While hangings were in the public domain, it was through there that the condemned stepped out on to the scaffold. That was one of the reasons why the planners left a large area in front of the new prison, to allow maximum viewing.

Apart from a few underground cells of the Friar Gate gaol, the only substantial remaining physical evidence today of capital punishment in Derbyshire is the looming, massive remnant of the new county gaol in Derby, now guarding a modern office complex. It is still easy to imagine the crowd gathered on the open space in front of its massive gateway, awaiting a public execution.

As a place where criminals were executed or incarcerated, its span was less than a century. Eight were hanged publicly, either in front or on top of the towering main gates, 11 more were judicially slaughtered within the high walls. Eighteen were buried with ignominy and no ceremony in the prison cemetery against the curtain wall, flanking the gateway's right or northern tower. The 19th rests in an unmarked grave in a secluded country churchyard.

With the opening of the new county prison, the old one in Friar Gate was sold to Derby Borough, thus allowing the small prison in Willow Road, little more than a hovel, to be closed down. In 1840, the Friar Gate establishment followed suit and the criminals of the borough were incarcerated with the county's at Vernon Street.

* * * * * *

A CONSEQUENCE of the decline in public executions was the increase in crowds flocking to watch them. With just eight hangings in 29 years, the opportunity to see some wretch kicking his life away became decidedly rarer. However reprehensible the behaviour of the spectators of past years, it now took a decided downwards spiral. Dickens, who witnessed several hangings, described it memorably as a 'tumultuous demonstration of indecent delight'. Seldom did the *Mercury* comment on the elemental ugliness of the crowd, but when it did it showed that Derby's mobs were just as objectionable. Nor were they made up just of the lower orders. As elsewhere, there were now onlookers from the more polite classes. Women were far more in evidence; children and pickpockets were ever-presents. It was as if people sensed that the age-old barbarity was reaching its closing phases, and they wanted to be there to gloat at death. Those holding the view that public killings were a deterrent

finally learned in those last years they certainly were not. They were just an ugly, riotous, drunken, vulgar, tumultuous, brutish spectacle.

Vulgarity was not a prerogative of the rabble. Commerce, seldom choosy as to where it trod in search of profit, made its own killing at the hanging fairs. Pickpockets, prostitutes, tricksters plied their trades. Ballad mongers followed their time-honoured trade; the *Mercury* was not averse to supplying them. Newspaper supplements described the life, trial, and execution of the murderers, augmented with sketches. Bakers with their gingerbread men, daubers with crude paintings and pedlars with crude statuettes, all purported representations of the victim, never failed to find a credulous market.

No less averse to exploiting the potential were the railway companies. Since on one occasion when no fewer than three were to be executed, the thought must be expressed that the reason why the top of the gates was chosen for the gallows was to facilitate all those extra spectators coming in by rail. Up to now, people walked to Derby, cluttering up the few roads with their carts and carriages. Of the seven killers to mount the scaffold, only one was from Derby. The others were from Heage, Chesterfield, Belper and Ilkeston and special excursion trains were laid on to ferry people in, anxious to see justice done as well as have a boisterous, rumbustious day out, well fuelled by drink. On one occasion, returning passengers, many excited by what they had seen and drunk, fought a pitched battle on Derby station.

DERBYSHIRE NEW COUNTY PRISON.

Some particulars of the Life, Behaviour and Execution of

JOHN LEEDHAM,

Who was hanged in front of the New County Jail, Derby,

On *FRIDAY, April 12th,* 1833,

FOR BESTIALITY.

The first known broadside to depict the new County Prison in Vernon Street, Derby. It tells the tragic story of John Leedham, the first to be hanged there and the only one not buried with the prison walls. He was also the last to hang for a crime other than for murder.

THE *Derby Mercury's* remark that John Leedham died at the rope's end 'in a state of the most perfect ignorance' was particularly well chosen. Of all the unhappy hangings at Derby, his must surely qualify as the most tragic. For perhaps the only time, the newspaper criticised not only the system but also the judge, for sending this 20-year-old man to his death. His crime, bestiality, was loathed and shuddered at by society, but there were reservations.

Commented the newspaper:

'The detestable crime for which the youth suffered is abhorred, but the human and religious feeling of society will not sanction the hurrying of a mere boy into eternity, when other punishments would promote virtue, deter from crime, and secure the ends of public justice as well or better.'

Leedham went to his death on 12 April 1833. As well as arousing the passions of the newspaper, he also achieved the unwanted distinction of being the first to hang at Vernon Street and the last to be judicially slaughtered in Derbyshire for a crime other than murder. Born at Yeldersley, near Ashbourne, he was the son of a labourer and a mother who died when he was eight. His education came from the Yeldersley Sunday School, which he attended until 13. For the next few years, he worked for local farmers. Described as of a roving disposition, Leedham decided, on reaching 18, to sample life in London. The capital was no place for this simple country lad. He led a dissolute life, and, 'much distressed, and impoverished', returned to his native Derbyshire. In February 1833, he was charged with bestiality.

No details are known of Leedham's 'detestable crime.' Unappetising though it was, that he was sentenced to death for it aroused the compassion of many. That he should have to die at all elicited a feeling 'from all classes in favour of mercy to the culprit'. It was evident 'that there is a growing dislike in the public mind to come of the sanguinary enactments of our laws'. At the assizes, Leedham, a short but strongly built youth of weak understanding, had been one of 53 cases tried. The death sentence was recorded for nine offenders, who were later reprieved and transported. A murderer was acquitted on the grounds of insanity and ordered to be detained during His Majesty's pleasure. Two men charged with committing unnatural offences (not specified) were acquitted. Leedham, it would seem, drew the short straw.

The inequality of judicial application troubled the *Mercury*. Leedham heard the court's verdict from the lips of Sir Bernard Bosanquet, and the paper lost no time in comparing the judge with Sir Thomas Denman, by then Lord Chief Justice:

'Dislike to what is considered an unnecessary waste of human life, has been greatly increased in this instance from a knowledge of the fact, that at the late Assizes in Northampton, the Chief Justice, Sir Thomas Denman, transported for life a young man, capitally convicted of an offence of the same disgusting nature, as that for which Mr Justice Bosanquest has thought proper, on the same circuit, at Derby, to execute a sentence of death pronounced by him on John Leedham!!! The wretched convict was only 20 years old – was not known to have committed any former crime – was a youth of very weak intellect – in a state of the most perfect ignorance – and scarcely capable of distinguishing between right and wrong. Can this be equal justice?'

Strenuous efforts were launched to secure a reprieve. One petition, signed by some 200 of Derby's principal inhabitants, had been hastily despatched to Justice Bosanquet, by then sitting at Warwick. He refused to ameliorate the sentence. A second petition was no more successful. Forwarded to the Home Office, it bore, according to a news sheet, the signatures of no fewer than 4,000 people 'of all classes, including nearly all members of the medical profession'.

Leedham's execution proved the highlight of the Easter Fair. Over 6,000 crowded into

South Street and Vernon Street to see him die. From the time the youth was arrested, the Revd George Pickering, aware of his likely execution, had paid particular attention to his religious instruction. The chaplain brought solace to a mind barely able to grasp what was happening. As his calling required him, the Revd Pickering persuaded the youth to make his confession, which he duly signed 'in a fair legible hand'. On the morning of his execution, a Friday, Leedham sat in the prison chapel and heard Pickering preach the funeral sermon and afterwards expressed himself ready to meet his doom.

Oh pray while you may to your Maker –
His mercy, not justice implore,
Said the priest, while the tears fill'd his eyes,
And his chok'd voice could utter no more;
You asked me to pray, said the felon,
But no one e'er show'd me the way;
'Tis too late, 'tis too late now to teach me,
I can't understand what you say.
(Song of the Scaffold)

Leedham claimed to be devoid of fear, and the *Mercury's* representative, who spoke to him half an hour before going to meet the hangman, noted:

'There was an air of perplexity and trouble in his mien, but his countenance was florid, and considering his youth the fortitude he displayed was wonderful.'

Midday was the time for dying. There was a little, hopeful delay while everyone waited for a messenger to arrive back with a Home Office response to the petition for mercy. There was none. Accordingly, the ritual was played out. Escorted by javelin men, the Under-Sheriff arrived at the prison gates, knocked and demanded the body of the convict. Leedham was taken from his cell and paraded around the wards. Behind their iron grilles, prisoners watched the sad procession pass by. The condemned youth called out his last farewells. As the party entered the hangman's room within the gateway, the victim's face 'assumed a deadly paleness'. The unknown executioner (elevated by the reporter's description to 'the last officer of the law') pinioned the victim's arms and when all was ready, the group ascended the spiral staircase and emerged on the scaffold.

By this time, Leedham was clearly distressed. Two turnkeys had to hold him up as they positioned him beneath the gallows. It had been the victim's intention, doubtless encouraged by the Revd Pickering, to speak a few words to the crowd, giving the almost statutory warning to avoid the crime that had brought him to such an ignominious end. However, such was his piteous condition, that prescription had to be abandoned. A few more prayers and the chaplain stood aside. The final moments had arrived. The executioner drew the white cap over Leedham's face, then stepped back, pulled the bolt and another victim was launched into eternity. The time was a-quarter-to-one. According to the *Mercury*, he did not appear to suffer much: 'A few struggles ensued, and life seemed extinct'.

After an hour, John Leedham's body was removed and handed over to friends waiting

A crude illustrations much used by publishers of execution sheets, with the result that it did not necessarily agree with the details of the murder.

A chaplain prays for the condemned man. In the background stands the grieving wife. A woodcut from a broadside dealing with the life and crimes of the Belper murderer, Anthony Turner (1852).

nearby. They took him away from Derby and up to Bradley where he was buried in All Saints' Churchyard. The rector, the Revd Evan Thomas, conducted a simple ceremony and later recorded in the parish register the name and date of death, with no additional comment. There was no headstone; at least none survives.

Apart from Crosland many years before, the identities of executioners have remained unrecorded. Leedham was the last to die with no report of who pulled back the bolt. With the decline in public hangings after 1830, there were fewer hangmen. As a result, those remaining in the business became quite famous (or infamous), some almost household names. The man who despatched

Leedham might have been William Calcraft. Appointed in 1829, his record of being the longest serving as well as the most prolific practitioner must now be unassailable. Beyond dispute is that he was incompetent almost beyond belief.

Derbyshire's course of capital punishment changed. From now on, only those found guilty of murder would die. The sudden, though not unexpected, drop in executions was highlighted by the fact that ten years elapsed before workmen's hammers again announced the erecting of the scaffold. That was the longest gap since 1741, when Peter Bowler died on Nuns' Green for the offence of dangerous wounding.

Hanging Them on High

THE accession of the Whig government in 1830 heralded far-reaching changes in the country's penal system and attitudes towards capital punishment. While much could be attributed to the new battalions of politicians, some of the changes were a culmination of public opinion and shifting perceptions from earlier times finally breaking the surface.

Effectively, by the end of the 1830s only those who had murdered mounted the scaffold. There still remained other capital offences, but they being whittled away, and where they applied the death sentence was commuted to either terms of imprisonment or transportation. Gone were the days when mutilating the corpse of a murderer was the only means whereby the comparative serious-ness of his (or her) crime could be broadcast.

Alongside the reforms there arose much debate over the use of the gallows. By the 1840s, alternatives were being seriously aired. There were those who saw nothing wrong with the time-honoured system of public hangings. At the opposite end of the scale, an influential grouping thought the time had come for the total repudiation of the scaffold. Others, while abhorring the employment of hangmen, conceded that there were crimes for which only they provided the answer. Then there were those who wanted the State's killings done in private, behind prison walls. This latter group declared that since public executions had proved to be no deterrent, then private ones would, although where they obtained their evidence is uncertain. Their theory, however, was that knowing that death would be a secretive, lonesome affair, far from the public gaze and gruesome levity, where last speeches went unheard, would further enhance the terror of being hanged. Certain officials would have to be present, of course, to witness that death was summoned in the prescribed manner.

The call for secret executions found an attentive and growing audience. Public executions had deteriorated into occasions that did nothing but bring the law into disrepute, and perhaps make the condemned something of a martyr. More to the point, the crowd's behaviour gave rise to strong feelings of disgust.

As the *Mercury* was to comment:

'*...the less sentimental care so little for the awful spectacle, as to look upon it with the same feeling as they would gaze upon a brutal fight, and indulge in all sorts of libidinous ribaldry, and ferocious ruffianism, and obscene mirth, under the shadow of the gallows itself.*'

The 1840s saw the movement for abolition reach its height. While there had been such demands in the late 18th century, it was not until Sir Samuel Romilly took up cudgels did it attain more prominence in the public agenda. Romilly, who nevertheless accepted that there would always be the gallows for a few most serious felonies, devoted his energies in seeking to have the death penalty removed from transgressions such as petty property offences. Although successful in getting Bills through Parliament, they came to grief in the Lords. There, as far as the Church was concerned, his compassion fell on stony ground. Romilly's death in 1818 saw the Quakers taking over the cause, and they were determined to have the gallows abolished altogether.

By the middle of the decade, the anti-hanging lobby had achieved its widest support. The tide appeared to be running in its favour. Gone were the Bloody Code, gibbeting and dissecting, along with the Black

Act. Their banner had attracted such luminaries as Dickens and Thackery, although they were to later march under a different banner. Pro-abolition letters besieged newspapers, sermons thundered from pulpits of the mainly nonconformist churches, pamphlets were everywhere.

Then the movement began to lose its impetus. There were too many persuasive arguments for keeping the gallows, if only for the crime of murder. The agenda changed, the course became confused. Debates began to centre on whether or not hangings should continue in public. This put the abolitionists in a quandary. They realised that once the gallows went behind prison walls their cause was lost: out of sight out of mind. This obliged them to take up the stance that if there were to be hangings, then they must be in the public arena. That was the only way to keep their ultimate aim to the fore. The retentionists, capitalising on the miasma rising from public killings, pressed for private slaughter.

* * * * * *

IN 1843, there was a triple hanging at Derby. Although by no means the first multiple slaying, it had been a few years since the last two, both in 1817. In any case, it was the first time the scaffold had been erected for ten years. Thousands poured into town to seize this rarely offered opportunity. From Chesterfield, Ambergate and Belper, people crowded on two Derby-bound excursion trains laid on by the North Midland Railway. While estimating crowds was never a precise science, the execution of Bonsall, Bland and Hulme

Bonsall, Bland and Hulme who were hanged in 1843 for the murder of Miss Martha Goddard of Stanley Hall. It was estimated that nearly 50,000 watched the hangings which were unique in that they took place on top of the gateway to the County Prison in Vernon Street.

was claimed to have attracted an audience approaching 50,000. Such a figure would have been noteworthy even for London's Newgate. Derby's population at the time stood at just under 33,000, so the calculation should be treated with caution.

For whatever reason, the decision had been taken that the scaffold be built on the top and to the left of the gaol's main gateway. From such a vantage, the outlook was impressive and the view from the ground was greatly extended. As far as the eye could see, people were massing for the killings. A *Mercury* correspondent standing at the scaffold site reported that roads, gardens, yards, windows, housetops, anything, anywhere commanding a view of the gallows had their 'separate crowd of gazers'. Vernon Street, South Street and Friar Gate buzzed like beehives.

What brought this huge assembly together was the savage murder of Miss Martha Goddard in September 1842. Found guilty of the crime were Samuel Bonsall, aged 26, William Bland (39) and John Hulme (24). Bonsall and Bland, both colliers, were natives of Heage; Hulme, a sweep's apprentice, hailed from Leek. Two of his brothers had already been transported. All three were burglars and sometime members of a larger gang. Violence came natural to them, and, if necessary, murder. Bonsall was to admit that he, with another, had planned to rob a woman who kept a tollgate between Matlock and Bakewell. They took with them a crowbar stolen from a Matlock forge, since it was accepted they might well have to take her life. Only the unexpected arrival of a carriage foiled their plan. Hulme, in his wandering daytime profession, would earmark possible places to rob. One such target was Stanley Hall at Stanley, the home of two elderly maiden sisters, Martha and Sarah Goddard.

On the night of 30 September, the three broke into the Goddards' home. From their subsequent confessions, sometimes confusing and at times tending to blame each other, it would appear that Bland stood guard on the landing between the two bedrooms occupied by the sisters. Bonsall and Hulme were in Martha's room, rummaging through the drawers for items to steal. She woke up, leapt out of bed, screaming 'Sally!' meaning her sister, and ran to the door where Bland caught her and pushed her back. Bonsall seized the terrified woman and ended her life with three blows of a crowbar. According to the other two, Bonsall had every intention of killing Sarah, who had now arrived on the frenzied scene. Seizing her by the hair, he dragged her to the floor and drew a knife. Hulme asserted that had he not interfered, Bonsall would have slit the woman's throat. Bonsall's version was that he sought only to intimidate Sarah into silence.

There was an outcry when the murder was discovered, for the sisters were well regarded in the neighbourhood. It was not long before the three burglars were arrested and charged. The trio stood trial before the judge, Mr Baron Gurney, on 20 March 1843. Their statements left little doubt as to their collective guilt; whose hand actually ended Martha Goddard's life being of little consequence where such a crime was involved.

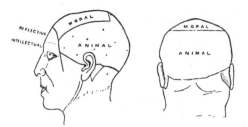

BONSALL, aged 26.

The phrenologist's 'map' of the head of Samuel Bonsall, the killer of Martha Goddard in 1842. The findings, that Bonsall's brain displayed a high development of animal, low and narrow of moral and retiring on intellectual, would not have come as any great surprise to those who followed the trial of Miss Goddard's murderers.

Bonsall, after stoutly refusing to admit his guilt, later confessed that it was indeed he who had brought the crowbar crashing down on their victim's head. The weapon was not available as evidence at the trial. Eventually it turned up, buried in a garden at Heage. Looking rather like a stunted walking stick, the ugly weapon was wrought from iron, three-quarters of an inch thick, 11 inches in length, turned over at the top.

From sentencing to the execution, the three, kept in separate cells, received religious instruction from the chaplain, still the Revd George Pickering and a Wesleyan Methodist Minister, the Revd William Vevers. Between them, they sought to bring the prisoners to a state of penitence and true repentance. The only way to save their souls was a full confession, acknowledgement and acceptance of the consequences of their sins. As the instruction proceeded, the whole story gradually came out of what happened at Stanley Hall. To the Revd Pickering, Bonsall finally admitted striking the fatal blows.

All was ready for the hanging day. Already within the prison walls was the hangman. From Appleby, Joseph Heywood is the first executioner to be identified with certainty since the reign of Crosland. This revelation may well be a result of hangmen having less to do. High sheriffs had always been responsible for appointing hangmen and generally they recruited locally. With lessening demand, they were more inclined to send for those appointed by the City of London. We cannot be certain that Heywood was one of those, or a practitioner from elsewhere and available for hire. Remember that Derby's scaffold had been in storage for ten years, and if there had been a local executioner, then his appointment may well have lapsed. What is sure, no other local volunteer was ever accepted.

What must surely be lost by now is the sketch made of Heywood while he waited in one of the gateway rooms for the condemned men to arrive. It was drawn by a Mr Bally of Manchester, a well-known phrenologist of the day, and the *Mercury* reporter, obviously a believer in Bally's calling, could not help but notice that the artist had caught well 'the lineaments of the executioner, whose expression of countenances was in perfect unison with his horrible calling'. Heywood, however, was not the principle reason for

Bally's presence. He had come to study the heads of the three murderers. One of the leading founders of the science of phrenology was an Austrian, Dr Joseph Kaspar Spurzheim (1758-1832) and Bally had worked under him for several years. Today, phrenology lies in the past, utterly discredited, but in the 19th century and well into the 20th, it enjoyed a wide and educated following. From studying the conformation of the human skull and mapping it, practitioners claimed they were capable of detecting a person's mental faculties and traits of character.

Bally published his findings, complete with scientific-looking diagrams. Bonsall's temperament he summarised as 'Lymphatic sanguineous, with a small portion of bilious', Bland he discovered to be 'Nervous sanguineous, and a portion of bilious.' Hulme turned out the worst of the three. Not only was the apprentice sweep 'bilious, lymphatic and sanguine', he also possessed 'a bad organisation, implying obstinacy, grossness, tyranny, cunning, murder and dishonesty'. None of which, reduced to everyday language, would have come as any surprise to those having already read the newspapers and circulating broadsheets. However, the findings, with their mapped profiles, would have been widely accepted with understanding nods. There was a very genuine, long-held belief abroad that criminals were a definite class if not breed, physically identifiable, their commonest trait being that they sprang mostly from the ranks of the lower orders. Much of the categorisation of the cells and wards of new prisons was based on such perceptions.

Also hovering in attendance was a Derby modeller and sculptor, William Barton of Parker Street, waiting to make casts of the prisoners' heads once Heywood had performed his tasks. Presumably Barton later sold plaster casts of the murderers' heads; it is known that they were presented to John Sims, Governor of Derby prison, to display in a museum maintained on the premises. There seems to be no record of what happened to those casts and the others that followed. A fine display still exists at Norwich Castle, of those hanged there. No doubt, it is basically similar to that once at Derby.

A few minutes before midday on 31 March 1843, according to custom, the Under-Sheriff, Mr Simpson, attended by the usual javelin men arrived in front of the prison's main gateway and formally demanded the bodies of the condemned. A few minutes later, Bonsall, Bland and Hulme left their cells to take up their places in the formal procession to the drop. At the head walked the Revd Pickering, reading the burial service. Condemned people were surely unique in hearing their own burial service before actually dying. As the group slowly made its way about the prison, other prisoners crowded at the grilled widows to watch it pass by. Occasionally, Bonsall stopped and addressed them. 'God bless you, lads, God bless you. Take warning lads, take warning.'

Entering the gateway rooms, the three were met by Heywood, who pinioned their arms. Then it was up a spiral staircase until the murderers stepped out on to the top of the prison portal. Even in their hideous situation, they must have been amazed to see the enormous crowd gazing up at them. Everywhere there were people waiting to see them die, their faces eager with anticipation. With their last moments one earth upon them, the three could clearly be heard praying on their elevated scaffold. The Revd Pickering reached the end of the service, Heywood drew back the bolt and the slayers of Martha Goddard went to eternity. According to the *Mercury*, Bonsall died almost immediately, the other two following after 'a very brief duration'. After hanging for the stipulated hour, the bodies were taken down and prepared for burial. Barton made his casts and returned to his studio. Bonsall, Bland and Hulme were the first of the condemned to be buried within the precincts of the prison, their bodies first covered with quicklime to hasten decomposition.

For years afterwards, the hanging of the trio was recalled in one or two local sayings in and around Heage. The village might be referred to as the place 'where they hang 'em in bunches'. A preacher, it is claimed, coined the phrase 'a Heage wash', meaning a hanging.

That Derby's theatre on Bold Lane chose to cash in on the triple event by displaying placards about town announcing it would be open for business after 2pm 'to accommodate the country people', drew censure from the *Mercury*:

'This was an offence against propriety and public morality, and deserves every

reprehension. Such a proceeding may for the moment perhaps bring a few extra shillings to the caterers of this species of amusement, but it is sure to create – and deservedly so – disgust in the estimation of all right thinking persons, and ultimately to materially injure those who are interested in this species of property.'

The *Mercury* could be accused of hypocrisy. Evidence suggests it was not averse to selling hanging sheets and ballads, first scrubbing out details of their publisher.

If the newspaper's account can be accepted, then the immense crowd was quite well behaved, at least up to the time the bodies were removed. Scenes more in keeping with the traditional hanging mobs took place later at Derby railway station. Something like 1,500 people, many in ascending degrees of intoxication and excitement, had swarmed down to the station, and saw no compelling reason why they should not be on the first of the special trains. A pitched battle was fought on the departure platform. 'A very disgraceful scene,' claimed the *Mercury*, with much fighting, wrestling and swearing. Railway officials finally succeeded in imposing some sort of order and in due course two packed special trains steamed away to their various destinations.

There is no reason to suppose that Derby throngs were any less rumbustious, noisy, drunken, blasphemous, or brutish than at other assize towns. That a crowd of over 40,000 watching three violent murderers die was comparatively restrained, somehow fails to ring quite true. As reports of these

occasions grew more detailed, it tended to reveal the average spectator as a member of the lower orders, people of the worst kind, coarse, disrespectful, idle, etc, etc, with little education or religious instruction. Persons not noted for their restraint. With the advent of the railways, emphasis was placed on the many coming from other towns in the county and the 'colliery districts'. This was perhaps fair comment, bearing in mind the location of many of the murders; Derby was comparatively peaceful. Mention was made of the more women attending, a national trend. Throughout the country, evidence was that executions were attracting those from the more so-called respectable classes of society. The explanation must surely be that since that public executions, a hallmark of English life for centuries, were getting fewer, then their appeal broadened. The morbid, the ugly, the darker recesses of human behaviour, have always exercised a strange fascination, even for the average person believing himself well adjusted.

*   *   *   *   *   *

FOUR years later Samuel Heywood was back in Derby. For him, the occasion had special significance, since John Platts was to be his 50th victim. However, the Chesterfield murderer was not accorded an elevated view for his last moments, the scaffold having being returned to its more usual location outside the prison gates. Nor was his end witnessed by anything like the numbers at the last time the hangman was in Derby, although a crowd of some 20,000 was still large enough to pack the approaches to the prison.

By August 1846, John Platts must have thought he had got away with the murder of George Collis. After all, it was nearly nine months since Collis had disappeared without trace. Then everything started to go wrong when workmen, employed to empty a cesspool in Chesterfield's Low Pavement, came across human remains. There were two leg bones, each with garters on (one red, one white), and thighbones as well as a quantity of human entrails. There were further shocking discoveries: part of a man's coat, trousers, a hat, silk handkerchief embroidered with the initials 'GC' as well as parts of a brace and stocking. At the bottom of the emptied pool was a fractured skull. The clothing was put on display in the hope that someone could identify it and give a name to the remains. The initialled handkerchief gave the authorities what they were looking for. Ellen Beresford of the West Bar recognised it as belonging to the man she was to marry, George Collis. The dead man's mother recognised the clothing as

The unfortunate George Collis, whose body was found in a Chesterfield cess pool in 1846. John Platts was hanged for his murder, before a crowd estimated at over 20,000.

that worn by her son the night he disappeared, 7 December 1845.

Collis and John Platts were once partners in a small butchery business, but their ways had parted. Inquiries soon pointed the finger of suspicion at Platts. He was arrested, charged with murder, and stood trial at the March 1847 assizes at Derby, before Mr Justice Patteson. The jury found him guilty.

John Platts was 22 years old, stockily built with a large chin and jawbone, lending him a heavy, morose expression. He stood an inch short of five foot. There was a twin brother and the two were nicknamed 'Gog' and 'Magog', John being the latter. They were born in a back room of a shop in Chesterfield's Shambles, owned by a man called Morley. Their mother never married, drank a great deal, was of negotiable virtue, and while the twins were still of tender years had another child, a girl. Giving birth to yet another illegitimate child annoyed the authorities. Hannah Platts was sent for a time to the local gaol to 'expatiate her offences against chastity'.

What happened to their sister is not known, but Gog and Magog were went to the parish workhouse. Reaching the age of ten, they were meant to be placed in parish apprenticeships. Maybe it was because of their tiny stature, but the three businesses approached preferred to pay the customary £10 to the parochial authorities rather than take the boys on and teach them a trade. Despite the setbacks and his size, coupled with an inoffensive nature, John Platts began to make something of a life for himself. Starting by running errands for the Shambles' butchers, he gradually progressed to serving apprenticeships. By then his mother had served her time in gaol and was earning a precarious living charring. John would visit her on Sunday evenings, usually to find her deep in her cups, a weakness that caused him a great deal of unhappiness.

By the time he was 20, Magog, having managed to save around £15, set up his own small butchery business in the Shambles. In 1845, he took George Collis into partnership. The pair did not stay together for long, Collis preferring to earn a living driving carriages. Platts worked on his own for a while longer, until he was taken ill and the business collapsed. Recovering, he returned to a former employer, a butcher named Robert Statham, who was probably glad to have him back, remembering the little man as quiet, and a hard worker who kept sober. He may have misjudged Platts. There were those in and around the Shambles who found him deceitful and untrustworthy. 'There was no believing a word he said,' was a commonly held opinion.

Before he died, Platts made a written confession, to which the *Mercury* did not attach too much credibility. In it, he claimed that Morley (behind whose premises he had

been born) was the killer, in partnership with another man. Since Morley had died of fever of the brain before the body was discovered, Platts obviously saw him as a means of escaping the rope. While admitting that he had been part of a plot to kill Collis, he claimed Morley was the leading light. Robbery was the motive, for they believed their victim carried a sum of money around with him, to pay for his forthcoming marriage to Ellen Beresford. However, Platts had been noticed shortly afterwards with blood on his hands, and a few days later was seen in possession of the deceased's watch. Moreover, he had already sold a pair of boots subsequently identified as his former partner's.

Reduced to the basic facts, it would seem that Morley and Platts, with a third person (whose name was withheld by the newspapers), met Collis and plied him with drink. When he was thoroughly intoxicated, they all went over to Platts' shop and there Collis was murdered. In summarising a case that was at times confusing, the *Mercury* arrived at the conclusion that Platts was the main perpetrator, with the slaying actually done at Morley's shop. First hit on the head with a hammer, then strangled, the unfortunate Collis's body was rifled and afterwards dismembered. A few hours later, the bloody remains were stuffed into a sack, placed on a wheelbarrow and trundled across the Market Place, to be jettisoned into the cesspool.

As the day dawned on 1 April, the crowds were already gathering. By 7am, the area in front of the prison was packed even though

The County Prison in Vernon Street. Its impressive façade has survived into the 21st century, now fronting a modern office complex but still a grim reminder of the last public executions to be held in Derby.

five hours were yet to elapse before the Under-Sheriff with his javelin men turned up at the main gateway. Since his trial, Platts continued to lay the prime blame on the late Morley, averring that his early death was caused by a troubled conscience bringing about the fatal fever. He himself displayed no contrition, indeed his fellow prisoners and prison staff, despite his fatal predicament, found him to be a character of 'sly deceit, and low craft, unparalleled in that receptacle of crime and wickedness'. That he had become the father of an illegitimate child not a month before did nothing to mollify that judgement.

The tolling of the prison bell signalled that Platts had left his cell and, with a turnkey either side, taken his place in the procession to the scaffold. Reaching the portal, he was ushered into the room where Heywood waited to pinion his arms. He requested heavy irons be fastened to his legs, to add weight to his small body and so hasten the end. Suddenly, he began to tremble. Up to then Magog had been calm and composed, at times almost indifferent to what was going on about him. Still shaking, he stumbled up the stairs that would take him to

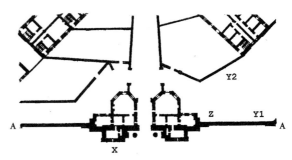

An extract from the original design of Derby Prison in Vernon Street. All that now remains are the wall section A-A, the flanking so-called Martello towers (not shown), and the front section of the main gateway. It is still possible to pinpoint former sites as follows: X – Scaffold site for public executions; Y1 – First scaffold site for private executions; Y2 – Second scaffold site or execution shed for private executions; Z – Prison cemetery where the condemned were buried.

the small external door in the portal wall and out on to the scaffold. Twenty thousand pairs of eyes feasted on his appearance. The cry 'Hats off!' rippled through the vast swarm. Platts never stopped shivering. Heywood, having put the white cap in place, drew back and pulled the lever. The trap doors yawned suddenly and down went the little man. For a while he struggled and then was still. Maybe Heywood, who would have immediately hurried down to beneath the scaffold, helped him on his way to eternity by pulling hard on the wildly kicking legs. The *Mercury* never noticed such horrible details, but the practice was common enough among the hanging fraternity. The statutory hour passed, the body was taken back inside the prison walls, to be smothered in quicklime to hurry Nature along and then buried. There were now four in the unadorned little cemetery.

Calcraft in Derby

MARCH 1852, as far as one can be certain, was the first time William Calcraft came to Derby. That he would come was entirely predictable; in fact he may already have done so, but unreported. After all, his career as a principle hangman spanned nearly half a century and he seems to have put in an appearance at some time or another wherever gallows were routinely erected. How many he sent to the next world has never been computed, even though his awesome career is quite well documented. A total of many hundreds would not be at all exaggerated. All those who had anything to do with him, who saw him strutting about his business on the scaffold stage, were all agreed on one thing: Calcraft was a bungler. Most hangmen were, but Calcraft outshone them all. In his defence, it has to be said that he was around for so long that it is doubtful that after a few years there were many execution watchers who remembered any of his predecessors. Dickens saw him at work, and voiced the opinion that he 'should be restrained in his unseemly briskness, in his jokes, his oaths, and his brandy'.

His name aroused the debased literary skills of the ballad writers:

My name it is Calcraft by every one known
And a sad life is mine to you I know own,
For I hang people up and I cut people down,
Before all the rebel of great London town.
For my old friend Cheshire he learned me the
trick
And I dine in the clouds tonight with Old
Nick,
For the people on earth do use me so bad,
That with tears I could drown them for I feel
now so sad.

William Calcraft, cobbler by trade, was born in 1800 at Baddow, Sussex. In his earlier years, he attended public hangings, not so much out of curiosity as to supplement a meagre income by selling hot meat pies. He was something of a contradiction to the popular image of a public executioner. Mild-mannered, he was a keen gardener, angler, a noted rabbit-fancier and regular churchgoer. Appointed as a hangman for London and Middlesex in 1829, he was the last salaried incumbent with a guinea a week, plus another guinea for each execution. Requests from the provinces earned him extra fees. More income came from the sale of pieces of the rope to the ladies (said to be good for the complexion) and the victims' clothing. While never a wealthy man, Calcraft enjoyed a comfortable life style.

On duty, he rarely dressed sombrely, more often than not appearing in a shooting jacket, and invariably with a fresh flower in his buttonhole. He considered it part of his duty to read newspaper accounts of those he was to kill. He held office for 45 years, the longest ever tenure, but brought few improvements to his craft. When he retired in 1874, the hanged still died by strangulation, slowly and painfully. Although the drop was the standard method, he hardly ever altered its fall to take account of the person's weight with the consequence that it was not unusual for spectators to watch him disappear under the scaffold and haul on the victim's legs. However, there was at least one improvement. Often, those hanged would lash out with their legs, somehow gain a foothold on the side of the trapdoor, and so delay their fall into the pit. Calcraft overcame that problem by introducing leg straps, to complement the pinioned arms.

While some successors to Jack Ketch

THE GROANS
OF THE
GALLOWS,
Or the Past and Present
LIFE OF
WILLIAM CALCRAFT.

THE LIVING
Hangman of Newgate.

" The Cross shall displace the Gibbet,
and all will be accomplished." Victor Hugo.

ENTERED AT STATIONERS' HALL.

Calcraft was the first hangman to publish his memoirs, in 1855. England's longest-serving executioner, he officiated at the last three of Derby's public hangings. By common consent he was a most inept craftsman, often causing his 'clients' untold suffering.

suffered mental horrors, sometimes leading to suicide, or, more commonly, excessive drinking, Calcraft seems to have remained relatively unscathed. That he did appear at times somewhat the worse for wear should not be wondered at, bearing in mind how long he slaughtered on behalf of the State. Whether he was ever affected by the manner in which he earned money is debatable. Some thought he showed as much compunction as if he were hanging a dog.

It fell to Calcraft to hang the last man and woman to be executed in public in Britain, in 1868. He also despatched the last three to mount the public scaffold in Derby. A few years after retirement, the longest serving hangman announced he would write his memoirs (a sketchy biography had been published in 1855), a proposal that found little favour with the *Mercury*:

'It cannot, it is feared, prove altogether an edifying or a very agreeable production…He always resented the idea that he had ever put anyone to death. He merely made the preliminary arrangements required by law as solemnly pronounced by an English judge, and allowed the culprit to execute himself by falling. With this somewhat peculiar, but very decided views as to his own part in a public execution, it is possible to imagine he might go through with it, as he affirms he has done for 40 years, without once experiencing any such qualms as would likely beset a weaker individual.'

In the event, he did not carry out the intention.

William Calcraft came to Derby in 1852 to hang Anthony Turner, who had attacked the throat of Phoebe Barnes with such fury and a knife that the head was almost severed from its trunk. Mrs Barnes of Field House, Belper, had employed Turner, a 45-year-old tailor living at Lane End, to collect the rents from her various properties. It was believed that he and his wife, a childless couple, had agreed, with a small weekly allowance, to raise the illegitimate child of Mrs Barnes' late brother, Thomas Walker, once a person of some influence in the town.

Whatever, Turner did not prove very satisfactory and Mrs Barnes felt compelled to discharge him from her employ. That was at Christmas 1851. Dismissal rankled with him. On 27 December, he took a carving knife from the provision shop of a Mr Haslam, telling that astonished gentleman that he was going off to kill Mrs Barnes. Turner hurried over to Field House (Haslam following some distance behind) and demanded of a servant girl that he be allowed to see Mrs Barnes immediately. That lady refused any such meeting. The maid delivered the riposte, only to be brushed roughly aside by a furious Turner, who dashed into the house and up the stairs to Mrs Barnes' room. Frightened, the girl fled to the next house, where lived the Revd J. Bannister, a relative of Phoebe Barnes. Maid and clergyman hurried back to Field House.

He was just about to go upstairs when he met Turner hurrying down, carrying a knife now dripping blood. A fight broke out and Turner was sent flying. He managed to run out of the house only to be confronted by the maid, waiting outside. Turner tried to use the knife again, but she fortunately managed to turn her head and evade the blow. Once clear of the house, he made good his escape, albeit short-lived. In the meantime, the Revd

Bannister had made the horrifying discovery of Phoebe Barnes' body lying in a pool of blood in her room. Her head had almost been cut from her body, and one of her thumbs lacerated from vain attempts to ward off the frenzied knife attack.

Turner's trial lasted three hours, the guilty verdict causing no surprise. Once Mr Justice Maule had delivered the death sentence, Turner was returned to Vernon Street, to wait for 26 March and Calcraft. While no particular place seems to have been designated as the condemned cell, it could have been one of the single cells in a ward specially built to house particularly troublesome inmates. Leaving there on execution morning, Turner made the obligatory walk to the gallows in a parade headed by the Revd Pickering, a ritual usually well covered by the *Mercury*.

There had been some changes, however. Whereas it had been customary to allow people to visit the condemned man on the morning of his death, be it for humanitarian reasons or simply curiosity, the practice was now forbidden. Only officials were allowed into the prison precincts. This may have been part of an effort to make executions as private and remote as possible. Press representatives (a category abused on occasions by wide interpretation) were included in the ban. To witness the demise of Turner, reporters were accommodated at the head warder's lodge standing outside the enclosing walls, officially assured that they would be informed of everything that went on inside, after death had taken place. An early example of the Press Release. It has to be admitted that the *Mercury*'s write-up did not differ in any great respect from earlier, eyewitness accounts. That newspaper's coverage of executions will be returned to later.

It was the report of Turner's death that supplied confirmation that condemned prisoners reached the scaffold through the small grilled doorway high in the wall of the left-hand tower of the main gates. Broadside drawings clearly indicate that this was so, but such illustrations can never be relied on. On reaching the gatehouse, Turner, the chaplain and some others, 'ascended to an apartment contiguous to the drop and Turner was then surrendered into the hands of Calcraft'. The executioner 'speedily completed the operation of pinioning', and a few minutes after midday the two stepped out on to the scaffold.

Perhaps the murder of Phoebe Barnes lacked the drama of the previous hangings, for the crowd that greeted Turner was by no means unusually large. Indeed, reported the *Mercury*, while there were several thousands gazing on, there had been neither the early morning rush for the best views nor any untoward behaviour. From the head warder's lodge the *Mercury* scribe judged the throng no greater than would have been found at a foot race or balloon ascent, other popular and established crowd pullers. In fact, the time was close to noon before the open ground in front of the prison was anything like crowded.

'As 12 o'clock approached, numbers of mechanics and labourers arrived from all directions, with the apparent intention of passing away the dinner hour.'

Illustration for an execution sheet about Anthony Turner, who murdered Phoebe Barnes at Belper in 1851. This is another example of a woodcut that could be adapted to show one or more persons in the dock or sitting on the judges' bench, to suit the occasion.

There were fewer females than on former occasions 'and the behaviour of the whole assemblage was silent, decorous, and orderly throughout'.

Beneath the gallows beam, Turner glanced down at the crowd but made no comment as he waited for the executioner to conclude the arrangements. Once satisfied, Calcraft pulled hard on the lever and the Belper killer plunged through the yawning trapdoors and 'instantly ceased to exist'. Within minutes, spectators began to drift away. By 1pm, with the corpse still hanging, Vernon Street was almost clear again. Nor did the *Mercury* observe any

instances 'worth noticing' of drunkenness, 'or other irregularity'. Turner's corpse was taken down and carried back into the prison. William Barton, the sculptor, was again on hand to take a cast of the head. Once finished, the remains, covered in quicklime, were interred in the prison cemetery. That sad little plot was filling up.

* * * * * *

WHATEVER drama was lacking in Turner's case, the execution of George Smith certainly made up for it. For one of those odd, inexplicable reasons, his crime made the

George Smith, the 'Ilkeston Parracide' a drawing taken from a newspaper supplement published to mark his crime and execution.

after the trapdoor had fallen. Calcraft, stated to be inebriated, tried to push him back. Failing, he threw himself at the man and the two of them ended up falling into the pit. This time, Calcraft succeeded in killing him.

George Smith, only 20, worked as a twist hand at one of the many Ilkeston lace mills. Home was a terraced house in Bath Street where he lived with his father, Joseph Smith, a shoemaker and small-scale property owner. A short, personable young man, George led a loose and debauched life, much of it revolving around drink. One newspaper wrote that he 'was seen in the street with a cigar in his mouth, was seen with a harlot; and the low theatres which so often frequent the town of Ilkeston was his element.'

You feeling Christians give attention
While to you a tale I tell;
For the solemn hour has come
When I must say farewell.
For the horrid crime of murder,
I must die a death of scorn,
Upon Derby scaffold high!
Oh! would to God I'd ne'er been born!
(from a popular ballad about Smith's crime)

national headlines, the Press dubbing him the 'Ilkeston parricide', although patricide would have been more accurate. Local newspapers published diagrams of the murder scene; one published a supplement carrying a portrait of the killer. Print technology was becoming more sophisticated. Smith's dying in 1861 has been generally accepted as drawing the biggest assembly of all to a Derby hanging. Some estimates went as high as 60,000, but that surely has to be an exaggeration.

Again, Calcraft was hired as the state's final judicial official. By this time, the hangman had achieved more odious notoriety through a bizarre incident that further enhanced his reputation for incompetence. In 1856, he had watched as one of his victims somehow managed to scramble back on to the scaffold

On 1 May 1861, George Smith, after several hours of heavy drinking, shot his father dead as he warmed himself by the fire at home. The tragic train of events leading to the murder had started a few days before. A Miss Emma Eyre had given birth to a baby, which she intended to 'father upon' Smith. He, while certainly the father, thought otherwise. With the promise of a gallon of ale, he persuaded some friends to visit Miss Eyre, but her mother would not let them see the baby. Returning, they recounted what had passed and advised him not to pay a shilling towards the child. Smith agreed and decided that France would be his next destination, where he could avoid paying any maintenance. Since that meant saying goodbye to his tavern friends, he bought them another gallon of beer.

Going to France seemed a good idea when deep in drink. In a more sober mood, Smith still chose to shake the dust of Ilkeston off his shoes but travelled no further than Belton in Leicestershire. After only a few days in exile, he was back in Ilkeston. He called on his father, shared a meal with him, and then sought out his drinking companions. Money, or lack of it, was proving a problem. He went back home, stole his father's bank book and caught the train to Nottingham. At a bank, he tried to draw £14 from his father's account, but was refused unless he could produce a note of authorisation. Smith confirmed later that the money was to have taken him to France.

Frustrated by his lack of success, Smith went on a drinking spree, got 'enticed with a girl' in a public house, an incident that provoked an unseemly row. The Ilkeston lace worker stepped further along the path to the gallows.

'I began to feel very bloodthirsty, and it here entered my mind that if my father said anything to me when I got home about the bank book or anything else I would blow his brains out.'

It was not a casual threat. Before leaving Nottingham, Smith bought a pistol, powder and caps. Back in Ilkeston, he made his final purchase, a pennyworth of shot. Two visits were made to his father's house. On the first, he opened the door and saw his father lying on a sofa, probably asleep. Closing the door, Smith walked to the bottom the garden, loaded the pistol and returned with the intention of shooting his father. By this time, however, Joseph Smith had gone out. George himself then left, went to a public house where, on reflection, he decided not to kill his parent. So, it was back to the house. Mr Smith had not yet come back, so George left the pistol in a drawer and made his way back to the public house. There was a lot of drinking and when Smith left to go home yet again, he was very drunk. An edgy temper was not helped any when he got into an argument with a companion and a fight nearly ensued. 'I was very vexed and excited with drink.'

When Smith arrived home and opened the door, his father was sitting by the fire, resting his head in his hands. An argument broke out, with Joseph telling his son that it was the last time he should come his house. George, preparing to go to bed, went over to the drawer and took out the pistol.

'I put my left hand up to the mantelpiece as if I was reaching something down, and with the other hand in which I held the pistol I shot my father.'

When the police came to arrest Smith, he sang 'a fearful ditty' –

'Here's heart that ne'er will fail; To swing under the gallows or under a rail.'

Those lines elevated the murderer George Smith to fleeting national notoriety and with it the sobriquet, 'The Ilkeston Parricide'. According to the *Derby and Chesterfield Reporter* (the *Mercury* now had strong competition), he learned those lines through frequenting Ilkeston's low theatres with their parading of 'robbers and the murders from the dirty stage, and (where) the mock kings stalk in fancied grandeur'.

Smith was arraigned at Derby assizes on 29 July before Mr Justice Willes. The evidence was overwhelming and he was sentenced to hang on 16 August. It was the first public execution for nine years.

Smith's appointment with Calcraft brought massive crowds into Derby. The railway companies laid on special trains which, as the *Reporter* sarcastically commented, 'brought in a considerable freight of human flesh of both sexes'. Both the *Reporter* and *Mercury*, provoked by competition, penned graphic descriptions of the scenes before the county gaol. The day dawned with great promise and from the earliest hours the streets were crowded, mostly with spectators from out of town, who had travelled by every means of transport available. The 'great bulk came from the colliery and other districts'. Some, having walked many miles, were lying on the grass in front of the gaol, catching up on lost sleep. Small boys, taken there by their fathers, appeared utterly exhausted by their exertions. Noticeable among the women were those burdened with large baskets packed with refreshments.

The *Reporter* described a scene that would have been familiar at any time in the previous century and a half:

'Itinerant newsvendors, with the "last dying speech and confession" of the parricide; elbow artists with penny portraits of the murderer; and sing-song bawlers of old cast-away imaginary confessions of great criminals "adapted" for the occasion, might be seen in abundance; and the wonder is that the public are so gullible as to swallow these "cheap and nasty" productions; but so it is. Scripture readers were busily engaged preaching and praying to all who chose to listen to them, but we are afraid, from what we observed, not to any advantage. We hope otherwise, but we fear not. In this midst of the exhortations of the Scripture readers, might be heard the cry, "Pork pie all hot – hot oh" – and untutored urchins laughed, and squealed, and were evidently in a fever of thoughtless excitement. The Scripture readers distributed tracts with various titles, and our curiosity being excited we asked several parties who eagerly clutched the tracts: "What are those printed papers about?" One "rowdy" answered: "I thought it was a ticket for drink." Another said "he thought it was another confession about another murder". And away they went, winking knowingly and laughing.'

The comments about confessions are a timely warning about relying on their contents too much.

As the hands of the prison clock above the gates reached 11.30am, the High Sheriff's retinue arrived on horseback. Javelin men were placed in a line to keep clear the ground before the 'black and ugly drop'. With other officials, the Sheriff entered the prison to demand the body of the prisoner for execution. It was at this moment that the ranks of the spectators began to swell further, and gave birth to the greatest mob ever gathered before the Derby scaffold.

The *Mercury* was on hand:

'*At this time the thousands, many of whom had been carousing in public houses, surged up Vernon and South-streets till acres of faces closely packed presented a remarkable sight, and a low murmuring sound rose from the crowd like the rolling of a heavy sea on a stony beach, as the prison bell tolled for the starting of the last earthly procession in which George Smith could take part.*'

In the days before that final procession, Smith paid his farewells to his two brothers, his sister and several aunts and uncles. There never was any mention of his mother, if she was still alive. The *Mercury* reported Emma Eyre and their baby as being among the visitors. Another to visit him was the High Sheriff, while John Sims, the prison governor, made regular calls to the cell. Both urged Smith to resist making any farewell speeches at the gallows. However, for much of the time he was absorbed by the ministrations of the chaplain, now the Revd Henry Moore, and the Revd S. H. Heron, a Dissenting minister from Ilkeston, whom the prisoner had particularly asked for. Both were painstaking in their efforts to prepare the Ilkeston Parricide, to make him accept the error of his ways and so

that when he ascended the scaffold he would do so in a state of genuine penitence.

Newspaper accounts would suggest that the clergymen succeeded in their task. It must be kept in mind that those accounts were based, necessarily, on statements issued by the Revd Moore and Revd Heron. It has to be remembered that the churches, especially the Church of England, in the urban and industrialised areas, never enjoyed the authority of earlier, more rural years. Consequently, they were not slow to take advantage of an opportunity to enhance their influence. That is not to say that the Ilkeston murderer was not swayed by their persuasiveness. When George Smith met William Calcraft for the one and only time, there is nothing to indicate that his penitence was not thoroughly genuine. When the last hours of one's life can be measured as accurately as Smith's, the mind, as Dr Johnson observed, can become wonderfully concentrated. That has to be kept in mind when reading the extremely long sermons that condemned prisoners listened to in prison chapels just hours before being killed. As 16 August drew nearer, Smith's attitude softened. He prayed regularly, concentrated on what the men of religion had to say and asked many questions.

On the final night, Smith saw the ministers before retiring to bed at 11pm and slept until four in the morning. Never alone in his last days, as four turnkeys or warders took it in turns to be with him day and night. Their presence was not only to bestow the comfort of company but also to ensure he did not usurp the State's prerogative.

The promise of a fine day was kept. As the prison bell tolled, bright, glorious sunshine warmed up the carnival atmosphere. Behind the high walls, Smith quit his cell and joined the procession. With a mournful voice, the chaplain began the funeral service oration. Prisoners pressed at the yard gates to call out last goodbyes. Smith advised them to avoid strong drink, most pertinent considering the part it played in his downfall. In just over five minutes, the main portal was reached. Smith was taken to the room where Calcraft waited with his straps. Then the few steps up the spiral staircase and out on to the gallows platform.

> *See what thousands are approaching*
> *To see a wretched culprit die,*
> *At the age of twenty years,*
> *Upon Derby scaffold high.*
> *Now the solemn bell is tolling;*
> *I must leave this wicked world;*
> *Tho' on the tree I die for murder,*
> *May God receive my guilty soul.*

The Revd Moore reached the last lines of the service. Smith advanced to the front, sank to his knees and with a loud, clear voice said a prayer. A responsive silence descended on the watching thousands. At 12.07pm, Calcraft drew back the bolt. As the trapdoors fell down, a scream went up from the crowd and George Smith died with the noise in his ears. One newspaper reported that for several minutes the body 'quivered'. There was no reference to Calcraft fitting leg irons to add some merciful weight. The murderer was a small man and it could be that he slowly choked to death.

Smith's body dangled for an hour, turning slowly in the warmth of the day. Later, Barton, the sculptor, made yet another cast to be placed with the other exhibits in the prison museum. After that, the routine burial in the murderers' exclusive graveyard.

> *For he has a pall, this wretched man,*
> *Such as few men can claim:*
> *Deep down below a prison-yard,*
> *Naked for deeper shame,*
> *He lies, with fetters on each foot,*
> *Wrapt in a sheet of flame.*
> (The Ballad of Reading Gaol)

* * * * * *

LESS than a year later, William Calcraft again purchased a railway ticket to Derby, carrying in his suitcase the appurtenances of his trade. Not only would it be last time a Derby crowd would see him on duty, but also the last time they would witness a judicial killing.

There was nothing in particular to distinguish the sordid, sadly mundane details surrounding Richard Thorley's killing of Eliza Morrow in her home at Court No.4, Agard Street, Derby, in February 1862. Not even the fact that it was one of the few murders in the final chapters of Derbyshire's history of capital punishment that did not take place in or around the Chesterfield area. Quite why that region should have been such a seeming cradle of violence is a subject that others might take up.

Thorley, aged 26, was born in Derby's Leather Bottle Yard, off Osmaston Street, the present-day Osmaston Road. There was an elder brother and two elder sisters. Their mother, a widow, worked as a washerwoman to help keep her family in a life of near-poverty. Young Thorley received little education and at an early age was put to work. Growing stronger, he found employment as a labourer in the foundries, a calling that developed him sufficiently to try his luck as a pugilist. After fighting several pitched battles in a sport noted for its brutality, he had earned something of a notorious reputation. There were also minor skirmishes with the law. Thorley eventually married, a change of circumstance that had some beneficial effect on him and his wild ways. Sadly, his wife died quite early. The loss embarked him on a lifestyle that revolved mainly around public houses and heavy drinking.

Eliza Morrow was a young mill worker whom Thorley had known for some time. In fact, she had visited him and his wife at their home. After Mrs Thorley's death, Eliza and Thorley began to keep company. That relationship had been established for some five months when Thorley's jealous behaviour put him on the road to the gallows. Eliza

Murderer Richard Thorley. Thorley was hanged by William Calcraft on 11 April 1862, the last person to be executed in public at Derby

enjoyed teasing him and making him suspicious. At times around Ford Street, she would be seen clearly enjoying the company of a young Irish soldier. Thorley once met him in a public house and challenged him to 'go out of doors', an offer sensibly declined. Eliza's seeming preference for a military escort goaded Thorley into a drinking bout lasting several days. In a swirl of drink and jealousy he went round to Court No.4, Agard Street, and stood beneath her window banging on a drum, demanding to know if she had the soldier in bed with her. In the end he went home, pocketed a razor, spent several more hours drinking, then went back to Eliza's house and slit her throat.

From the scene of the crime Thorley ran towards Abbey Street and arrived breathlessly at the Olde Spa Inn where he ordered two bottles of ginger beer. The landlord of the Spa, Thomas Chapman, saw that Thorley's hands were wrapped in bloodstained bandages. Thorley told him that he had been involved in a fight with an Irishman at the Abbey Inn, further down Abbey Street, at its junction with Monk Street.

By the time Thorley left the Spa, the Derby police were hunting him. Two women – Urania Morrow, probably a relative, and Emma Underwood, and a ten-year-old boy, Charlie Wibberley, had told police that they had witnessed the murder and that Thorley was their man. At midnight he was arrested in Canal Street by Detective-Sergeant Vessey. At once he confessed and was taken to the Lock-up off the Cornmarket before being transferred to the gaol in Vernon Street.

Just six weeks after Eliza Morrow's death, Richard Thorley was tried at the March assizes where Mr Yeatman QC, for the defence, unsuccessfully argued that the offence should be classed as manslaughter because it had been committed in an act of fervour. The judge, Mr Justice Williams, advised the jury not to consider it a crime of passion, but one of cold-blooded murder.

They took the judge's advice and Richard Thorley was found guilty and sentenced to die on 11 April, a Friday. The court in St Mary's Gate was packed with spectators among whom women were particularly prominent. The Under-Sheriff's office wrote a letter to William Calcraft to discuss terms and conditions for the execution. England's senior hangman was now 33 years into his appointment, inept as ever and with a steadily mounting death tally that remains uncalculated.

While Derby's last public hanging failed to draw a crowd as large as that of George Smith the previous year, it nonetheless was estimated that around 20,000 made their way along Friar Gate and up Vernon Street. Some chose to assemble the day before, anxious to get the best vantage point. A Mr Wood was busily employed erecting the scaffold, the sight and sound of his workmen with their hammers beating out a macabre staccato rhythm. The *Mercury* voiced its displeasure of the sight of young lads tumbling away in high glee in front of the gaol, as if one the eve of some holiday. Others also gave offence:

'There was, of course, a large sprinkling of the members of the short-pipe, coarse-mouthed school, who delight in lounging about and cracking lewd jokes. It is to be hoped the solemn lesson of today may have a salutary effect on some of them.'

By nightfall most of the idle curious had dispersed, leaving the gallows' arena silent and within the gaol's walls the condemned man with his last thoughts. As Thursday ended, there were some

Victim Eliza Morrow.

who could look back on a most profitable day. Opticians had done brisk business supplying telescopes and opera glasses for those who preferred watching the hangman at work from a distance. The *Mercury*, in a sarcastic mood, supposed that distance lent enchantment to the view. 'We cannot say that we admire their taste.'

On the Friday morning, the mob, the sights and sounds filled the ground outside the prison. 'Who that has seen a motley crowd at an execution can fail to fill up this hasty sketch?' asked the *Mercury*. The number of young lads drew more critical comment, and the fact they seemed utterly unimpressed with what the occasion was all about. 'The dregs were there in great abundance, and not a few of the "gentler" sex.' Plainly disgusted at the scene, the newspaper added that 'all the sum of Derby were there' as well, plying their various trades.

Within the gaol, Thorley had devoted much of his last days absorbing instruction and advice as clergymen strove to bring him to an acceptable state of grace. There was a great deal of hymn singing and saying of prayers, not only with the ministers, but at times the Governor, Mr Sims, the school-master, Mr Haynes and the various turnkeys detailed to keep watch. A notice had been pinned up in the prison chapel asking prayers for Richard Thorley 'who has but a few days to live'. Next day it was removed, but then replaced at his request. 'It touches me here,' he is reputed to have said, putting a hand on his breast. On the last day, for the sake of accur-

acy, a new notice went up, asking for prayers for Thorley, 'who has but a few hours to live'.

On the morning of 11 April, after a special service in the chapel, the prison bell began to toll. Richard Thorley took his last walk that ended where Calcraft waited with his straps. Immediately after noon, the prisoner appeared on the scaffold. An intense buzz from the crowd rose on the air, but quickly subsided. Sharing the scaffold with the victim and Calcraft were the chaplain, the Governor, the Under-Sheriff and other officials. Thorley threw back his head and in a clear voice was heard to pray 'most earnestly', offering up to Heaven pleas for forgiveness. Finishing, he took the few paces to the hanging beam. Calcraft fiddled with the noose; Thorley handed his prayer book to the Governor. Calcraft gave one last look and then sent Richard Thorley into the next world.

The last public execution in Derby had taken place. After hanging 'the usual time', the body was taken into the prison grounds. William Barton took another cast. After that, the quicklime and then interment in the grimly exclusive cemetery by the curtain walls. In his prayer book, Thorley had written on the first page:

Mrs Brierley,
With her brother's dying love,
April 11th, 1862.

The last page bore the message:

Hannah Brierley,
With her brother Richard's dying love,
April 11th, 1862.

HAD George Townley hanged, then Thorley would have been denied his only claim to dubious fame. While Townley strictly speaking could be said to have no place here, to omit him would mean excluding one of Derbyshire's more interesting and controversial murder cases.

There were some that stood in the dock at assizes and though found guilty of murder were not executed but detained in a secure establishment. They were held to be criminally insane, and as such protected by an Act of 1816. That Act was extended in 1840, and additionally laid down that those who became insane while serving a prison sentence were to be transferred to a lunatic asylum.

Whether or not he was insane when or after he murdered Elizabeth Goodwin in August 1863 was what thrust an otherwise unremarkable murder into the national limelight. She had been engaged to Townley but decided to break it off. She later reluctantly agreed to meet him at her grandfather's home, Wigwell Grange near Wirksworth. As they walked in the grounds, he stabbed her with a pocketknife, killing her almost immediately. Highly agitated, he carried the body back to the house and confessed to what he had done. George Townley made no attempt to flee and surrendered quietly to the police when they arrived.

His trial at Derby assizes in December caught the public imagination, for this was a killing from the more gentle reaches of society. Despite his confession, Townley pleaded 'not guilty', his defence based on the grounds of insanity. Evidence was produced to the effect that mental instability was not unknown in the family. However, there was no indication as to his state of mind at the time of the murder. Speaking for the defence was Dr Forbes Winslow. He examined the prisoner while in gaol and concluded that by then he was insane. The doctor could not with certainty say that was his condition when he took the knife to his ex-fiancée. There was no doubt in the jury's mind, however. Taking little more than five minutes to consider their verdict, they found George Townley guilty.

It was the train of events set in motion by the judge, Baron Martin, which led to a national outcry. The case was seen by many as the law being perverted by wealth; a working man, lacking Townley's family resources, would have hanged without any argument. Writing to the Home Secretary, Sir George Grey, the judge said that while he thought the jury's verdict quite correct, he had reservations about the wisdom of executing someone who was undoubtedly mentally disturbed. An independent commission consisting of two magistrates and two doctors confirmed that the Derbyshire murderer most definitely was insane. In accordance with the law, Townley was incarcerated in the Bethlehem Royal Hospital, more irreverently and famously known as Bedlam.

For many, Townley's treatment reeked of privilege and influence. Money had purchased a reprieve. That the family was wealthy enough to hire the services of Dr Winslow raised anger in many quarters. National and provincial newspapers, as well as medical publications, were alarmed, seeing wealth buying medical opinion (the 'professional mad-doctors') beyond the reach of the less financially able. Public outrage won the day.

Townley was re-examined, and now discovered to be sane. His sentence was commuted to one of penal servitude for life. Transferred from Bedlam to Pentonville Prison, he committed suicide there in February 1865, throwing himself over a staircase railing.

Return to the Shadows

BY THE time Derby staged its next execution, the setting would be very different. Public hangings were no more. No black, brooding scaffold stood before the main gateway to the prison. The great doors were closed; locked was the small grilled doorway in the tower. No more would prisoners step through it, to be greeted with raucous cheering and cries of 'Hats Off!' With the passing in May 1868 of the Capital Punishment Amendment Act, executions were exiled to behind prison walls. Gone forever were the hanging fairs with their swollen crowds, the drunken revelry, the blasphemy, the ribaldry and libidinous behaviour, the tatty commerce, the implied contempt for the law. The era of secret killing had dawned.

Once the Bloody Code collapsed, to be succeeded by much-needed rationalisation of punishment for criminal behaviour, attention focused on public hangings. Imprisonment now served as punishment for a great number of once capital felonies. Shaming punish-ments were on the way out. The pillory lasted until 1837, the stocks for a little while longer, mainly as a rural pursuit. Whipping, while much beloved by the military which steadfastly refused to look beyond the cat o'nine tails, gradually fell into disuse. Surprisingly though, it remained on the statute books until 1948.

The dramatic decline in public hangings, in effect now only for murder, had made their comparative rarity occasions for even vaster

A hawker, the seller of street literature such as execution broadsides and last-confession sheets, as well as the latest popular ballads.

crowds and more unruly behaviour. While estimates are notoriously difficult, the crowds outside Derby prison may well have averaged around 15-20,000 for the period 1833-1862. Not many have put forward the mob as the reason for making executions private matters, but at the end of the day, it was primarily the disgraceful behaviour of spectators and rampant opportunism of traders that tipped the balance. Public killings were a national blight, a residue from more brutal times. They were an embarrassment to a more civilised, and in some ways more hypocritical society.

There was several schools of thought leading to the Act of 1868. One sought total abolition. That never was a serious option, since its proponents were always fighting a defensive action. Even the suspicion that innocent people had been hanged (actually correct, but given discreet and limited circulation by a sensitive Home Office) could not win over large numbers of those disgusted by the public killings. Too many people of otherwise many shades of opinion had to be convinced that hanging was not the correct punishment for murderers. Cross currents forced the abolitionists to oppose those who sought to have the scaffold removed within the prisons, seeing only too well that once hangings were in secret, then their cause would be lost. People would simply lose interest. Not only that, officialdom would be less accountable. Any mishaps, any bungling, anything at all untoward, all could easily be whitewashed. Those who wanted to retain hanging, realising that the days of public

occasions were almost certainly ending, pushed for the secret slaughter. They could hardly lose. Hanging was bound to stay; inside or outside prison walls was the only issue.

The final moves came early in the 1850s. One of the leading lights in the debate was Samuel Wilberforce, Bishop of Oxford, who, in the House of Lords, raised the necessity of reviewing capital punishment. The good bishop was a keen advocate of hanging, absolutely essential to the maintenance of good law and order. He was acutely aware of the threat posed by the anti-hanging lobby. Therefore, he, too, pursued a policy of abolishment, only his was of the public spectacle. Within prison walls was the only place to execute criminals. He had little difficulty in getting supporters. Many in the Lords were becoming upset over an increasing tendency to reprieve women sentenced to death, mainly because of the feeling they should not die before crowds whose vulgar behaviour left so much to be desired. It was somewhat ironic; public hanging was proving a partial deterrent but for the wrong reasons.

For other reasons, Bishop Wilberforce worried over the inclination to commute women's death sentences. Should the trend continue, then it might not be too long before they stopped hanging them altogether and then the practice might spread to condemned men. In 1856, he asked that a Select Committee be appointed to inquire into the whole question. Approval was given, with the bishop appointed as chairman.

As the Wilberforce Committee, it

announced in its final report what had been blatantly obvious for years: public executions were no deterrent. Those hanged were often looked upon as some sort of martyr or tragic hero-figure, given a stage from which to make a dying speech, to protest their innocence or to rail against the State or religion. Wilberforce recommended that they be held in private. Recommendations were made to introduce the correct note of sombreness, dignity and solemnity into what was meant to be a most awful happening. A solitary bell should be tolled as the prisoner made his way to the scaffold and after he had been killed, a black flag hoisted above the prison would signal to those outside that the law had finished its grim work.

The streets of Derby had been disgraced by the behaviour of many that witnessed Thorley's hanging. The crowds, if the *Mercury* is to be believed, had at first conducted themselves well and 'very good order was preserved'. However, once the corpse had been removed, those same spectators, many of them 'low rascals and repulsive women', behaved in a most objectionable manner. The police courts were rarely as busy. Outraged, the *Mercury* used its platform to hold forth on public versus private hanging question. With what had been debated over the past few years, and now on the eve of a Royal Commission (yet to be announced), much of what appeared under the headline '*The Morality of Public Executions*', makes interesting reading:

'*There is a class, and we believe an increasing class, of moral philosophers who earnestly advocate the abolition of capital punishment, and the substitution of some other penal severity for death on the gallows. We are not of that class; but we frankly admit, that if any consideration could have the effect of inducing us to revise put opinions, and at least to advocate some other mode of inflicting the awful punishment of death, it would be the frightful scene of profligacy and demoralisation which the streets of Derby presented on Friday last after the execution of Richard Thorley.*'

That the *Mercury* normally turned a blind eye to the conduct of spectators was tacitly acknowledged. The editorial continued:

'*In all parts of the country it is evident that executions have no other effect than to produce the most shocking scenes of intemperance, indecency, riot, and desperation. The demoralising effects of these disgusting spectacles have often engaged the attention of Parliament, and men of different parties admitted the mortifying fact. Legislators who make laws of death, and Judges who administer them, utterly deny that the punishment has any connection with the principle of revenge or retaliation.*'

The newspaper then posed a question central to the whole issue:

'*Do these executions, then, fail entirely as a public example? Perhaps not; we cannot tell how many, or how few, may be moved by the terrors of a dying criminal's agonies to reform their vicious practices; but we fear that the many, as executions are now conducted and spoken about, are induced to regard the punishment rather as the fate of a hero or a martyr; while the less sentimental care so little for the awful spectacle, as to look upon it with the same feelings as they would gaze upon a brutal fight, and indulge all sorts of libidinous ribaldry, and ferocious ruffianism, and obscene mirth, under the very shadow of the gallows itself.'*

One solution suggested was that executions could be held in secret in the early hours, with no witnesses excepting a jury, sheriff and prison officers and perhaps visiting magistrates. Objectors, the newspaper realised, would be bound to point out that private executions would have no effect as public examples. They were only fit for states deep 'sunk in slavery or barbarism.' The *Mercury* disagreed:

'The execution would not be secret, though secluded from the noisy intrusion and fierce gaze of a brutal rabble; as we would have it conducted with every external indication of solemnly impressive ceremony, which would apprise the world outside the prison walls that the dread work of death was being done upon a fellow-creature.'

Public hangings were banished under the Capital Punishment Act Amendment of 1868. With the private execution established, the movement for abolishing hanging lost momentum. There was nothing visible on which public attention could focus. A solitary bell and a fluttering black flag, nor (later) a death notice pinned on the prison gates were not going to arouse any significant anger. Public opinion, to be a force capable of stir-

ring politicians into action, had to be outraged. Officialdom would take care of everything, now that the rabble and tawdry commerce had been moved off stage. So that the public at large would know what went on, the Press was to be allowed to attend hangings. Some newspapers did faithfully report executions in full, but authority's brow creased in predictable annoyance. Gradually, the newspapers were squeezed out. At first, the Home Office let it be known that reporters should be discouraged; later they were to be barred altogether.

Considering the lengthy accounts of the *Mercury* and the *Derby and Chesterfield Reporter*, it might be thought that Derby prison allowed unrestrained access to their representatives. Certainly, those two were reporting in much greater detail than some of their provincial contemporaries. But reading their accounts, it is apparent that officialdom had some influence over what was and was not written about. There were 11 private hangings at Derby prison, each was reported in quite similar terms. Details of the crime, the trial and the prisoners' last days. A great deal of the clergymen's activities, their sermons, their efforts to get the victims to repent and mount the scaffold in a true state of penitence.

On the killing day, the reporter would describe how he entered the prison, give something of its layout, an impression of the scaffold, mention the murderers' graveyard and maybe add a few details about the hangmen. Then came the victim's last walk, accompanied by several officials and clergymen, and so on to the scaffold. Not one hanged ever gave any trouble; all faced up to their final death agony with fortitude and died quickly. There were never any problems; there never would be officially. After an hour, the body was taken down and buried in the graveyard, first being smothered in burning quicklime. Proceedings concluded with the formal inquest, each newspaper carefully listing all those present.

Newspaper coverage of hangings, be they public or in secret, nearly always avoided those last few dreadful moments, when the trapdoor dropped and the victim followed, to be brought up short by the dull, sickening thud of the rope reaching full stretch. The behaviour of those about to die seemed remarkably similar. The vast majority of those executed at Derby died truly penitent, often with a prayer or hymn on their lips. Their final speeches were suspiciously eloquent (given the circumstances), as were the printed confessions; exhortations to others to mend their ways and not follow their example, or else a similar fate would surely be their lot. Of course, some did depart like that. But, from other places, more realistic and reliable sources attest to those, far from few, who kicked and screamed away their last few minutes on earth, who cursed and swore, blasphemed and renounced God, and protested their innocence to the end. We learn that some, almost incapable of standing (not a few from generous helpings of drink), had to be supported by turnkeys as the hangman slipped on the noose and white cap.

Accounts and other histories tell how some were sat upon a chair to await death, or had to be helped stand by prison warders. Such scenes seemingly never happened at Derby. Nor did victims choke or strangle to death, or had to be helped on their way by the executioner hanging grimly on to their kicking legs beneath the scaffold's platform. Derby's victims had the knack of passing over into boundless eternity almost immediately the noose tightened, or gave a slight struggle before 'the world for ever closed upon him'. It simply could not be true.

Missing throughout Derbyshire's chronicle of capital punishment are statements or reflections from private individuals, maybe clergymen, prison officials, or the more observant bystander. There are examples from other places. Surely someone in those vast crowds in Friar Gate or Vernon Street must have returned home and wrote down what they had witnessed and what they thought. None have so far surfaced; perhaps they rest hidden in some private archive. Until something turns up, then Derbyshire's account has to be set against the overall experience and conclusions drawn. Whatever else can be said, it cannot be unique.

* * * * * *

WITH the disappearance of the scaffold, and the isolation of executions, the hangmen themselves began to feature more prominently in the public eye. People began to learn more about the men who carried out the slaughter of those who had offended the system. Calcraft had become a household name, not just for notorious ineptness, but also the sheer length of time he officiated on the scaffold. How many he executed remains a mystery. In 1855, a sketchy account of his life *The Living Hangman of Newgate* appeared under the aptly titled *The Groans of the Gallows*, which really revealed little. He was pensioned off in 1874 and soon reports circulated that England's longest serving executioner planned to publish his memoirs. For some reason, what should have been a minor best seller never reached the printing press. William Calcraft, last of the salaried hangman, died in his bed in 1879, in his 80th year.

Hangmen came from two sources. Those appointed by the City of London, who were available for hire, and others who were locally recruited. High Sheriffs were responsible for the hiring of executioners, and, technically, should they fail to find one then they personally would have to do the killing. There were always enough volunteers. As the hangings decreased, the Home Office gradually took over responsibility for their appointment and training. There was always more than one hangman, usually a principal and a few others who acted as assistants,

Unlike Calcraft,

William Marwood never had his experiences committed to paper. Which is to be regretted, because of all hangmen, he must surely rank as the most interesting personality, as opposed to controversial. Appointed in 1874, he died in 1883 of inflammation of the lungs, still in office. With a declining market, he had in that time despatched 164 to the next world. One can only wonder just how many Calcraft executed in this time. He and Calcraft had at least two things in common: both were from East Anglia and both cobblers by trade. As far as Marwood was concerned, that was all. He never passed up an opportunity to ridicule his predecessor. 'He came from a family of slow worms,' was one assessment, but the most reported was, 'He throttled them, but I execute them.'

While he may not have actually invented the long drop, Marwood certainly perfected it and made it the standard method of killing for as long as capital punishment remained in Britain. Evidence suggests that it first came from Ireland. What certainly did come from there was a treatise published in 1866, titled *On Hanging*. The author was an extraordinarily versatile polymath, the Revd Dr Samuel Haughton. Forever inquiring into things, the physics involved in the swift hanging of a

William Marwood, hangman.

human being intrigued him. The result was the recommendation of killing by breaking the neck rather than strangulation, being far quicker, simpler and more efficient. While it is extremely unlikely that Marwood ever read *On Hanging*, let alone understand it, his long drop theories and practice undeniably trod the same path and almost simultaneously.

What Marwood did was extraordinarily simple: he merely lengthened the fall of the standard, or short drop. That had been around for something like a century and no one had come up the idea before (least of all Calcraft). However, the fall was not to be a standard measure, but vary according to the victim's height and (at last) his weight. During his career, Marwood evolved a ready reckoner, a table of drops and weights, that at least one of his successors (James Berry) would continue to refine in accordance with experience.

What is even more extraordinary, is that Marwood was working on ideas for more efficient executions even before being appointed. Apart from living next to a cemetery in his home at Horncastle, there was nothing to perhaps explain this macabre interest. He never even attended a public execution. Moreover, he had not been content just to let ideas buzz around his head. Letters were posted to numerous officials, prison governors being among the more obvious, explaining how hangings could be carried out so much more efficiently. Instant death was possible, he assured the recipients. Such confidence led to an invitation to Lincoln Prison in 1871, where he executed his first prisoner and did so by breaking his neck.

Three years later he became a permanent hangman, paid a retainer of £20 a year by the Sheriff of the City of London and allowed to charge fees for individual executions. As a perquisite, he was permitted to sell the clothing and personal belongings of his victims, as well as pieces of the rope. Marwood was an innovator. More improvements followed. Among others was the rope itself, exchanging the thicker less pliable grade generally used, for softer Italian silk hemp. A more efficient noose came with the introduction of a metal eye. That the scaffold trapdoors be at floor ground level with a receiving pit or cellar dug beneath was a suggestion that anticipated (or inspired) the eventual Home Office recommendation.

Much of our knowledge of executions comes from the man regarded as Marwood's successor. James Berry in his

James Berry, sometimes know as the 'reluctant hangman'.

159

autobiography, *My Experiences as an Executioner* (1892), not only gave particulars of some of his more famous killings, but considerable detail on how they were arranged, the methods employed, and being responsible for supplying his own ropes. They were 13ft long and would be used more than once; one ended a life on no fewer than 16 occasions. Economy was not the reason, but the acquired knowledge that a fully stretched rope was far more effective for its deadly mission. Berry was a Lancashire man, born in 1852 at Heckmondwike. In 1874, he joined the Bradford Borough Police Force and it was probably during that time he first met Marwood. The two became friendly and while the hangman expressed no shame over his profession, he was not inclined to discuss it. However, it must have been from him that Berry first conceived the notion of becoming an executioner. In 1884, with Marwood dead, the Sheriff of London appointed Berry.

Berry was a complex character. He admitted that he did not like being an executioner (he was known as 'the reluctant hangman') and yet took great trouble to do it efficiently as possible. Like his predecessor, he too believed that a man should never die facing east. He studied Marwood's hanging tables and set about making them even more reliable. As his base he chose a man of 14st and gave him a drop of 8ft. An 8st man would require 10ft. Every half-stone lighter weight would require a two-inch longer drop. Berry was of a tidy mind. Before becoming a policeman he had found employment as a

clerk and what he learned he applied to his latest profession. Calling cards were printed, careful to point out that he was an executioner and not just a hangman. High Sheriffs seeking his services would receive a printed form setting down terms and conditions. Each carried its own reference number.

On the other hand, Berry was something of a thorn in the flesh of authority, not least for the excruciating verse he was prone to compose and read out to his victims. One example, which might have caused a ballad writer to blush, read:

My brother, sit and think
While yet on earth some hours are left to thee;
Kneel to thy God, who does not from thee shrink,
And lay thy sins on Christ, who died for thee.

James Berry, described by one newspaper as 'the direct instrument that produced death', resigned in 1892. He had had enough and sometimes drank a little too much. In later years remorse set in and he eventually became a preacher, regarding himself as an evangelist. He died in 1913.

While Berry visited Derby several times, he never thought any of the doomed worthy of comment in his memoirs. He did, however, describe the typical procedure of a hanging day. It is worth giving since, with slight variations, it was generally followed in all gaols; virtually all ritual had been erased from the ceremonies, a ploy by the authorities who wanted state slaughters kept as low key as possible.

Hangings were scheduled for 8am, and a few minutes before the authorising document would be handed to the executioner by the High Sheriff, Under-Sheriff or some other designated official. The hangman then entered the condemned cell. Present would be the chaplain and two attendants who had remained overnight with the prisoner. After pinioning, the prisoner left his cell and with others made up the procession to the gallows. Led by the chief warder, the victim walked between four other warders and by the side of the chaplain. Then came two principal warders, followed by two more warders, behind which came the prison governor and the sheriff. A doctor and an attendant brought up the rear. As the procession moved off, the hangman placed the white cap in place but would not pull it over the victim's face. The chaplain began reading the burial service. With the scaffold reached, the cap was pulled over the condemned man's face, and the leg straps fastened on. After a last check, the executioner pulled the lever to release the trapdoor.

As had been the practice for centuries, the corpse remained hanging for an hour. Taken down, it was placed in a coffin and carried to the prison mortuary to await the findings of the inquest. That generally took place around 10am and was a mere formality but required by law. Then the quick burial in the prison grounds, the body covered in quicklime to ensure swift decomposition. Often there was nothing more than a set of initials and a date scratched on a wall to record a last resting-place. There is some proof that the names and date of Derby's triple hanging of Bonsall, Bland and Hulme in 1843 were inscribed on a slate to mark where they lay. Maybe it was because they were the first to be interred there. It disappeared after the prison was demolished in the 1920s, although it is believed to have found its way to Derby Museum some 30 years later.

After Berry, the next executioner to visit Derby was James Billington, another Lancashireman, from Bolton. Appointed in 1884, he hanged 147 people, and in between managed a barber's business (popular with the morbidly curious) and later became a publican in his hometown. Other occupations had included that of a miner, a mill worker and a wrestler. On scaffold duty, he had the habit of wearing a dark suit and a black skullcap. While it would have been only of passing interest to the victims, Billington had three sons, Thomas, John and William, all of them appointed executioners. The four were not averse to making something of a mockery of their profession by swapping jobs, much to the confusion of officials and newspaper reporters. What is not beyond dispute is that it was James who hanged Charles Thomas Wooldridge, the Royal Horse Guards trooper whose execution inspired Oscar Wilde's evocative *Ballad of Reading Gaol*, surely the most moving of all writings in the library of anti-hanging literature.

James Billington was the last executioner to die while still in post, on Friday 13 December 1901. Next on the scene was a member of a family for many still synonymous with the gallows, the Pierrepoints. First was Henry, more familiarly Harry, in 1905 who at first assisted Billington. The only one of the family to have worked in Derby, he retired in 1910. His elder brother, Thomas, entered the business a year later and retired as late as 1946. The last of the Pierrepoint dynasty was Albert, son of Harry, who served from 1940 to 1956.

It is yet another Lancashireman, James Ellis from Rochdale, who completes the list of relevant hangmen in Derbyshire's history. Appointed in 1907 to principal executioner, he occasionally worked as assistant to both the Billingtons and Pierrepoints. In their reports of the related executions, the *Mercury* stated that Ellis was assistant to Pierrepoint, but neglected to identify which one, although in fact it was Harry.

Behind Closed Doors

WITH the arrival of private executions, the curtain rose on Derby's last act. The final 34 years would become little more than a litany of hangings. Judicial slaughter at Vernon Street aroused little public reaction, which is not too surprising for none of the 11 hanged were for murders that stirred the public appetite for sensation. Hanging no longer was a national issue; the total abolitionists would remain in the wilderness of indifference until well after World War One. Politicians had other causes to pursue, and the bishops could rest in conscience with their chosen Biblical authority. Derby actually held its last execution several years before World War One; indeed the prison had more or less ceased to operate by then. Those found guilty of murder in the county would be sent to be killed on gallows at other assize towns.

* * * * * *

DERBY had to wait 11 years for its first execution within the prison walls. Though Calcraft was still in employment (he had another year to go), it was William Marwood who caught the train to bring him to preside over the initial hanging under the new regime. According to the *Mercury*, this would be his second, the first being at Warwick. This was incorrect, for as we have seen the Horncastle man's debut was at Lincoln in 1871.

Benjamin Hudson, just 24, from West Handley near Chesterfield, murdered his wife, Eliza, in April 1873. The background was familiar to so many murders: an unhappy marriage, frequent quarrels, problems with the children, bills unpaid. The Hudsons had been married for three years, and Eliza bringing three illegitimate children to the home did not augur well. In fact, her husband soon had reason to suspect that she had resumed an affair with a former paramour. Not that he himself greatly helped matters. Prone to violent outbursts of temper, Hudson treated his wife so badly that she had been obliged approach the local magistrates to seek some protection. After one particularly savage episode, a terrified Eliza fled from the home for good and went to stay at her father's house at Eckington. She sought and obtained a legal separation and Hudson, advised by his solicitors, agreed to pay maintenance. He then smashed up the family home, sold the furniture and went off to live with relatives.

To earn money, Eliza Hudson went out washing. One evening she was returning home when her husband, who had been following her about for some days, confronted her. An argument broke out and Hudson, seizing a convenient hedge-stake, attacked and killed her. He made no attempt to escape, and actually was sitting by the fireside of a relation when the police turned up an hour or so later to arrest him. There was no disputing his guilt and after his trial, Hudson was sent to Vernon Street. Alterations were in progress at the gaol, resulting in the temporary lack of a suitable condemned cell and so Hudson was accommodated in a cell in the old debtors' block, there to wait for 4 August, a Monday, and the gallows.

Since this execution was the first in private, 'the anxiety of the curious', as the *Mercury* expressed it, found people loitering at the prison gates on the Sunday evening, even though Hudson was not due to hang until 8am next day.

'But their watching and waiting were in vain, and they had to content themselves with conversing about the murder, which together with the youth of the prisoner, formed a fruitful topic of gossip.'

Work on erecting the scaffold 'in all its horrid nakedness' had begun the previous Friday night. Standing in the outer patrol, a paved circular walkway bounded on one side by the outer walls and the other by the main buildings, and some 20 yards to the right of the portal, it was the same one used for public executions since 1833 and the hapless Leedham. A square wooden platform standing some 4ft above the ground, the underpart had now been skirted in, except for a aperture through which the trapdoor lever could be operated.

Marwood had arrived at Vernon Street on the Saturday. If the *Mercury* is to be believed, the rope selected and already tied to the cross beam was 'about two yards in length'. This is doubtful, considering that Marwood calculated the drop at 4ft 6ins. He was still in the early days of computing his long drop table. The day Hudson died on the rope was in keeping with his dreadful fate. The *Mercury* was on safer ground:

'Rain had been falling from an early hour, and as eight o'clock approached the shower increased, and a thick fog prevailed. The bell continued to toll until the hour of doom. A few minutes after eight o'clock the condemned man was conducted to a small private office situate about 200 yards from the scaffold, and there he met by the hangman, who put the question. "Are you Benjamin Hudson?" to which he replied, "Yes." This was all he said, and in a standing position he quietly allowed his arms to be pinioned with leather straps by the executioner. When the chimes of eight had commenced, the procession set off for the scaffold.'

In his left hand Hudson carried a bouquet of flowers given to him by an aunt on her last visit. In the right, he clutched his prison cap. He did not appear agitated. Even when standing on the trapdoor with Marwood placing on the white cap, his composure did not falter. Some of the spectators 'were thrilled with an undefinable feeling of awe at the dreadful solemnity with which his life was to be forfeited'.

The chaplain finished the burial service. Marwood pulled the lever, and Hudson plummeted to his death. He had dropped the flowers but his right hand still clasped the cap. Above the main gateway a black flag unfurled in the slight wind. According to the *Mercury*, Hudson took two and a half minutes to die, adding, illogically, that he did so 'quite easily'. That comment despite the chest distending to 'a great size' and the slight twitching of hands, arms and legs, nor any appreciation of just how long two and a half minutes was when alone with the last dreadful pain.

Hudson had been denied the Church's last sacrament, 'as the chaplain thought he did not sufficiently understand its nature'.

> *The Chaplain would not kneel to pray*
> *By his dishonoured grave:*
> *Nor mark it with that blessed Cross*
> *That Christ for sinners gave,*
> *Because the man was one of those*
> *Whom Christ came down to save.*
> (The Ballad of Reading Gaol)

After that, the removal of corpse, the formal inquest presided over by the coroner, Mr W. H. Whiston, and displaying of the statutory notices. Bearing in mind the careful though shorn ritual, it was only as the inquest opened that three or four prisoners began the digging of Hudson's grave, close to where Thorley lay. With the inquest over, Benjamin Hudson was interred, the flowers and cap placed on his chest, and quicklime thrown on top. In front of the gaol, a small knot of people waited. Once the notices had been pinned up and then read, they then slowly dispersed, 'and the small square was soon left to its wonted quietude'. Behind the brooding walls, the grey world of retribution regained its grey, monotonous rhythm.

* * * * * *

SEVEN years later, Marwood returned to Derby. On 3 August 1880, he had written to B. Scott Currey, the Derbyshire Under-Sheriff, to confirm his arrival on 14 August, and 'I Will Bring Rope and Straps and Cap when i Com.' His fee would be £10 plus travelling expenses, and a sign of the cost of living, the same as for the 1873 visit. There was no charge for his time, or for the rope and straps since they were now provided by the Home Office. John Wakefield was the man he had contracted to hang and for that most appalling of crimes, the murder of a little girl.

The killing of nine-year old Elizabeth (Eliza) Ann Wilkinson was one of the few murders in this period that did not take place around the Chesterfield area. With an elder 16-year old sister, she was hawking cardboard comb boxes, as their father had told them.

With just one box left, Eliza tried her luck at 13 Tanyard Court, off Green Street in Derby. John Wakefield opened the door, asked what she wanted and was offered the box for a halfpenny. He handed her the money, took his purchase and then seized the little girl. Dragging her into the house, he stabbed her twice in the neck with the knife he had been using to peel potatoes. One blow was so strong that the weapon penetrated the innocent neck from one side to the other. Wakefield's next actions were out of keeping with the bloody violence. After washing his hands, he walked over to the police station where he told an astonished Inspector Barnes: 'I have committed a murder.'

Today John Wakefield would have been classed as mentally sub-normal. Living with his mother, he was not capable of getting employment and in fact their domestic arrangements were something of a role reversal. She went out to work while he stayed at home doing the housework. Weighing only 10st, his outstanding physical characteristic was a head large in proportion to his slight body. Taciturn and moody, he never spoke to anyone if he could avoid it.

The *Mercury* claimed he possessed considerable mental ability. This suspect verdict was delivered on discovering that he could quote lengthy passages from a book entitled *History of the Jews* and was fond of the books of Kings and Joshua in the Old

An execution contract is concluded. A letter from William Marwood, the hangman, to the Under-Sheriff of Derbyshire, B. Scott Currey, confirming details for the hanging of John Wakefield, a child murderer, at Derby on 16 August 1880. Marwood's fee was £10, plus travelling expenses, but the rope and straps were free, being supplied by the Home Office.

Testament. Moreover, 'he was a frequent visitor to the Derby Free Library'.

Wakefield's trial produced no surprises. After the judge, Baron Huddleston, had summed up, the jury, without leaving their box, returned the not unexpected guilty verdict. Back in Derby gaol, Wakefield's taciturn mien did not alter. He received religious instruction to prepare him for the ordeal to come, but the chaplain could do little to banish the customary moodiness. A petition on the grounds of insanity was despatched to the Home Office, but the reply was negative.

On Monday, 16 August, Wakefield was the centrepiece of the ritual cortege to the scaffold. The only thing out of the ordinary was that only one reporter (from the *Mercury*) had been admitted to witness proceedings, a decision of the Sheriff's office not elaborated on. Since arriving on the Saturday, Marwood had inspected the scaffold, and calculated a drop of around 9ft. Clearly, his tables were getting more precise. Wakefield arrived at the gallows, and climbed the steps. While the chaplain completed the funeral service, the hangman fitted the cap and checked the rope for the final time. When all was ready, Marwood pulled the lever and the child-killer was dropped to the next world. 'Death was to all appearances, instantaneous,' wrote the sole representative of the Press.

That the murderer was a Derby man probably accounted for the fact that a crowd of some 2,000 stood watching as the black flag fluttered above the main gate. Some were already aware that he had died, for the sudden rattle of the trapdoor had been clearly audible despite the thickness of the intervening walls. The spectators were quiet enough, the only notable incident being the sighting of a young man believed to be Wakefield's younger brother, Arthur, standing nearby. Some began to close around him out of curiosity but he walked away, whistling carelessly and warning that something else would 'happen that day if they did not look out'. Shortly after that, the official notices were pinned on the gates and as if that was their signal, the people moved off.

* * * * * *

MARWOOD paid his third and final visit in November 1881 and, tragically, to execute another child killer. It was the all too familiar tale of a young girl being lured away by a strange man with something of interest to entice her.

Alfred Gough was a rag collector living in Chesterfield. He had become a familiar figure in that part of Derbyshire, pushing his handcart and, in addition to his principal trade, selling coloured paper flags. One day in August, as he arrived in the village of Brimington, he attracted the attention of some children playing by the roadside, in particular six-year-old Eleanor Windle. Telling her friends that her mother had a halfpenny of hers, she trustingly went off with Gough. Later they were noticed by a woman who saw that the rag collector was behaving improperly with the child and, grabbing a broom, chased after them. Both moved away at her approach. When Eleanor failed to return home, a frantic search was organised. Her outraged body was discovered next day hidden in a plantation, with a piece of sackcloth wound tightly around her neck. Nearby lay a piece of coloured paper such as used in making toy flags.

Gough came under immediate suspicion and later that same day was apprehended by the police in a Chesterfield public house. He hotly denied committing the murder, and continued to do so vehemently almost to the very end. The summer assizes at Derby had just finished so he was tried at Leicester before Mr Justice Mathew, where the jury refused to believe his story and found him guilty of the crime.

Little enough was known about Gough, believed to be a native of Derby. There was no evidence of a criminal record. Until he met Eleanor, he appears to have led a blameless life. When a young boy, his father went abroad where he died, leaving his wife to rear Alfred and his sister. Mrs Gough moved to Leeds and later Nottingham, working hard to bring her children up properly. When old enough, Alfred went out to work, taking various jobs until he decided to join the Leeds police force. How long he remained in uniform is not known, but he was regarded as being a steady, industrious man who looked after his money. What had clearly disturbed him was being jilted by a young woman, to such an extent that he quit the police force and enlisted in the Army, serving in the 17th Regiment of Foot. There was a period of service in India and

after completing his six-year engagement, Gough returned to England. But he was now a changed man, still in his early 30s and unable to settle down. He took to the wandering life, earning a precarious living as a rag collector.

His offence was a dreadful thing, and as the Mercury put it, not a finger 'was raised in Gough's favour, or a voice heard asking for mercy towards him'. Much of the time left to him was spent in spiritual preparation, with breaks for exercise in the yards and a cigarette. Nearly 1,000 spectators turned up on the morning of his execution, despite the wet and tempestuous weather. Within the prison precincts, officials were making the final preparations 'with disciplinary calmness'. The emotion behind the blank official façade is perhaps best left to Wilde:

At six o'clock we cleaned our cells,
At seven all was still,
But the sough and swing of a mighty wing
The prison seemed to fill,
For the Lord of Death with icy breath
Had entered in to kill.
He did not pass in purple pomp,
Nor ride a moon-white steed.
Three yards of cord and a sliding board
Are all the gallows' need:
So with the rope of shame the Herald came
To do the secret deed.
(The Ballad of Reading Gaol)

Clearly words had been spoken about the degree of Press representation, for no fewer than six reporters received permission to witness Gough die. They saw Marwood make his appearance, 'a little wizened old man with fresh complexion and a pleasant face', who wished a polite 'Good morning' to a passing warder. When Gough made his entrance, the *Mercury*'s scribe seemed surprised by his bearing. He was nothing like the ferocious-looking individual other newspapers had stated, seeing someone who seemed kindly disposed. Had his clothes been anything but old and much-mended, then 'his appearance would have been that of a respectable artisan, than rag gatherer'. Perhaps that was what deceived Eleanor Windle.

One incident more common than its lack of reporting would imply was spotted by the *Mercury* man: just before reaching the gallows, Gough 'drank eagerly' from the flash put to his lips by a warder. It could only have been a strong drink to ease him through the next few moments.

In the end, Gough had admitted his guilt. On the morning of his death, he wrote a letter to the chaplain making the confession. There had been other letters which caused him much distress. He had written several that had fallen into the hands of some of his relatives, and they had handed them over to the Sheffield newspapers, presumably in exchange for money. Gough learned that his sister was among the sellers, and declared he would never have written any them had he realised how they were going to be treated. There seemed to be a lively market for his correspondence. A letter to him at the prison came from his brother-in-law asking if there were any further letters. The gutter press is

nothing new. Displaying more propriety, Gough asked the prison governor, Captain Farquharson, to destroy a confession he had already written for this bother-in-law.

William Marwood left Derby for the last time. Within two years he was dead, through inflammation of the lungs complicated by jaundice. He had succeeded in bringing some credit to his gruesome profession, as well as much-needed expertise. But what he was doing had preyed on his mind. In the latter stages of his career he was reputed to have taken to drink, a well-recognised hazard of his calling.

* * * * * *

JAMES BERRY came to Derby in 1888 to hang his 127th victim, a man named Thomas Delaney. He had been in Manchester the day before and the rope used there would be employed again, to send yet another killer from the Chesterfield area into the next world. While there was little to distinguish the ruthless murder of Mrs Delaney from dozens of other domestic slaughters, the hanging of her husband possessed one or two, by then, unusual features.

The Delaneys had been married four years and there were two children of a union more noted for casual violence and heavy drinking than its bliss. One night in April, the couple had been indulging at the Red Lion public house and routinely fell to quarrelling. Delaney was heard to threaten his wife, 'I will do for you before the night is over,' to which she retorted that it was more than he dare do. A foolish remark that ignored experience.

There were times she had been physically ill-treated, and after one particularly bruising assault had appealed to the law for protection.

Preferring not to listen any more to the Delaneys' squabbling, the landlord ordered them off the premises. They went, still abusing each other. It was to be their last difference of opinion. Reaching home, Delaney grabbed a poker and thrashed his wife so severely that she collapsed at his feet in a pool of blood. The noise of their fighting brought neighbours to the door. Delaney was arrested while his unconscious wife was hurried to Chesterfield Infirmary. Despite the most appalling wounds, particularly to the head, she clung on to life for six weeks before succumbing. Charged with murder, he stated that he attacked her for telling him she had been with another man. That confession he later withdrew, confessing that what had really rankled was her appealing to the law for protection against him. One wonders if the irony of that remark occurred to him.

Delaney stood trial before Mr Justice Hawkins, who listened to the defence barrister Mr Heztall pleading on the grounds of hereditary insanity. In view of the evidence, it may have been the only defence available, although it was established that Delaney's father had committed suicide while confined in a lunatic asylum. The prosecution had little trouble in demolishing the defence's case and the jury took only ten minutes to find the prisoner guilty of murder.

Since the last execution, the Home Office had introduced a rule that no hangings were to take place on Mondays, while still allowing the statutory three Sundays to elapse between sentencing and the date set. For Thomas Delaney, the wait for 10 August was broken by a visit from his sister and brother-in-law and, at his own request, the Revd G. Windram, a Primitive Methodist minister from Chesterfield. On his last Thursday, he spent the day quietly and in the evening stayed looking out of the window of his cell until it was too dark to see anything. Perhaps on the night air he heard the sound of hymns being sung outside the main gate by Mr White's Gospel Hall choir, an interlude that drew a large appreciative crowd. A lot of time was spent in prayer and contemplation and all the while two warders sat with him.

Or else he sat with those who watched
His anguish night and day;
Who watched him when he rose to weep,
And when he crouched to pray;
Who watched him lest himself should rob
Their scaffold of its prey.
(The Ballad of Reading Gaol)

Friday morning dawned. By 6.30am, Vernon Street began to fill with early arrivals. They, no doubt, were pleased that the day promised to be fine and so made the wait to see the black flag break that more bearable. Some from Chesterfield had actually walked to Derby. Interest was aroused when the gates swung open to allow five time-expired prisoners, three men and two women, to hurry out and thankfully disappear. Not long afterwards, various officials arrived and were admitted to the prison to perform whatever tasks they had.

Any hoping to see Berry were frustrated. He was already within the walls, having arrived the previous day to check the scaffold and estimate the drop. He decided on one of 5ft, which for a victim weighing just 10½st, was a short descent. According to his tables, it ought to have been around 9ft (Marwood had similar figures). Berry would explain his intention later to the Press. As 8am drew close, the spectators numbering close on 2,000, many of them women and children, grew more attentive. Hoping to hear the thud of the trapdoor more clearly, several had ranged themselves by the wall behind which the scaffold stood. They were not to be disappointed, for it would plainly be heard 'at the Vernon Street end of the lawns furthest from the gaol'.

Some accommodation had been reached with the newspapers, and four reporters were allowed to attend, two from Derby and two from Chesterfield. Had any attended a killing before they would have noticed one obvious change. No longer was the scaffold open to the sky. It had come to someone's attention that it was possible to overlook the gallows from roofs of nearby houses. The structure was accordingly roofed in, giving it the appearance a large wooden shed. One reporter commented on the graves close by and, perhaps confirming that identifying markers were once in place, noted there were nine in number. There would have been ten.

What could hardly have been missed was the 11th grave. Only that one was open, waiting for the latest victim, who would have to pass within a few feet on his way to the hangman.

With yawning mouth the yellow hole
Gaped for a living thing;
The very mud cried out for blood
To the thirsty asphalte ring;
And we knew that 'ere one dawn grew fair
Some prisoner had to swing.
(The Ballad of Reading Gaol)

Just before 8am Delaney was taken from his cell to march in the gallows' procession. Berry pinioned his arms and put on the white cap. Off they all went, officials, warders, executioner, doctors, chaplain and murderer. If he saw the yawning hole, Delaney made no sign. The covered scaffold was reached. Stepping on the platform and dropping through the trapdoor occupied Delaney less than 30 seconds.

Death, however, was not so swift. Two surgeons, Dr C. A. Greaves and Dr F. E. Taylor, spent almost ten minutes gazing into the pit at the dangling body. Greaves later spoke to reporters and said that while the victim must have become unconscious immediately, the body's muscular action did not cease for some seven minutes. That was when Delaney actually died. Cause of death was strangulation not dislocation, caused by the comparative short drop decided on by Berry.

There must have been times at Friar Gate and in the long ago of Nuns' Green when such things were quicker.

Berry also spoke to the reporters and confirmed that the drop was shorter than would have been usual, but he admitted that he intended death to be by strangulation. Dislocation, he had observed, caused blood to appear. Since the white cap was for hiding such manifestations, he may have been on the defensive. He had already been involved in controversies over his methods. On two occasions, the drop chosen was too long with the result that one victim had been decapitated and the other nearly so. With each incident there had been a dispute with the doctors over the length of the fall.

Berry spent some time talking to the Press. He revealed that sometimes he shook hands with the condemned before the pinioning. However, nothing would have induced to him to do so with such a man as Delaney, saying there were 'some circumstances in connection with the assault on the woman, which it was impossible to publish'. One can only wonder at what special information the hangman of all people was privy to, if any. Warming up to his subject, Berry said that he sought to bring about death as quickly as possible, even though it was difficult to forget that murderers gave their victims no mercy and added, somewhat incongruously, no time for preparation. The *Mercury* found the executioner a fresh complexioned, pleasant featured man, of a sympathetic disposition, who took pride in his awful employment.

Remarking that this was his first visit to Derby, he patted himself on the back by expressing satisfaction at the manner in which the sentence of the law had been carried out.

* * * * * *

THROUGHOUT his eight-year career, Berry proved something of a headache for Home Office officials. No one doubted his expertise and the soundness of his improvements, but he could be cantankerous and his relationship with the medical men was not always of the best. Apart from that, there was the suspicion that he was drinking more than was advisable, and there was nothing he enjoyed more than playing the role of raconteur in public houses. Usually willing to chat to the Press, he may have been right when he voiced misgivings that not all representatives were genuine, but the morbidly fascinated who had somehow contrived a pass. His comments at the Delaney hanging perhaps came to the ears of the Home Office, for when he next came to Derby, his last visit, the drop selected was with the express intention of dislocating George Horton's neck.

Again, the occasion was child murder. The victim was Horton's own daughter, Kate, aged seven. The method was poison, the motive, to collect the insurance on her life for £7. While Horton was caught and punished, it has to be wondered how many similar killings went undetected or lacked sufficient evidence on which to proceed. Over the years, the *Mercury* reported mysterious deaths that could have been brought on by those seeking financial gain through insurance policies. Child mortality rates were high and, for the poor at least, taking out policies on their children's lives was an obvious if sad investment. For the same reason, parents would have their children baptised with the same first names, so that family tradition might be maintained against the threat of early burials.

George Horton's story was founded on drink, poverty, the coal miner's poor pay, and his fecklessness. The father of several children, he was a man of shiftless temperament who wandered around the Nottinghamshire and Derbyshire border area with his family in tow. At this time, they were sharing a house with another family at Swanwick Lane, Alfreton. His wife was dead and her husband had been unable to afford even the cheapest coffin for her last rest. Because of their nomadic lifestyle, the children were denied what little schooling was available. Their diet for days at a time would be nothing more than dried bread. Everything was coming to a head. Whatever sort of home the Hortons had, it was on the verge of breaking up – and payments on Kate's life policy were in arrears. A few weeks before his daughter died, Horton was said to have remarked to a fellow miner: 'I have got shut of two of my children, and I shall soon be shot of the lot. Then I shall take my hook.' It was about that time he went into a chemist's shop at Ripley and purchased some vermin killer of which the most active ingredient was strychnine.

On 20 May 1889, Kate Horton died in terrible agony. As she did so her distraught father was wandering about in the fields. Already he had discarded the little blue bottle that had contained the poison. When he returned home and saw Kate dead on the sofa, he claimed that if he knew anything like that was going to happen he would never have gone to work. Remorse overtook him, and as he lent over the little body, his tears fell on her still face.

Quite how and when he managed to poison his daughter was never fully established. The suggestion was that she had been given some the day before – a Sunday – when she complained on feeling unwell on her return from chapel. Horton was arrested and his family broken up. One daughter had already left home, and now the remaining children were packed off to Belper Workhouse. He was tried at Derby and sentenced to die on 21 August. An unsuccessful attempt had been made to obtain a reprieve on the grounds that he had not been seen to administer the poison.

James Berry travelled down from his Bradford home the evening before. His last appointment had been in Ireland, at Tralee, where he hanged Lawrence Hickey who, by coincidence, had committed the same crime for the same motive as Horton, except that the victim was not a daughter but another relative. Another coincidence was that Horton would die on the same rope. This was not a case of economy but the fact that nooses became much more efficient when stretched through use. Berry had also made a suggestion that saw a change in the Derby gallows. Gone was the iron structure used since 1833, and a strong wooden beam put in its place. Just as stretched rope was more effective, so too the natural resilience of wood. At first, Berry had estimated a drop of 5½ft (Horton was 5ft 8in and weight just over 10st). However, the miner was a powerfully built man with a strong, muscular neck. Berry added another six inches.

In the days leading up to the scaffold, Horton ate well and listened attentively to the vicar of Swanwick, the Revd J. E. Matthews, to whom he finally admitted his guilt. There being no condemned cell, his last days were spent in a cell adjoining the prison's infirmary, just a short distance from the gallows.

Horton went to his Maker without any undue fuss. The usual procession marked by the passing bell escorted him to the scaffold, now reached by an incline rather than steps (another Berry innovation) and within 20 seconds was dead. Above the gateway the black ensign of death shivered its message to those waiting below. Executions were not what they were. Where once thousands stood, now some 800 had gathered before the prison. Listening to a bell, waiting for the flag and, for some, crowding against a wall to listen for the sound of the trapdoor was a poor substitute for the days when slaughters were full-blooded public events.

The *Mercury* saw on the upturned faces the signs of pity for the poor wretch 'whose last moments on earth were so few'. Others displayed 'only the hard, stern features of the ordinary rough who seemed to regard the whole proceedings as a capital pastime and an opportunity of letting off some "tall talk" about executions and murderers in general'. Their opportunities were getting rarer – in fact there were to be just six more.

The Last Scaffold

DERBY had retained its scaffold for several years after the ending of public executions. In fact, the one used essentially was the same one on which John Leedham ended life in 1833. In 1885, the Home Office decided that a uniform construction should be introduced into prisons, and the recommendation incorporated many improvements suggested by Marwood and Berry. A rare example of civil servants heeding the advice of experts.

The new design did away with the familiar raised scaffold on which stood the cross beam from which victims were hanged. The gallows were to be housed in a plain brick building with double doors; not unlike a garage in appearance which, in fact, many prisons used it for when it was not otherwise engaged. Inside, a pit was dug into the floor and guarded by large trapdoors, which dropped when released by a lever and were caught by spring catches to prevent any rebound. The waiting noose dangled from an iron loop placed in the centre of a massive beam set either into the walls or rested on two stout uprights. Executions were now as secret as could reasonably be arranged. At Derby the new building was built in the outer patrol, not on the original scaffold site, but some 20 yards away and close to the gaol's inner wall. It was all a far cry from the Tree on Nuns' Green.

First to die under the new arrangement was William Pugh, the Brackenfield murderer, on 5 August 1896. Robbery was the motive behind his slaying of Elizabeth Boot on 9 May. The location was Lindway Farm, home of Thomas Limb of a well-known farming family, in the parish of Brackenfield, midway between Matlock and Alfreton. Elizabeth, a young woman of 20, was the daughter of a neighbouring farmer and worked at Lindway as housekeeper and dairymaid. On the day of the murder her employer went off to the cattle fair at Matlock, leaving Elizabeth on her own except for two daytime workers and her niece, Beatrice Emma Boot, who had come over to keep her company.

In the afternoon, Pugh, a collier lodging in

the neighbourhood, called at the farm. He spoke to Elizabeth but what about was to remain a mystery. Young Emma saw her aunt and Pugh walk together towards a barn at the bottom of the farmyard. Elizabeth Boot was never seen alive again. A short while afterwards, George Hitchcock arrived at the farm. Another farmer, he had called to borrow some weights to measure straw. As he entered, he noticed Pugh walking across the farmyard. Seeing Hitchcock, he turned and disappeared into the farm buildings. Hitchcock thought nothing of the matter and went off to the barn to fetch a hayfork, in the company of a farm labourer named Bryan. It was the latter who discovered Elizabeth Boot, lying on the barn floor, her throat savagely cut from blows clearly delivered by a bloodstained billhook found lying nearby. There had obviously been a struggle, the deceased being pursued around the barn by her assailant. There was no sign of Pugh.

News of the dreadful deed quickly spread and people living about rushed over to the farm to see for themselves. Among them was Pugh, who had gone to the home of a man called Sanders with whose daughter he was keeping company. Next on the scene was the police and after a few inquiries they apprehended Pugh and placed him in the lock-up at Alfreton. At first, he denied any knowledge of the crime, but later confessed and stated that his motive was robbery. He knew Thomas Limb kept cash at the farm; he presumably knew Elizabeth Boot and attempted to learn from her the whereabouts

of the money. At Derby assizes, the jury took just 20 minutes to find him guilty of murder.

Again, as there was no cell designated for the condemned, they housed Pugh in one close by the prison infirmary. As was usual, much of his time was spent in the company of a clergyman, in this case the Revd J. B. S. Watson, the prison chaplain. He had an attentive audience and indeed Pugh, as the *Mercury* learned, seemed overtaken by a 'religious monomania', spending a great deal of time singing hymns. The watching warders thought him an ideal prisoner. Nor did his predicament diminish his appetite any, dinner usually consisting of roast beef and vegetables followed by egg pudding. Efforts made to obtain a reprieve were in vain. When the chaplain broke the dreaded news, Pugh apparently took it calmly enough.

There was a new hangman on the scene, James Billington. Berry had resigned in 1892 and pursued a career of evangelist and lecturing on his experiences as an executioner, in the meantime arriving at the conclusion that hanging was all wrong. Billington had been in Manchester the day before, sending a Derby man named Joseph Hurst to his fate for murdering his illegitimate child. In contrast to the good relations enjoyed by the Press with Derby prison authorities, no reporters were permitted inside Manchester gaol.

Billington brought with him an assistant, William Wilkinson, a spindly man who sported a long black beard. Despite his calling (or perhaps because of it), Wilkinson appears as a man of stern principles. He had made the shocking discovery that his parents had actually got around to marriage some time after he was born. Such profligate behaviour upset him so much that he had his name changed to Warbrick. The two executioners had first worked together that same year, at Newgate's last triple hanging. Billington never took kindly to the Home Office ruling that he had to have an assistant, seeing it as a reflection on his capabilities. For his part, Wilkinson (or Warbrick) raged against the Billington family, claiming they were preventing him getting more work.

There had been a spontaneous change in tradition outside the prison. In the days leading up to the execution, several hundred people would turn up to talk about what was to happen and perhaps gaze up at the soon-to-be employed flagpole above the main gate. Sensing a ready-made congregation, the Salvation Army also put in an appearance and 'with voices pitched at their shrillest and highest key endeavoured to make their presence heard within the gaol'. Whether they succeeded in their objective the *Mercury* did not discover, but they did manage to make themselves 'a decided nuisance'. So much so that at times the area around the prison and Vernon Street resembled a fairground. Local residents complained with the result that the Salvationists were moved on. Undaunted and used to surmounting far greater obstacles, the army marched only as far as nearby Old Uttoxeter Road where they continued 'their noisy service with renewed vigour'.

On 5 August, his final day, Pugh rose early,

breakfasted on bread and butter with tea, then sang a few hymns, including *I Was a Wandering Sheep*. A few minutes before eight he joined the procession to the new execution shed. As always, he seemed calm and possessed. Billington and Wilkinson pinioned him and when the chaplain reached the Burial Service with the lines 'I am the resurrection and the life', the scaffold bolt was withdrawn and Pugh went down to his Maker. The drop was 8ft and death was said, as ever, to have been instantaneous. Outside, a large crowd, mostly silent, waited for the raising of the black ensign. As it fluttered out on the morning air, a general murmur of 'Oh!' was heard. A few raised their hats. For a few minutes there was a profound silence. Then the spectators scattered to their various destinations.

* * * * * *

DERBY'S final execution of the 19th century proved a little out of the ordinary in that had the age of the murderer been verifiable, he might not have hanged. Establishing when John Cotton, the Bugsworth killer, was born was seemingly beyond the capacity of the authorities. In an editorial comment, the *Mercury* referred to the understanding that the Home Office refrained from confirming the death sentence for those whose years were past the symbolic three score and ten. On the assizes' calendar, Cotton's age had been entered as 75; police inquiries indicated he was ten years younger; the inquest on his body learned that in fact he was approaching his 72nd birthday. Cotton himself was not sure.

Continuing its ruminations, the *Mercury* pointed out that if he had been able to prove when he was born, he might have:

'*passed the closing years of his life in the comfortable seclusion of one of Her Majesty's convict prisons without being overworked, having no care for tomorrow, food and lodging provided by the State, together with medical necessities and the occasional supervisions of the chaplain*'.

It would not have all been such near-paradise since, as the writer pointed out, the prisoner would have suffered an absence of beer and tobacco.

Cotton was not an endearing individual. There was a long criminal record of drunkenness and cruelty to horses. Married three times, he boasted that he had killed his first two wives. He certainly did his third, on board their narrowboat on 26 October 1898 while moored at Bugsworth, a canal basin near Whaley Bridge on the Peak Forest Canal. (The name Bugsworth no longer appears on maps, a long history of jibe and ridicule aroused local pressure to have the name changed to Buxworth in 1934). For many years, Cotton had earned his living as a boatman. On the night of the murder, he spent the night drinking with his wife in a nearby public house. They fell to quarrelling. When he seemed about strike her, the landlord intervened. Soon after, the couple left and returned to their boat. The fighting and squabbling continued and it all ended with Cotton beating his wife to death with a poker. His drunken condition was used as his

defence at the subsequent trial in Derby, but it carried no weight with Mr Justice Mathew or the jury.

James Billington was hired as executioner, with one of his sons as assistant, but which one was not given in newspaper reports. There was little enough to distinguish Cotton's execution on 21 December from the others. There was the usual procession, the pinioning of arms and legs and then the last few yards to the execution shed and, finally, oblivion following a 6ft drop. Although the August morning was cold and cheerless, the waiting crowd was a little larger than before, but its only excitement was a morbid fascination with the tolling bell and the running up of the black ensign.

* * * * *

AS THE new century dawned, there were changes to the execution ritual. Nothing of any major consequence, but they did make such events even more a secluded performance. Until the end, Derby's hanging days remained more open than at other prisons, mainly through the High Sheriff's office continuing to agree to newspaper reporters being allowed within the walls. Elsewhere, the independent eye was slowly being closed. Most noticeable of the changes was the disappearance of the black flag ritual. Home Office policy thought it best done away with. The same fate was suffered by the tolling of the bell signalling the start of the melancholy procession from the prisoner's cell to the execution shed. Only when the victim had actually hanged was a bell to sound, to announce the slaughter to those who patiently waited outside for their dubious vicarious pleasure. The only other official gesture to remain was the display of appropriate notices at the prison entrance. Of the four more hanging days to come, all were for murders committed in the Chesterfield region; the last three within the town itself.

* * * * * *

IT WAS James Billington's son, William, who put the rope round John Bedford's neck on 30 July 1902. The role of assistant was filled by the founding father of the Pierrepoint dynasty of executioners, Henry Pierrepoint. Both knew what they were there to do, and did it with the minimum of fuss, allowing a drop of 7ft.

Styled by the newspapers as the Duck-manton Murder, the case followed that well-known pattern, the eternal triangle. John Bedford lived at nearby Calow. A single man, he had been on what the *Mercury* described as 'intimate terms' with Nancy Price, the 48-year-old wife of a fish and chip shop owner in Duckmanton. On 25 June, while Mr Price was away in Chesterfield, his wife met Bedford in a public house. Both were stated to be sober when they left the premises and went to the Price home. Nancy Price was never seen alive again. The next morning, Bedford returned to the public house, his boots and clothing smeared with blood, and told a friend that he had killed her. The body was found on a sofa. There was a smile on her face, while in one hand she held a darning needle and in the other a stocking. Death had been sudden,

brought on by Bedford smashing in her skull with a poker. He acknowledged his guilt, saying that jealousy was his motive. Apparently, he had seen Nancy with another man, three years before. He later told the police: 'I ought to have been married, and then it would never have happened. I know my doom, I shall have to swing.'

The absence of a tolling bell and black flag, and the fact there really was nothing to witness, probably accounted for the small crowd outside Derby prison. As 8am approached, around 200-300 people had assembled. Many were women and children, while the majority clearly were 'workmen and others of the artisan class'. As the fatal hour struck, everyone fell silent until the ringing bell beyond the prison wall announced that Bedford had gone. With nothing more to detain them, the spectators dispersed.

* * * * * *

THERE WAS even less of a crowd to comment on for the next execution, that of John Silk on 29 December 1905. A 'few hundred' hung around the massive prison gates, but the *Mercury* reporter put that down to the mistaken belief that the black flag remained part of the ceremony. A feature of the reports of that newspaper had been the decline in space devoted to the religious instruction and prison chapel services. Where once the efforts of clergymen and their final homily would often occupy a column or more, now little more than a few lines were devoted to the spiritual aspect. It might be conjectured that a correlation existed between the less coverage and the lessening influence of the church in general. It has been well established that religious authority went on the retreat in regions where the long-term effects of the Industrial Revolution were obvious, if indeed that authority had ever really existed.

Silk's slaying of his mother on 5 August was a savage business, fuelled by excessive drinking and the hint that service in the army had, as his defence counsel suggested, 'affected his head'. He lived with his mother in Chesterfield's Spa Lane. Separated from her husband, she was known as Mary Fallon. She suffered some disability, being obliged to use crutches.

Her son had enlisted in the army for eight years and was discharged with a very good record. He returned to Chesterfield and his mother. Generally regarded as a good son, his behaviour could become violent and unpredictable when he indulged an unfortunate fondness for alcohol. Silk started drinking heavily just after midday on the day of her death. There must have been some bitter disagreement since he was heard by several people declaring that there would be a murder in Spa Lane that night. On at least two occasions he returned home, very drunk, and was overheard quarrelling with his mother. The last time he returned it was nearly midnight, and in such a drunken stupor that he had to be helped back. There were more rows, mostly over a lamp that ended up shattered on the floor. Next day a newspaper delivery boy on his rounds discovered that a shocking murder had been committed. Mary Fallon's body lay on the floor, her head terribly injured by blows from one of her crutches and a broken chair. Five ribs were broken, the medical evidence concluding that she had been jumped on repeatedly. As for John Silk, he was shaken into reality by a policeman who found him in his room, deep in an inebriated sleep, his face hands and wrists smeared with blood.

There was never any doubt over the outcome of his trial. Indeed, once he realised the enormity of the crime, Silk accepted his fate and swore he would go to his death like a soldier, which he did. From letters written in gaol and statements by those who had known him in earlier years, Silk had been well liked and was most appreciative of the help given to himself and his mother by neighbours. Drink had been his downfall. Henry Pierrepoint was the hangman, assisted by John Ellis. The latter was going through a busy period, Silk being the third he had helped cross into the next world in three days. On 27 December, he had been at Stafford gaol, the next day Leeds, before taking a train to Derby.

* * * * * *

DESPITE rumours that Pierrepoint and Ellis did not always see eye to eye, the two worked together for the last two executions at Derby prison. A year after Silk died, the pair passed into the gaol, this time to hang another ex-soldier, Walter Marsh. His crime, while extreme, had a dreadful familiarity about it.

Marsh had reached the rank of sergeant in

the North Staffordshire Regiment when he completed his 20 years' engagement. A soldier of good character, he saw service overseas and being of a thrifty nature, returned to civilian life with sufficient money to set himself up in business as a publican in Sheffield. In the closing years of his army career he had married Eliza Gascoyne who, at 18 years of age, was probably far too young for a retiring soldier of 38. From the start, the marriage proved far removed from heaven. There were frequent quarrels, the root cause of which was his jealousy, which at times turned to violence. Unable to make a success of the public house, the couple moved to Chesterfield where they set up home at Goyt Terrace. That turned out to be no cure for their ill-starred union and the arguments and violence continued. In June 1906, Mrs Marsh petitioned the Chesterfield magistrates for a separation order on the grounds of persistent cruelty. Lacking any corroborative evidence and bearing in mind her husband's military record, the application was rejected.

Marsh did not mend his ways, and relations worsened. A few weeks later the landlord called to the house on some business. Marsh happened to be absent and when he learned of the visit, immediately rushed round to the man and soundly berated him. The result was that the Marshes were ordered to quit their home. Despite such a lesson, Marsh's behaviour did not improve. A day or so after he was seen assaulting his wife, and not much longer after that, by now thoroughly, frightened, she slept at a neighbour's house.

Foolishly, Eliza Marsh returned to her husband. On 9 July he picked up his razor and slit her throat. After his arrest, Marsh said that his wife had been guilty of neglect and that in one argument she had thrown things at him. At the time of his wife's death, he insisted he had been shaving when they started arguing and in the ensuing struggle she was cut so badly that she died from the wounds. Neither Mr Justice Ridley nor the jury accepted Marsh's explanation and he was sentenced to die on 27 December.

Snow had fallen heavily, which may have explained the few dozen people waiting outside the prison portal when Pierrepoint and Ellis killed Marsh. Within the walls, the prisoner gave no trouble and observed the prescribed ritual. Since the trial he had put on weight and grown a beard. His eyes were red from crying, and there were more tears as he stepped on to the trapdoor. Seconds later, Pierrepoint jerked the lever and Marsh dropped into the next world. The prison bell sent out its sad message and a little later the notices publishing the event were posted. Now, just one more slaughter remained.

* * * * * *

FOR the third time in a little over 18 months, notice of an execution was pinned to the outer gate of the prison in Vernon Street.

*Capital Punishment Amendment Act,
   1868
31 and 32 Vict. C.24.S.7.
The sentence of the law passed upon Wm.*

Edward Slack, found guilty of murder, will be carried into execution at 8am tomorrow.

Dated 15 July 1907, the brief note was signed by Francis Nicholas Smith, Sheriff of Derbyshire, and Charles Murrell, Chief Warder in Charge of HM Prison Derby. Normally, the Chief's name would not have appeared but the Governor, Captain C. E. Farquharson, late 21st Hussars, was away on holiday. It would be the first execution missed by him since taking up office in 1880. William Slack would be the last person to be judicially hanged in Derbyshire. While the fact itself warrants a footnote in the county's history, the deed itself was nothing exceptional. However, there were some grim coincidences. Slack was the last of three successive murderers who had killed in Chesterfield. Each had served in the Army, their victims were all female (as were all of those whose murderers were hanged in private at Derby) each was executed by Henry Pierrepoint and his assistant, Ellis.

William Slack, aged 47, was a painter by trade. A man with a prickly temper, his behaviour was such that Mrs Slack thought it prudent to leave their home and go and live elsewhere in Chesterfield. She did not tell her husband where. For his part, he would at various times approach the police in an attempt to find out. Once, while questioning an officer, he suddenly attacked him with a carving knife and a cobbler's knife, inflicting 16 wounds. A term of penal servitude in

Portland Prison was his reward, and then to be placed under police supervision when he eventually returned to Derbyshire. Domestic problems apart, Slack was also conducting an affair with Lucy Wilson, a married woman. There was a child said to be born of the liaison. Although Slack claimed the baby as his, Mr Wilson may have been telling the truth when insisting his wife had never been unfaithful in what had been, on the whole, a happy marriage.

On the day of the murder, 18 March, Slack warned Mrs Wilson that he wanted nothing more to do with her; if she failed to heed him then he would 'cut her head off'. Later he would assert that she had urged him to go away with him, with the persistence associated with an unscrupulous and designing woman, as he described it. Slack met and talked with Lucy Wilson outside the theatre where she worked as a cleaner, and expected to see her again later in the day. That meeting came in Highfield Road. Mrs Wilson was pushing the baby in its pram, making towards the house where Slack was working. He met her as she walked along. They stopped and chatted and, according to the statement of a passing postman named Bennett, there was nothing about their conversation or behaviour to attract attention. A few minutes later Bennett heard a noise he would describe as 'the chopping of wood'. Looking back, he saw Slack striking Mrs Wilson about the head with a hatchet. She died almost immediately, her lifeblood flowing down the gutter. Throwing the weapon over a wall, Slack walked off only to turn back and return for the pram. As he reached the dead body, he knelt down on his hands and knees and kissed it. He then stood up and went off with the pram and its baby, which never woke throughout the whole vicious episode. As for the police, they had little trouble in tracking down Slack, arresting him and rescuing the baby.

Slack stood trial before Lord Justice Coleridge, during which the painter worked himself into an uncontrollable rage, uttering blasphemies that shocked the court. As the trial drew to it close and the judge began summing up, Slack became more uncontrollable, frequently interrupting despite several warnings from Lord Coleridge. He continued the same outrageous behaviour right up to when he was led away by the warders, his execution set for 16 July. Maybe Slack's conduct in court led to the far greater crowd than was usual collecting outside the prison on hanging day. They might have been anticipating a 'scene' as the *Mercury* reporter thought; although how they would ever know was questionable.

As it turned out, the final execution officially went without a hitch. Slack marched quickly and jerkily to the shed without faltering, head erect and the burial service sounding in his ears. Immediately facing the open doors of the shed was his grave, covered by planks, but obvious in purpose by the fresh earth piled alongside. Whether the condemned man saw and understood, he gave no intimation. Once inside, Slack stood on the spot marked by a chalk-marked 'T' and died instantaneously. Pierrepoint gave a drop of 7ft 7ins. For the last time, the Derby prison bell tolled for a victim, the official notices went up on the gates, and the inquest arrived at its expected verdict. Then the corpse, smothered in quicklime, was unceremoniously buried.

The Derby Mercury's *report of Derbyshire's last execution, the hanging of William Slack on 16 July 1907.*

EXECUTION AT DERBY.

CHESTERFIELD MURDERER HANGED.

SLACK MEETS HIS END WITH FORTITUDE.

THE SCENE IN THE PRISON.

Capital Punishment Amendment Act, 1868. 31 and 32 Vict. C. 24. S. 7.

The sentence of the law passed upon Wm. Edward Slack, found guilty of murder will be carried into execution at 8 a.m. to-morrow.

(Signed) Francis Nicholas Smith,
Sheriff of Derbyshire,
Charles Murrell,
Chief Warder in Charge.

H M Derby Prison, 15 July, 1907.

Thrice within a period of a little over eighteen months has a notice to the effect that the extreme penalty of the law was to be carried into execution been posted on the outer gate of His Majesty's Prison at Derby, and thrice has the condemned man, who has suffered the unhappy fate hailed from Chesterfield.

On Tuesday, shortly after the prison clock had struck eight, Wm. Edward Slack, the Chesterfield painter, found guilty of the awful murder of Lucy Wilson, a married woman, at Chesterfield on March 18th, paid forfeit with his life for the crime. From the first it was practically certain that there would be no reprieve, and when the Home Secretary's letter was received on Saturday stating that he saw no reason for an interference with the sentence passed by Lord Coleridge, the intimation came as no surprise. ... is given a description of the extraor-

"You must be quiet," Lord Coleridge said, "I beg your pardon," replied the prisoner; "I'll have what's right, and then I'll stand the consequences."

When he again shouted across the court, and once more a warder asked him to calm himself, he answered, "If it does me harm I'll have to stand to it. I don't care if it does me harm—the worst is the worst. I shall have to stand to all that now, shan't I?"

And Lord Coleridge impressively remarked: "I believe your best friend would advise you to be quiet."

After he had been found guilty he used a most disgusting expression to the judge, and freely interrupted the course of the sentence.

Lord Coleridge fully felt the painfulness of the situation, and when Slack once more attempted to turn aside his lordship said with some emotion: "I will not add to your distress by one unnecessary word. I am not your judge. I am only a temporary minister of human justice."

"I have been judged by a lot of old farmers," Slack interrupted just afterwards, and as the last words of the sentence were uttered, he lifted up his hand as though to pull a hair from his head, blew between his fingers, and shouted, "You see that. I don't care that —— much. That's the sort of man I am now."

And as the Judge pronounced the final prayer—"And may God have mercy on your soul," Slack answered back, "There's no God, else I should not have been here. There is no God."

Events in Chesterfield.

This dramatic scene followed the story of the crime, which took place in Chesterfield on

For where a grave had opened wide,
There was no grave at all:
Only a stretch of mud and sand
By the hideous prison-wall,
And a little heap of burning lime,
That the man should have his pall.
(The Ballad of Reading Gaol)

After a while, the final gathering of watchers went their different ways. There was nothing more to see.

Abolished for Ever

WITH the execution of William Slack, Derbyshire's history of capital punishment came to an end. Between 1903 and 1953, 16 men who had committed murder within the county were hanged as punishment, but since they were killed at either Nottingham or Leicester gaol they have not been included in this history. The execution shed continued to be used for garaging the prison van, its primary function confined to history.

The prison itself did not survive for much longer, just managing to reach its centenary. No more prisoners were accepted at Vernon Street after 1916. During the Great War of 1914-18, the establishment was used as a military detention centre. Gradually the great hulk fell into disuse and was sold off in 1929. The cells and most of the blocks were demolished and the area cleared and turned into a greyhound racing stadium, a function that survived until the 1980s. Still surviving are most of the impressive front walls with the gateway intact and two of the Martello towers.

To the left of the entrance can still be seen, a few feet above ground level, the iron grill door through which the condemned stepped directly on to the scaffold in the days of public hangings. While the wall against which the small graveyard lay remains in place, there is nothing to show where the murderers' remains once lay. The remaining edifice has been handsomely restored and named Vernon Gate. Despite its dismal origins and sometimes violent history, the structure is a handsome relic that can be said to enhance a city which has seen its architectural heritage steadily eroded by city planners and replaced by buildings that do little to elevate nor contribute to the city's identity.

Relics of the hanging days are comparatively rare, although efforts have been made to preserve what survives. The old county gaol in Friar Gate exists in part underground and a small museum created. A skull claimed as that of Anthony Lingard grins from an exhibition case, while various ballad and broadsides adorn the walls of former cells. A replica of the planks on which the Pentrich rebels were beheaded after death is on view, while the original is stored in the city's museum. Also in store may be the simple headstone commemorating Bland, Bonsall, and Hulme the three murderers hanged on the top of the Vernon Street prison gateway. Kept at the Derbyshire Constabulary Memorabilia Museum in St Mary's Gate are the handcuffs used on William Slack, as is the hatchet with which he slew Lucy Wilson.

The death penalty itself survived many more years, and it has to be admitted because of traditional opposition to have an ancient barbarity consigned to the dustbin of history. As already stated, once judicial killings became private occasions, those opposing capital punishment found it increasingly difficult to arouse public feelings on the subject. Out of sight, out of mind and visible only to the eye of officialdom, public apathy could only follow. There were some reforms. In 1908 hanging of persons under 18 was abolished; in 1933 an Act was passed whereby a person who was under 18 when the offence was committed would not hang, but be detained during His Majesty's Pleasure. Mothers who killed newborn babies could not be hanged after 1922. Nine years later, pregnant women were given immunity from hanging.

The name most synonymous with the abolition of hanging was the Labour MP Sydney Silverman. He battled long and hard against the politicians (mainly in the Conservative ranks) and the Church of England. Under the Labour Government he sought to have hanging suspended for an experimental period of five years. He persuaded the Commons to support him but was defeated in the House of Lords. Silverman in 1956 tried again. The then Conservative government advised him against presenting his Death Penalty (Abolition) Bill, but he nevertheless pressed on. The Bill was given a second reading by 286 votes to 262. Again, the Lords threw it out. It was during this period that the Lord Chief Justice gave his opinion: *'There are many cases where a murderer must be destroyed. I believe it is a sign of a healthy conscience in a country if they are determined to avenge crime.'*

He also believed in hanging the insane. Such a measure was never invoked even in the darkest days of the Bloody Code.

Eight years later Silverman tried again. His Bill passed its second reading in the Commons by a majority of 185. Old habits die hard. Hangings for all categories of murder were suspended only for five years. That enactment, The Murder (Abolition of the Death Penalty) Act of 1965, was approved on 9 November. However, Sydney Silverman had finally won through. Before the trial period had expired the Commons finally abolished the death penalty for murder on 16 December 1969 by 343 votes to 185. Two days later the Lords gave their approval by a majority of 46. Among those who voted for the legislation was the Archbishop of Canterbury and 18 other bishops. The final winning over of the Church was little more than a nominal gesture, for what turned out to be the last executions had taken place five years earlier.

With the abolition of capital punishment for murder, only two hanging offences remained on the statute book, treason and piracy with violence. Dating from 1351, the Treason Act had last been used in 1946 while the Piracy Act had not been invoked since 1860. Even those two crimes eventually followed suit. If there were any remnants of the Bloody Code, they were finally washed away in May 1998 when the Commons voted to block any future attempt to reinstate the death penalty for murder in Britain, in

peacetime. In January 1999, Parliament renounced the right to restore capital punishment by signing a European convention against the death penalty.

There will always be those who wish to see the hangman being re-employed. Since the last judicial executions in August 1964, the occasional newspaper survey has shown a preference for their return while the occasional Tory MP has attempted to raise some enthusiasm. In 1984, the House of Commons, by a massive majority of 116 votes against, decisively rejected the restoration of hanging. There were several pro-hanging Conservative MPs who, having

observed that they could not win the vote despite their party having a parliamentary majority of 140, then suggested that the subject should be laid to rest for good. Of the eight Derby and Derbyshire MPs, the five Tories were in favour of bringing back hanging while the three Labour members were against. Yet even as this book was being prepared, a local newspaper carried an interview with a retiring judge. He was reported as backing those who called for the death penalty to be re-introduced. He believed that the existence of capital punishment was allowable in a civilised society, that people should know there was a sanction. Executions would be confined to premeditated murder and murder of officials such as prison and police officers.

Public opinion swung as far as it can away from the clusters of gallows spawned by the Bloody Code. Now the pendulum rests at the other extreme, to where it was when William the Conqueror abolished capital punishment nearly 1,000 years ago.

Appendix A
List of Executions in Derbyshire

HERE is a list compiled from all known sources of those executed in Derbyshire in accordance with the Law. Unless otherwise stated, it can be accepted that before 1812 executions were carried out at Nuns' Green in Derby. From 1812, and still public events, they were moved to Friar Gate with the county gaol serving as backdrop. From 1833 until 1862, the scaffold was erected in front of the new prison in Vernon Street. In 1868 judicial killings became private events, carried out behind prison walls. The last took place in 1907. Executions were by hanging unless noted otherwise.

After some years the *Derby Mercury*, first published in 1732, began listing previous executions (some prior to 1732) at the conclusion of reports on the latest hangings. While not complete, they are quite comprehensive and much referred to. Their main usefulness is as the essential cross-reference to court cases reported in the *Mercury* and later the *Derby and Chesterfield Reporter*.

Before 1732, sources are scarce and then scanty in content. Two useful ones are the books by Derby historian William Hutton (1723-1815) and William Woolley (died 1716), both of whom would have had access to material since lost, mislaid, forgotten or destroyed. Not automatically thought of are the catalogues and listings of the noted Derbyshire antiquary, Thomas Bateman (1821-1861) whose magnificent collections of diverse material and archaeological finds were housed at Lomberdale Hall at Middleton-by-Youlgreave. Bateman amassed a great number of ballads, broadsheets, broadsides, and execution sheets, some now available in Derbyshire libraries. Those publications, well called street literature, while extremely useful, must be approached with caution and some knowledge of their history. Tabloid journalism is not a recent innovation. Also surviving are some assizes' calendars.

(* Executions mentioned in text)

1341*   Two men and a woman gibbeted on Ashover Moor for murdering one of the King's purveyors.

*   The bodies of three men hung in chains at Chapel-en-le-Frith for robbery with violence.

16thc*   Unidentified pedlar summarily hanged at Ashford-in-the Water on the orders of Sir George Vernon.

1556*   Joan Waste, 1 August, burned for heresy at Windmill Hill Pit, Derby.

1578   Peter Graves of Bubnell, Thomas Robinson of Wirksworth, Edward Morris of Chesterfield, Christopher Harrison of Monyash and Eleanor Wright of Bakewell, at Derby, crime(s) unknown.

1588*   25 July, three Roman Catholic priests, Nicholas Garlick, Robert Ludlam (the Padley Martyrs) and Richard Simpson, hanged, drawn and quartered at St Mary's Bridge, Derby, for treason.

* A woman hanged at same time as the priests, said to be for murder.

1591 Seven hanged, no other details.

1599 A man named Okey hanged outside Derby Town Hall, no other details.

1601 Woman burned at stake at Windmill Hill Pit, Derby, for poisoning her husband. No other details.

1608* Five men and a woman at Tapton Bridge, near Chesterfield. No other details.

* Mrs Stafford and another female, the Bakewell Witches. Date and venue not known.

1609 Henry Bennett, hanged at Derby for murdering Roger Moore, a serjeant. Bennett's mother and brother said to be involved. No other details.

1645 Richard Cockrum, for killing Mills, a servant at The Angel Inn, Rodney Yard, Derby.

1660c* Crosland, father and son, for horse stealing. Executed by youngest son, John, who then took on job of official hangman.

1665* 14 March. Young woman pressed to death at County Hall after refusing to give evidence; regarded by court as being 'mute of malice.'

1679* August. Ten highwaymen known as the Bracy gang. Executed were John Barker, Richard Bracy, Roger Brookham, Daniel Buck, Joseph Gerrat, Thomas Gillat, William Loe, Thomas Ouldome, John Robottom and Andrew Smedley. The other gang members, Richard Piggen and John Baker, turned King's Evidence and escaped execution. (Possibly the biggest mass hanging in Derbyshire)

1693* A farm girl from Swanwick burned at the stake for murdering her master, a farmer. (Last reported case of burning in Derbyshire)

1723 Man, for horse stealing. No other details.

1725 Rock, Lyon and Shaw, for counterfeiting. No other details.

1726 Man, for horse stealing. No other details.

1727 Man, for horse stealing. No other details.

1731* William Billings, 9 April. Crime unknown.

1732* John Hewitt and Rosamond Ollerenshaw, 29 March, for murder.

1735* John Smith, 8 August, for burglary and felony.

1738* Richard Woodward, 30 March, for highway robbery.

1740 William Dolphin, 9 April, for highway robbery.

* George Ashmore, 29 August, for counterfeiting.

1741 Peter Bowler, 1 August, for dangerously wounding.

1754* Mary Dilkes, 29 March, for murdering her baby (dissected).

1755* Ann Williamson, 1 August, for picking pockets.

1756 John Ratcliffe, 2 April, for horse stealing.

1757* Thomas Hulley, 29 April, escaping from transportation.

1759* Charles Kirkman, 24 March, for murdering an infant child (dissected).

1763 John Perry and Amos Mason, 12 August, for highway robbery.

1768* John Lowe, 20 April, for house breaking.

* Charles Pleasant, 4 May, for forgery. An on-off execution as many efforts were made to obtain a reprieve.

Bloody Code Era

1776* Matthew Cocklayne, 21 March, for murder. (Last person to be gibbeted at Derby)

1780* James Meadows, 31 March, for highway robbery.

* William Buxton, 25 August, for highway robbery.

1782* James Williams, 28 March, for horse stealing.

* John Shaw, 2 August, for breaking out of gaol and escaping transportation.

1784* Thomas Greensmith, 8 April, for house breaking and robbery.

William Rose, 16 April, for horse stealing.

1785* William Grooby, George Grooby and James Pitts (or Peat), 1 April (Easter Fair), for burglary.

1786 John Sheppard and William Stanley, 7 April, for house breaking.

James Halliburton, 1 September, for rape.

1787* John Porson, 9 April, for picking pockets.

1788* Thomas Grundy, 22 March, for poisoning his brother (dissected).

1790 Joseph Allen, 12 August, for shop breaking.

1791* William Rider, 1 April, for robbery.

1794 James Murray, 4 April, for house breaking.

1795 Thomas Neville, 10 April, for robbery.

1796* James Preston (70), 17 March, for murder of male bastard child, born of Susannah

Moreton (24). Both sentenced to death and dissection. Woman reprieved morning of execution. (Preston dissected)

1800 Thomas Knowles, 5 September, for uttering a one guinea Sheffield Bank note.

1801 George Lacey Powell and John Drummond, 14 August, for highway robbery.

James Grattan of Heage, 14 August, for burglary.

* John Evans of Duffield and John Dent of Coleorton, 14 August, for sheep stealing.

1802 James Mellor and Thomas Spencer (cousins), 27 August, for burglary.

1803* William Wells, 19 March, for murder at Barlborough (dissected).

1804 Richard Booth and John Parker, 6 April, for horse stealing.

1807* William Webster, 20 March, for poisoning eight people, two of whom died (dissected).

* Joseph West, 8 April, for uttering forged bank notes. (Last execution at Nuns' Green)

Executed in Friar Gate

1812* Percival Cooke and James Tomlinson (alias Fruz), 10 April for burglary. (First hangings on the new drop)

1813* Paul Mason, Richard Hibbert and Peter Henshaw, 9 April, for burglary.

1815* Anthony Lingard, 28 March, for murder. (Last gibbeting in Derbyshire)

1816* Joseph Wheeldon, 9 August, for murdering his niece and nephew, Isaac Wheeldon and Mary Ann Wheeldon (dissected).

1817* John Brown of Nottingham, George Booth of Chesterfield, Thomas Jackson of Woolley Moor and John King of Matlock, 15 August, for burning stacks of corn.

* Jeremiah Brandreth, William Turner, and Isaac Ludlum, 7 November, for high treason. Hanged and then beheaded. Leaders of the Pentrich Revolution.

1819* Hannah Bocking (16), 22 March, for murder (dissected).

* Thomas Hopkinson of Ashover, 2 April, for highway robbery.

1822* Hannah Halley, 25 March, for murdering her

infant. (Last woman to hang in Derby and last victim to be dissected)

1825* George Batty of Norton Woodseats, 8 April, for rape. (Last person to be hanged in Friar Gate)

End of Bloody Code Era

Executed in Vernon Street, outside the new County Gaol

1833* John Leedham, 12 April, for bestiality. (Last person to hang in Derbyshire for a crime other than murder)

1843* Samuel Bonsall, William Bland and John Hulme, 31 March, for murder.

1847* John Platts, 1 April, for murder. Crowd estimated at over 20,000.

1852* Anthony Turner, 26 March, for murder.

1861* George Smith, 16 August, for murder.

1862* Richard Thorley, 11 April, for murder. (Last public execution in Derbyshire)

Hanged within the County Gaol, Vernon Street

1873* Benjamin Hudson, 4 August, for murder of his wife near Eckington

1880* John Wakefield, 16 August, for murder of Elizabeth Ann Wilkinson (9) at Derby.

1881* Alfred Gough, 21 November, for murder of Eleanor Windle (6) at Brimington.

1888* Arthur Thomas Delaney, 10 August, for murder of his wife at Chesterfield.

1889* George Horton, 21 August, for murder of his daughter, Kate (8) at Alfreton.

1896* William Pugh, 5 August, for murder of Elizabeth Boot at Brackenfield.

1898* John Cotton, 21 December, for murder of his wife at Bugsworth.

1902* John Bedford, 30 July, for murder of Nancy Price at Duckmanton.

1905* John Silk, 29 December, for murder of his mother, Mary Fallon, at Chesterfield.

1906* Walter Marsh, 27 December, for murder of his wife at Chesterfield.

1907* William Edward Slack, 16 July, for murder of Lucy Wilson at Chesterfield. (The last execution in Derbyshire).

―――――――――

Between 1903 and 1953, 16 men were executed for murders committed in Derbyshire. However, since they hanged at either Nottingham or Leicester prison they have not been included in this listing.

―――――――――

Below are listed those who were either sentenced to death and died before their due date, or may have been executed but no records have survived.

1431* Peter Swordman. In delivering its verdict in another case, a jury named him as being responsible for the murder of William Woderove.

1589* Father James Clayton, for high treason, but died in Derby gaol from typhoid, 22 July.

1596* Alice Gooderidge, for witchcraft, but died in Derby gaol.

1616 A man named Sheldon suspected of having murdered his sister Jane at Martin Lane (Derby?); no further details.

1621 Thomas Stringer 'killed his man' at Derby; no further details.

1734 Thomas Bennett sentenced to death at Derby Summer assizes for murdering his wife at Crich; no further details.

* Woman, for rick burning. While this execution is included in the *Derby Mercury* list, there is no report of any such case at the assizes for that year. Maybe an example of quoting a catchpenny ballad.

1784* John and Benjamin Jones (brothers), convicted of burglary, hanged themselves in Friar Gate gaol on 4 August. Their execution had been set for 20 August.

Unknown date

  A woman named Isoult or Isolda strangled her husband, a baker, at Middleton. Tried to dispose of the body by burning in the bakehouse oven. Her nerve failing, she fled only to be captured later. No other details.

A BALLAD catalogued in Bateman's library gave details of a crime and execution that has proved impossible to verify. All too often these publications failed to give a year, let alone a date. Possibly early 19th century, it dealt with a William Wild who murdered two small children by drowning at Church Broughton.

Discovered by the author, a second murder ballad gave not only the year, 1823, but also the month, July. A young girl, Ann Williams, in service at Wirksworth, had fallen in love with William Jones. She became pregnant, looked for marriage, but met death instead. It has not been possible to confirm this all-too common story. No one hanged that year in Derby. Maybe the sheet was another example of a catchpenny publication. Such publications were usually broadsides, reporting details of murders in most lurid detail, only to be discovered later as fictitious, being dreamt up by the printer when trade was slack. Such efforts were also known as 'cocks'.

Another ballad surely from the same dubious origin was *The Cruel Gamekeeper*. Date and publisher unknown, nor names given, it recounted the sad history of a farmer's daughter who lived at Buxton. The ballad actually placed that town 'in Staffordshire', which immediately arouses suspicion. The story followed the familiar routine, seduction, pregnancy and murder; her killer (who told the story) finished with the statement, 'So the gallows proved my marriage bed.'

Appendix B

Capital Convictions and Executions
1731-1830 (by decade)

BELOW is a breakdown by decade of all known capital convictions and actual executions, for the period 1731-1830. Before 1731, records are so scarce that it would be pointless to include those known. What follows was culled mainly from newspapers of the day. For that reason alone, they can be treated only as a fairly reliable guide. Crimes are as stated in their reports, not as far as is known, from court records.

Finishing at 1830 was decided upon since after that year the death sentence was virtually monopolised by the crime of murder and therefore would have little meaningful bearing. Where a convicted criminal was reprieved, it has to be assumed that they were transported; the lesser sentence was rarely reported.

Crime	Sentenced	Executed
1731-1740		
Murder	5	2
Highway robbery	3	2
Counterfeiting	1	1
Burglary	1	1
Not specified	1	1
Stealing horses	1	-
Stealing deer	1	-
Forgery	1	-
Robbery	1	-
	15	7
1741-1750		
Dangerous wounding	1	1

Crime	Sentenced	Executed
Sheep stealing	7	-
Horse stealing	4	-
Stealing	1	-
Stealing plate	1	-
Horse wounding	1	-
House breaking	1	-
Coining	1	-
	17	1
1751-1760		
Murder	2	2*
Horse stealing	2	1
Picking pockets	1	1
Escaping from transport	1	1
Sheep stealing	9	-
Entering dwelling house	1	-
Robbery of person	1	-
Highway robbery	1	-
Forging notes	1	-
Housebreaking	1	-
	20	5

* dissected

Crime	Sentenced	Executed
1761-1770		
Highway robbery	4	2
Housebreaking	2	1
Forgery	1	1
Horse stealing	3	-
Sheep stealing	2	-
Cattle stealing	2	-
Breaking into dwelling	2	-
	16	4
1771-1780		
Highway robbery	3	2
Murder	1	1**
Horse stealing	8	-
Sheep stealing	2	-

Hanged For Three Pennies

Crime	Sentenced	Executed
Cattle stealing	1	-
Burglary	1	-
Setting fire to coal store	1	-
** gibbeted	17	3

1781-1790

Crime	Sentenced	Executed
Burglary	10	4+
Horse stealing	14	2
Housebreaking	3	2
Murder	1	1*
Rape	1	1
Shop breaking	2	1
Picking pockets	2	1
Breaking out of gaol, escaping transportation	4	1
Sheep stealing	10	-
Stealing from inn	2	-
Cattle stealing	1	-
Stealing from church	1	-
Breaking into dwelling	1	-
Stealing	1	-
	53	13

+2 who committed suicide not included *dissected

1791-1800

Crime	Sentenced	Executed
Robbery	2	2
Murder	2	1*
Housebreaking	6	1
Uttering bank note	1	1
Sheep stealing	7	-
Burglary	5	-
Stealing	2	-
Rape	1	-
Assault and robbery	1	-
Horse stealing	1	-
Stealing clothing	1	-
Entering dwelling	1	-
Fraud	1	-
	31	5

* dissected

1801-1810

Crime	Sentenced	Executed
Burglary	12	3
Sheep stealing	11	2
Horse stealing	10	2
Highway robbery	5	2
Murder	2	2*
Uttering forged notes	1	1
Breaking into dwelling	2	-
Stealing	2	-
Returning from transportation	1	-
	46	12

* dissected

1811-1820

Crime	Sentenced	Executed
Burglary	13	5
Firing haystacks	5	4
High treason	4	3
Murder	3	3* **
Highway robbery	1	1
Breaking into dwelling	25	-
Sheep stealing	11	-
Horse stealing	9	-
Stealing	4	-
Robbery	4	-
Shop breaking	3	-
Housebreaking	2	-
Intent to murder	1	-
Horse wounding	1	-
Uttering forged cheque	1	-
Escaping from transportation	1	-
Cattle stealing	1	-
Breaking into weaving shop	1	-
	90	16

* 2 dissected, ** 1 gibbeted

1821-1830

Crime	Sentenced	Executed
Murder	1	1*
Rape	1	1
Breaking into dwelling house	27	-
Horse stealing	22	-
Sheep stealing	15	-
Stealing in dwelling house	14	-
Highway robbery	7	-
Burglary	6	-
Assault/stealing from person	6	-
Shop breaking	4	-
Stealing cheeses	3	-
Malicious wounding	2	-
Robbery of person	2	-
Forging of bank notes	2	-
Grievous bodily harm	1	-
Escaping from transportation	1	-
Returning from transportation	1	-
Firing haystack	1	-
Stealing from person	1	-
Breaking into office	1	-
Stealing geese	1	-
Stealing shot gun	1	-
	120	2

* dissected

Appendix C
The Bloody Code (1770-1830)
Capital convictions and executions

Crime	Sentenced	Executed
Horse stealing	64	4
Sheep stealing	56	2
Breaking into dwelling	55	-
Burglary	47	12
Highway robbery	16	5
Stealing in dwelling house	14	-
House breaking	11	3
Murder	10	9
Stealing	9	-
Shop breaking	9	1
Escaping from transportation	6	1
Assault/stealing from person	6	-
Firing haystacks	6	4
Robbery	6	2
Uttering forged notes	5	2
High treason	4	3
Rape	3	2
Stealing cattle	3	-
Stealing cheeses	3	-
Stealing from inn	2	-
Picking pockets	2	1
Returning from transportation	2	-
Malicious wounding	2	-
Robbery of person	2	-
Intent to murder	1	-
Grievous bodily harm	1	-
Assault/robbery	1	
Fraud	1	
Horse wounding	1	-
Stealing from church	1	-
Setting fire to coal stock	1	-
Breaking into weaving shop	1	-
Stealing from person	1	-
Stealing geese	1	-
Stealing shot guns	1	-
Breaking into office	1	-
Stealing clothing	1	
Entering dwelling	1	
	357	51

Executed: 14.25%

Crimes and sentences were taken mainly from the *Derby Mercury*, which did not necessarily report all assizes in full. As for the crimes themselves, the descriptions are again the *Mercury's*; actual court records and findings are rare. While many of the offences are broadly similar, their diversity and preciseness clearly indicate what helped to bring the Bloody Code into such ridicule and the Black Act's eventual abolishment in 1823.

Over the Code's 60 years, Derbyshire executed 14.25% of those sentenced to death. That compares with 22% for London and Middlesex where the 1723 Act would have been implemented with more vigour. The hangman was at his busiest at Derby over the period 1785-1810 when slightly over a quarter (26%) of the condemned mounted the scaffold. That slaughter rate was actually higher than London's *and* Middlesex's at 23%. However, if that figure is to assume any significance it would first have be compared with other assize towns, since it may have been an overall provincial trend.

Statistics became more available and reliable after 1805.

Appendix D
Street Literature

MUCH of the information on Derbyshire's history of capital punishment comes from the pages of the *Derby Mercury*, joined later by the *Derby and Chesterfield Reporter*. Indeed, in the absence of most of the court records, those two publications effectively are the prime sources. That they are proves to be a drawback when researching. Compared with other counties (particularly Nottinghamshire and Staffordshire in this context), Derbyshire has been poorly served. Whereas other counties have libraries on whose shelves appear the works of local historians and commentators – usually in the 19th century – dealing *inter alia* with crime and punishments in their regions, Derbyshire can display none on any significant scale. Alternatively, if they did once exist, they have since become lost to view and reference.

It might be argued that such an absence is not great loss, since the two newspapers mentioned can surrender such a lot of information if trawled diligently. However, when searching through the libraries of Nottinghamshire and Staffordshire, since Derbyshire is often mentioned, it soon becomes apparent that their local historians had access to sources other than the two newspapers quoted. While it can now only be conjecture, those other origins most likely lay within the realms of what conveniently is termed street literature. That heading covers such publications as ballads, chapbooks, broadsides and broadsheets, confession sheets, and execution sheets, generally covering the more prominent and infamous crimes. Those publications go back as far as the 16th century and really did not go out of fashion until around the middle of the 19th, when the popularity and cheapness of newspapers brought about their demise.

While they are an invaluable source, it pays the researcher to treat them with care. Dates, when not missing altogether, can be incorrect. Locations and specific detail, especially in the earlier examples, are often vague. The reason for that is simple. Until the advance of the printing press, the main printers of street literature were to be found in London. While details of crimes and executions in the capital were easily acquired, those of events in the provinces were not. Those printers had to rely on the hawkers, the ballad mongers, the higglers, the street singers, who travelled all over the country. They learned of local crimes and sensational trials and, committing to memory as much as they could (memories were far better exercised in those days than now), gave the particulars to the printers on their return. As the presses became cheaper, other centres sprang up. Newcastle was one, Bristol another, and then Nottingham. Derby was a long way down the line, although its present-day collection of street literature is rated among the finest in England.

Those local chroniclers of years ago would have had far more examples of such literature to refer to than is the case today. There were people who made a hobby of collecting the sheets, or at least making a faithful copy of them, for the paper used was not of the best quality, nor the ink. The printers were not in the market for posterity or archival survival, but quick profit. The result was that much was lost as age, if nothing else, took its toll. For example, the Pentrich Revolution was a happening that excited national interest and yet comparatively little of its known street literature has survived.

In the 19th century, Derbyshire had several who took the trouble to collect and catalogue local ballads and broadsides. Principal among them was the noted antiquarian Thomas Bateman (1821-1861), more famous for his archaeological digs and reports. Bateman housed his extraordinary collection at Lomberdale Hall, Middleton-by-Youlgreave. His library, carefully classified and catalogued, was a treasure house not only of street literature but also hundreds of other earlier records of Derbyshire. Bateman's accumulation came up for auction at Sotheby's in London in 1893. There were volumes of broadsides; Lot 174 alone amounted to 240. Lot 814 ('a large collection', reported the auctioneers) consisted of 'Derbyshire ballads, songs and criminal literality'. There were many more. All went under the hammer over

a five-day period; just a few are now housed in Derby Local Studies Library.

That sale might be the explanation why, in 1902, the *Mercury* was suddenly able to add to its list of executions. Up to then, the litany started in 1732 with the hanging of Hewitt and Ollerenshaw. Now it was going back to 1341, although there were enormous gaps. Where the newspaper obtained its information it did not state, but the possibility has to be allowed that it stemmed from the Bateman sale. Nor must the search be given up. As recent as 1996, some execution sheets turned up unexpectedly in a strongroom and are now lodged in the Derbyshire archives. Bearing in mind the sheer quantity housed in Bateman's library at Lomberdale, there must be more just waiting to be found.

Curiously, the *Mercury* never mentioned the execution of the Bakewell witches. The story has been told many times, but where the contemporary evidence is, or was, remains a mystery. The only remaining, fleeting source seems to be Hutton in his history of Derby, and even he was writing years after the event. Maybe it was to be found in Lot 814. Another surprising omission from the *Mercury* listing is Crosland, the hangman who executed his father and brother around 1660.

Since many of the illustrations included in this history were taken from street literature, a word about them would be in order. Except in extremely rare exceptions, those pictures were not true representations of the events described beneath them. Every printer would have a stock of woodcuts of typical scenes, such as the hanging, going by cart to the scaffold, prison scenes such as a prisoner writing out his confession or listening to the exhortations of a clergyman.

So often were the pictures at variance to the events that those who have studied this form of literature have concluded that they were used merely to make the publication more attractive. A court scene was a court scene, and the printer would have a standard woodcut with the bench and the dock empty, to have moveable figures inserted to agree with the narrative. Felons hanging from the gallows could be amended in the same way.

A close attempt to portray the scene as it happened can be found on execution sheets dealing with public hangings outside the Vernon Street prison. The first time it appeared was with the description of the unhappy life and execution of John Leedham in 1833. Several subsequent hangings carried the same illustration, which would be quite acceptable. The omission of the Martello towers erected after the Reform riots two years before Leedham died, could suggest the picture was a production woodcut circulating among printers and by a happy coincidence looked like the standard Derby scene. In the writer's opinion, the illustration was cut in anticipation soon after the prison opened in 1827, and then had to wait six years before being used. After that, the printers could not be bothered to update it.

Bibliography

Berry J.: *My Experiences as an Executioner* (Percy Lund 1892).

Briggs J. et al.: *Crime and Punishment in England* (UCL Press 1996).

Emsley C.: *Crime and Society in England, 1750-1900* (Longman 1987).

Gatrell V.A.C.: *The Hanging Tree* (Oxford University Press 1996).

Glover, S.: *The History and Directory of the Borough of Derby* (Derby 1843).

Hay D. et al.: *Albion's Fatal Tree* (Allen Lane 1975).

Hutton W.: *History and Antiquities of the Borough of Derby Town Down to 1791* (Derby 1791)

Potter H.: *Hanging in Judgement* (SCM Press 1993).

Stevens J.: *England's Last Revolution – Pentrich 1817* (Moorland Publishing 1977).

Stevenson J.: *Popular Disturbances in England 1700-1832* (Longman 1979).

Taylor D.: Crime, *Policing and Punishment in England, 1750-1914* Macmillan Press 1998).

Thompson E.P.: *The Making of the English Working Class* (Penguin Books 1991).

Woolley W.: *History of Derbyshire* (Ed. Glover C. and Riden P.).

Newspapers

British Spy or Derby Postman
Derby Mercury
Derby and Chesterfield Reporter
Leeds Mercury (1817)

Other Sources

Ballads, Broadsides, Execution Sheets (collections located in Derby and Nottingham Local Studies Libraries)

Derbyshire Miscellany (Derby Local Studies Library)

Notes and Queries (Derby Local Studies Library)